THE FLEET MARRIAGES

"… in these houses, it was enough that the victim was provided; the priest was always ready for the sacrifice; the incautious youth, inflamed with lust and liquor, incentives to both being regularly furnished in the same places, might there at all seasons and at all hours, seal his final ruin, … and the inexperienced virgin, deluded from her parents' protection, … be irreparably betrayed into a surrender of her honour and fortune to the abandoned libertine, or infamous sharper, under the appearance of a marriage, which might be afterwards destitute of legal proof; seeing the seducer, having once served his particular purpose might prevail to have the register suppressed or cancelled. The licentious prostitute, who had contracted large debts to support her extravagance, was in these places furnished with a plea for coverture, whereby she was enabled to elude the honest demands and escape the just resentment of her defrauded creditors; and it has happened that an industrious tradesman has been totally undone, under the pretence of a matrimonial engagement, to which he was utterly a stranger, and which, on his part, had no real existence. These are not merely possible or imaginary evils, but such have been really known in many instances."

Sir Tanfield Leman, *Matrimony Analysed*, 1755.

Roger L. Brown is also the author of:

The Followers of Jeroboam, 1983
The Welsh Evangelicals, 1986
Irish Scorn, English Pride and the Welsh Tongue, 1987
The Tribulations of a Mountain Parish, 1988
Lord Powis and the Extension of the Episcopate, 1989
*Reviving the Clergy, Renewing the Laity: Archbishop
    Benson's Mission in Wales*, 1994
A History of the Fleet Prison, London, 1996
David Howell: A Pool of Spirituality, 1998
Llandaff Figures and Places, 1998
Pews, Benches and Seats, 1998
Reclaiming the Wilderness, 2001
A-Z of Welsh Clerics, 2002
Parochial Lives, 2002
*The Letters of Edward Copleston, Bishop of Llandaff,
    1828-1849*, edited for the South Wales Record Society, 2003.
Ten Clerical Lives, 2005
In Pursuit of a Welsh Episcopate, 2005
John Griffith, the Unmitred Bishop, 2007

THE FLEET MARRIAGES

A History of Clandestine Marriages
with particular reference to the Marriages
performed in and around the Fleet Prison,
London

Roger L. Brown

TAIR EGLWYS PRESS
WELSHPOOL
2007

ISBN: 0-948780-17-7

Dedicated
to the memory of those who encouraged my love of history:
Ada Florence Watts
Clifford Evans
Professor Douglas Chandaman
Professor Thomas F. Reddaway

Published by the TAIR EGLWYS PRESS
Welshpool Vicarage, Powys, SY21 7DP

CONTENTS

ILLUSTRATIONS

INTRODUCTION

This study is concerned with clandestine marriages, and, in particular, with those celebrated in and around the Fleet Prison in London. There, between two and three hundred thousand marriages were solemnized within the period 1694-1754, a fact which suggests that the vast majority of English people have at least several ancestors who married at the Fleet. A study of these marriages has, therefore, an immediate genealogical appeal. The circumstances in which they took place gave rise to considerable concern. In order to end them Lord Hardwicke, then Lord Chancellor, was forced to bring in legislation which brought about a major theoretical change in the English law of marriage. This change was one which was of vital interest to every family in the country, as it was to the State itself, for it ended the old concept of marriage as being formulated by consent alone. Thereafter the State insisted that its own consent to any individual marriage was required before it would protect it, and began to regard matrimony more as a legal contract than as a sacramental state. Such a change permitted the divorce laws of the following century.

In recent years genealogists have tended to make a distinction between clandestine and irregular marriages. For example, a distinction has been made between "clandestine" marriages openly solemnised, and therefore regarded as irregular, and those marriages conducted in secret, and consequently seen as clandestine. Others have suggested that a marriage celebrated in the parish church of a couple without the previous calling of banns or the obtaining of a licence, or solemnized with a valid certificate of banns or a valid common licence but in a parish church other than their own, was irregular rather than clandestine in form. Ecclesiastical law, however, regarded all such marriages as clandestine, whatever their circumstances, and I have followed suit.

The major sources for a study of these marriages are the Fleet registers. These are at the National Archives at Kew, London (formerly known as the Public Record Office), and their class number is R.G.7. This is by no means a complete collection of these registers, for many

1

have been lost and destroyed, and a number are found elsewhere. These registers contain many duplicate entries, not only because many of these "registers" are rough notebooks whose entries were written up into more permanent registers, but also because many of the clergy, as well as the marriage house keepers, maintained their own registers. In addition many "registrars" made collections of entries from numerous other registers. As a result one particular entry might be recorded in three or more registers (with varying degrees of accuracy in transcription), besides being included in various "notebook" entries, often with additional information about the cost and circumstances of the marriage.

The printed *London Sessions Papers* contain much material of interest, for few years passed without there being at least one trial recorded within its pages in which a Fleet marriage was concerned. The more notorious cases were written up and included in the various legal case books, and these have provided valuable material as to the abuses perpetuated by these clandestine marriages at the Fleet. The same is also true of the records of the Consistory Court of the Bishop of London. By contrast the other diocesan records have provided little of interest save for particulars of some of the Fleet clergy, as have the books of the Fleet Prison, which are also at the National Archives. Of the printed sources the most valuable is that of the debates of the 1753 Marriage Act included in Corbett's *Parliamentary History*. A scrapbook in the British Library entitled *Humours of the Fleet*, compiled sometime in the mid-nineteenth century and devoted to the history of the prison and its marriages, has been of great value. Only two books have been written about the Fleet marriages in particular. J. S. Burn's *The Fleet Registers* of 1833 was written to show how far the registers could be regarded as legal evidence, while John Ashton's *The Fleet, its River, Prison and Marriages* of 1889 adds little of interest. Reginald Haw discusses the implications of clandestine marriage at the Fleet and elsewhere and its consequences in English law in his study *The State of Matrimony*, published in 1952; much of the legal argument found in chapter one is derived from this work. An article relating to the Fleet registers, mainly from my pen, although wrongly attributed (as was later acknowledged), will be found in volume 1 of *The National Index of Parochial Registers*, edited by D. J. Steel for the Society of Genealogists, and published in 1968.

Until recently the only modern study of these marriages was my thesis entitled "Clandestine Marriages in London, especially within the Fleet Prison, and their effects on Hardwicke's Act, 1753." This was accepted for the M.A. degree of the University of London in 1972. In the writing of this thesis I received much encouragement from the late Professor T. F. Reddaway, sometime Reader in London History at University College, London, and from Professor Douglas Chandaman, sometime Professor of History at St David's University College, Lampeter. In addition I received financial help from the Pantyfedwen Trust of St David's University College, and I was privileged to hold the Goldsmiths' Company's Studentship in London History for 1964-5. A synopsis of this thesis appeared in a symposium entitled *Marriage and Society: Studies in the Social History of Marriage*, edited by R. B. Outhwaite, and published in 1981 by Europa Publications of London.

In more recent years a number of studies have appeared in which the Fleet Marriages are discussed, while a substantial debate has arisen about the effects of the 1753 Marriage Act. Lawrence Stone's *Road to Divorce* and *Uncertain Unions* appeared in 1991 and 1992 respectively; R. B. Outhwaite published his study *Clandestine Marriage in England 1500-1850* in 1995; Tony Benton's *Irregular Marriage in London before 1754* was published by the Society of Genealogists in 1993, with a second edition in 2000, and Mark Heber has already published three volumes of his transcripts of the Fleet Registers from 1999 onwards, *Clandestine Marriages in the Chapel and Rules of the Fleet Prison: 1680-1754*. It may be worth noting too that my own book, *A History of the Fleet Prison, London*, was published by the Edwin Mellen Press in 1996 as volume 42 of its Studies in British History.

There are many who have assisted me in the writing of this book, and I am indebted to my former colleagues in the London Seminar of the Institute of Historical Research, the Librarians and staff of the British Library, the City of London Library, and the Keeper and his staff of the National Archives. I express too my gratitude to the many people who have suggested that my thesis should be published in a more popular format, and to my wife, Phyllis, whose help, patience and encouragement has made this possible. My only regret is that it has taken so long – nearly forty years since I first embarked on this undertaking, but parochial commitments, and a change of direction into Welsh ecclesiastical history, arrested progress. A period of sabbatical leave has given me the space I needed to complete it, for which I express my gratitude to the Rt. Revd. John Davies, Bishop of St Asaph. The final proofing of the text was completed in the relaxing atmosphere of Penpaled, Criccieth, by courtesy of Martin and Ruth Canning, to whom I express much appreciation.

AN EDITORIAL NOTE

Where necessary, the dates have been changed to New Style.

The spelling and capitalisation of the quotations have been changed to modern English usage wherever necessary.

The term "rules", indicating the rules or limits of the liberty of the Fleet Prison, permitted to selected debt prisoners, is always distinguished in the text by the use of italics.

An examination of all known register entries of the Fleet marriages was made for the years 1700, 1710-13, 1720, 1730, 1740 and 1750. An estimate of the number of marriages was drawn from this examination, but due to the difficulty of eliminating all duplicated entries, combined with the uncertainty about how many registers have been lost, this estimate must be regarded as provisional rather than exact.

1
THE OLD LAW OF MARRIAGE

An apocryphal story is told about Dean Swift. It is said he came across a man and a woman sheltering under a tree from a storm. They were rushing for all too obvious reasons to a town in order to be married. Discovering the dean's ecclesiastical position they begged him to marry them and, this completed, requested a certificate to establish the "proof" of their marriage. The dean thus wrote:

> Under an oak, in stormy weather,
> I joined this rogue and whore together.
> And none but he who rules the thunder,
> Can put this rogue and whore asunder.

We, with our notion of marriage as being permitted only after the completion of due formalities, and taking place before a legal official in a duly appointed place within specified hours, find the above anecdote very strange. Yet however apocryphal the story may have been it accurately sums up the state of English marriage law before the Marriage Act of 1753. Salmon could thus write in 1724, in his *A Critical Essay concerning Marriage*, "neither the want of banns or licence, or the being perform'd at an uncanonical hour, or in a closet, by night or day, will divest the parties of any of the rights, privileges or advantages of a marriage solemnized in the face of the Church." It may be surprising, but it is true, that an age which recognised the importance of marriage, with its attendant civil rights about the legitimacy of issue and the right of succession to property, still permitted a system of marriage that was neither simple to understand nor certain of absolute proof, and that failed to put obstacles in the way of sudden, clandestine or youthful unions, which tended to undermine the well-being of marriage itself. Why, then, were such marriages allowed?

The answer is complicated, but part of it is to be found in the fact that the laws of matrimony had been formulated, and were still regulated, by two separate jurisdictions, these being statute and common law, and canon law. That which at one time had satisfied the Church's canon law, regarding the basis of matrimony, has also satisfied common law, but by the beginning of the eighteenth century this was becoming an obsolete principle as theory outstripped practice, and as each began to accept different principles by which to establish the validity of any given marriage. It is necessary, therefore, to examine the requirements which both jurisdictions necessitated before they would declare a marriage fully valid, although both tolerated a marriage performed without all these requirements.

The free consent of two people to be man and wife together was the essence and basis of matrimony. Henry Swinburne thus declared that it was "but a present and perfect consent ... which alone maketh matrimony", while the civil law had a maxim, "consensus non concubitus facit nuptias": it is not the bedding which makes the marriage, but the consent of the parties. A promise to marry a person in the future, followed by sexual intercourse, was also held to be a valid marriage. Without this requirement of consent no form of marriage could be upheld as valid, but if a marriage was deficient in every particular save that of consent it was, stated Lord Chief Justice Holt, "as much a marriage in the sight of God as if it had been *in facie ecclesiae*", that is, in the face of the Church, with the full requirements of ecclesiastical law. Secret marriages, because of the fear of a subsequent denial by one of the parties to it, were regarded by Swinburne as being "in effect as if they were not".

Such consent needed to be completely free, and to be given by two people who had no legal impediment to their marriage. Such impediments were outlined by the ecclesiastical Canons of 1603, the main ones being those created by the relationships exhibited in the Table of Kindred and Affinity, and the prohibition of minors from marrying without the consent of their parents or guardians. The age of consent was fixed at fourteen years of age for males and twelve for females. However, if a marriage had been celebrated before that age had been reached in one or both of the parties to it, the marriage was considered to be no more than a solemn betrothal (called a marriage *per verba de futuro*) which could be repudiated when the parties to it had reached the age of consent. Nevertheless, the marriage of a child over this age without parental consent having been first obtained was still upheld as valid in law, although severe penalties were laid against those who seduced infants into marriage. An act of 1557-8 ordered that a person who had married a "maiden" under the age of sixteen should be imprisoned for five years and the estate of the "wife" forfeited to the next of kin for the lifetime of the seducer. This was both to punish the seducer and to remove temptation. A further act of 1596-7 made it a felony without benefit of clergy to abduct a minor under the age of sixteen. Several persons were convicted and executed under this enactment.

The second main requirement imposed by both Church and State was that the performance of the ceremony, and the steps leading to it, should be accompanied by publicity. This was in order to proclaim that a marriage was to take place, to ensure that no impediments to it existed, to check clandestine marriage, and to remove any doubts as to its validity or performance. The method used to ensure that this requirement was met was to publicly announce in the parish church or churches of the couple the forthcoming marriage by the calling of banns on three separate Sundays or holy days (which could allow the banns to be completed within a week in some cases), and by performing the ceremony openly in the place of public worship where the banns had been read during the time of divine service. Many shrank from the publicity this gave, as Misson in his *Memoirs and Observations in His Travels over England*, written in the 1690s, noted. He wrote:

> To proclaim banns is a thing nobody now cares to have done; very few are willing to have their affairs declared to all the world in a public place, when for a guinea they may do it all snug and without noise, and my good friends, the clergy, who find their accounts in it, are not very zealous to prevent it. Thus they buy what they call a licence, and are married in their closets, in presence of a couple of friends, that serve for witnesses, and this ties them for ever.

As a result, Misson added, people were "amaz'd to see women brought to bed of legitimate children, without hearing a word of the father".

These licences mentioned by Misson were the episcopal or common licences of marriage, issued by the bishop's appointed surrogates. These licences dispensed with the requirement of banns by taking security against the existence of any impediments to the marriage. They still required that the marriage should be solemnized in the parish church of one of the parties, and the issuing of the licence was restricted, in theory at least, to those of good estate. As Misson hints, their granting had become a matter of ecclesiastical revenue, so that the provisions and restrictions laid down in the 1603 Canons for their control were never properly performed nor enforced. The special licence of the archbishop of Canterbury permitted a far greater dispensation from canonical requirements, for it included not only a dispensation from banns, but also from the necessity of marrying in the parish church of one of the parties to the marriage. Its application was strictly limited and its cost prohibitive.

By the end of the seventeenth century, statute law enforced these requirements and made their absence into a civil offence. It did so for financial reasons, namely the better to collect and regulate the revenue which derived from a stamp duty of five shillings placed on all licences and certificates of marriage issued, and a tax placed on all marriages performed. This tax was graduated according to the social position of the bridegroom: a duke was required to pay fifty pounds, an esquire five pounds, a gentleman one pound, and all others not in receipt of poor relief two shillings and sixpence. These duties and taxes were imposed in the 1690s for the express purpose of obtaining revenue "for carrying out the War against France with vigour". These acts also imposed statutory penalties on those clergy and others who offended against their provisions. Consequently those marriages, which were performed without the calling of banns or the issuing of a licence, became offences against the civil as well as the canon law, for the absence of such banns and licence was now considered to be a fraud upon the revenue.

In order that witnesses might be present at the marriage, that greater publicity might attend its celebration by daylight, and to ensure sobriety in the parties to it, the 1603 Canons ordered that marriages were to take place only between the hours of eight in the morning and twelve noon. Not even an episcopal licence could dispense from this requirement. This matter, however, was challenged in the civil courts, and the judgment of Lord Hardwicke in the case of *Middleton v. Croft* of 1736 became crucial for determining and limiting the jurisdiction of ecclesiastical law as opposed to common law. Hardwicke argued that the 1603 Canons, which had never received statutory force, only affected the laity in so far as they were in conformity to the laws of the realm or to that custom upon which common law rested. All the 1603 Canons regarding marriage, with one exception, were validated by this ruling. The one exception was the restriction in the hours of marriage, which by this ruling were declared to be non-binding upon the laity, although binding upon the clergy. This judgment has been seen as the commencement of the challenge to the ecclesiastical prerogative of marriage by the civil lawyers.

Apart from the requirement of ministerial intervention, which will follow later, the other requirements may be briefly mentioned. The service was to be in accordance with the service prescribed in *The Book of Common Prayer*, which gave to the service a uniformity and dignity it otherwise might have lacked. As the Church had always upheld the doctrine that a marriage to be fully effected needed to be indissoluble, English law presumed upon the mutual understanding of this by the partners to a marriage. In fact the only form of divorce then available was that of *a mensa et thoro*, awarded in cases of adultery, which was no more than a legal separation and did not allow a subsequent remarriage within the lifetime of the first partner. Lord Rosse, however, in 1669 obtained a private act of Parliament which while described as "an act of grace, a mere dispensation", permitted him to remarry within his first wife's lifetime. Between 1719-69 sixty similar bills were presented to Parliament, although the expense of obtaining such an act was substantial.

A further requirement was that the marriage should be consummated, and this, together with free consent, was considered to constitute marriage both complete and indissoluble.

The 1549 *Book of Common Prayer* had ordered that the newly married couple should receive Communion on their marriage day, but the rubric of the 1662 Prayer Book exchanged this order for the more plausible words, "it is convenient that", and hence this provision was universally neglected. Yet the fact that the rubric provided for the subsequent celebration of Holy Communion is sufficient indication that a priest was required by the Canons of the Church to solemnise a marriage. The ecclesiastical courts thus refused to protect the marriages or to grant the full rights of matrimony to couples until they had been married in the presence of a priest and according to the prescribed regulations of the Church.

To an ever-increasing extent the common law or civil lawyers were taking the attitude that a marriage performed without the presence of a priest or a person in deacon's orders was neither good nor effectual. This was because these lawyers were increasingly dealing with cases involving matrimonial offences and rights, and, as a result, they began to insist on better evidence of marriage being produced than the words of a party to it or the testimony of a witness. Without the production of more tangible proof they were declining to administer the civil rights of marriage to those who applied for them, or to convict those who contravened the law of matrimony. Consequently, during the

seventeenth century the lawyers began to accept for convenience the
old notion that where the priest was, there was the Church. They began
to consider that a marriage conducted by a clergyman met that standard
of proof which they required. Nonconformist marriages, once regularly
accepted as valid, were now being questioned if brought before the
courts. An act of 1694-5 refused to recognise that because "Papists,
Jews and Quakers" paid the taxes required on their marriages these
marriages would be regarded as effectual in law. In 1703, Samuel
Harris, a dissenting minister of Stepney, was accused of "having taken
upon himself to solemnize marriages" when he was not in priest's or
deacon's orders of the Church of England, and in Haydon's case in
1710-11 a husband was refused letters of administration in his wife's
estate until he had proved himself a husband by the law through which
he claimed such letters. He had been married by a layman.
Paradoxically, in the case of *Elmes v. Elmes* of 1711 the Master of the
Rolls decided that by common law Henry Elmes was not the husband
of Anne Ordway. They had been married by a Fleet parson in a
distiller's shop. Elmes was not liable, therefore, for his wife's debts. A
year later the ecclesiastical Court of the Arches reached a different and
contrary conclusion, namely that Elmes was her husband in law and
liable for her debts. Such was the uncertainly at that time over what
constituted a valid and recognised marriage.

Marriages solemnized before a Roman Catholic priest were
generally accepted as valid.

A marriage that was celebrated without the requirements depicted
above, termed a clandestine marriage, was still upheld as a valid
marriage and as an indissoluble union, unless it failed to meet the
requirements of free consent. However, until that marriage was
solemnized according to the rules of the Established Church, that is, *in
facie ecclesiae*, the marriage was alleged to be in a state of nullity in
respect of its civil rights. This was because the proof of such marriages
was often so precarious that neither the Church nor the State could
admit the parties concerned to the civil privileges of matrimony. The
reason for this position was because all the ecclesiastical requirements,
after free consent, were directory and not negative in the sense that
their absence could void a union. Consequently, clandestine marriages
were tolerated by both Church and State, for as Lord Stowell stated,
"everything is presumed to be complete and consummated in
substance, but not in ceremony". The ecclesiastical courts often
required that those married in this form should be "remarried"
according to the Canons of the Church, but this was not because it

considered that first marriage invalid, but rather to give publicity to the fact that a contract had already been made.

Consent may have been the essence of marriage, but on its own it gave no legal protection whatsoever. There was thus a serious theoretical conflict between ecclesiastical law and common law. The Church accepted marriage by consent as the lowest denominator for recognition of a union, but only admitted a marriage *in facie ecclesiae* to the benefit of its protection and to the privileges of matrimony. However, the common law by accepting a position between these two extremes for a marriage which the State would protect and support, ended the old notion that that which had previously satisfied the Church with regard to matrimony would also satisfy common law. Indeed, to determine whether a marriage was valid, one had first to enquire as to whether it constituted a marriage according to ecclesiastical law, and then enquire as to whether that marriage was recognised as valid by the common law lawyers and courts. Under this development the doctrine of consent alone had been replaced by one of consent with ministerial intervention, and this alone, to the common law lawyers, constituted matrimony.

Thus those marriages, which while clandestine, were yet performed in the presence of a priest, came into a middle position between those who were married *in facie ecclesiae* according to the Church's requirements, and those who were married without any ministerial intervention. As such this "middle type" of union lacked the full ecclesiastical privileges of the former, and yet possessed the legal completeness demanded by the common law lawyers which was wanting in the latter; and while punishable in law for the manner of its celebration, was still regarded as a complete union with the full legal or common law rights of matrimony. Neither authority was happy with this position. The ecclesiastical courts endeavoured to deprive those married in such a fashion of the legal benefits of matrimony in those cases which came before them, and considered all those so married, or who assisted in such marriages, to be *ipso facto* excommunicated, and thus liable to further ecclesiastical censure. The clergy who officiated at these marriages could be punished by suspension from or deprivation of their livings or curacies. The common law courts also deplored the existence of these marriages, and often severely punished those who permitted such irregularities to continue. However, they could do little to prevent them, for the theory which the lawyers had found to distinguish between those marriages which the State was prepared to recognise, and those which it declined to protect, could not exclude the clandestine marriages performed at the Fleet and other such places, with the intervention of a priest, from the terms of what they considered to be, and would support as, a valid marriage. This is the reason why the apocryphal marriage solemnized by Dean Swift was perfectly acceptable in English law.

The Abbé le Blanc, another French traveller in England, observed that "the laws of England ... tend all to favour even the most indecent marriages", and he noted that where the utmost simplicity and clarity were required, obscurity and perplexity prevailed. There was simply no consensus as to what constituted a valid marriage. This situation remained until Lord Hardwicke altered the whole course of marriage law by his Marriage Act of 1753.

2
EARLY CLANDESTINE MARRIAGES

Clandestine marriage was one of the most persistent problems faced by the medieval Church. A decree of the Council of Trent ended this problem for the Roman Church, for it insisted that every marriage was to be performed in the presence of a priest and two witnesses, or else be regarded as null and void. The bishop of Nazianzum considered this decree to be of such great importance that he held that it alone was sufficient reason for the Council to meet, irrespective of its work in counteracting the influence of the Protestant Reformation. The decrees of this Council were never accepted in England, for obvious religious reasons, so that clandestine marriages were still regarded as valid and continued to be celebrated in this country.

Even a casual study of seventeenth and eighteenth century social history will reveal that clandestine marriages were extremely common. The bishops continually reminded their clergy about their obligations regarding the law of marriage, as did Bishop Godwin of Llandaff in his Injunctions, written at the beginning of the seventeenth century:

> Item 6: Whereas many marriages clandestine and otherwise unlawful are daily made, and then ignorance is alleged for excuse of the fault; you shall understand, that you ought not to marry any persons but in the church, and that between the hours of eight and twelve in the forenoon, none within the compass of those times that are forbidden by law, none whose banns have not been lawfully asked three several holy days, without a dispensation for the same first had under the hand or seal of me, or Mr. Doctor Trevor my chancellor and none other. If you shall hereafter offend in the premises, you are to be suspended *ab officio et beneficio per triennium*; wherein I advise you to hope for no favour.

The bishops also included articles regarding these marriages in their visitation queries, sent to the clergy and churchwardens of each parish in their dioceses, requesting information as to whether the clergy were faithful to their calling and the church fabric in good repair, whether there were any papists or nonconformists within that parish, and other similar concerns. The 1682 Articles of Visitation for the diocese of Canterbury were typical of many such articles for this and other dioceses throughout this period. Its fourteenth clause required the churchwardens to answer regarding their minister:

> Hath he presumed to marry any persons in private houses? Or such, as being under age, hath not the consent of their parents, or without the banns first published on three Sundays or holy days in the church? Or at any other house, than between eight and twelve in the morning unless he had a licence or dispensation to so do, granted by such authority, and in such form, as the canons direct?

The episcopal registers for this period show that many clergymen were required to answer charges as the result of these returns or other sources of information. Francis Davies, bishop of Llandaff 1667-75, dealt with nine such offenders out of a total of thirteen clerical delinquents. Most received a sentence of suspension, which was generally lifted a month or so afterwards providing bonds were entered into to secure good behaviour for the future. In the archdeaconry of Chester between 1676-99 fifty-eight clergymen were prosecuted for similar offences, their bishop stating that their activities had caused discomfort and unhappiness to many parents, had led to the ruin of many young people, had given an evil example to others, and occasioned a great scandal to the Church and government.

Peter Roberts, a legal official in the diocese of St Asaph, kept a commonplace book during the period 1607-46. In this he records 157 marriages, of which one seventh, twenty-six in number, are either described as clandestine or may be so regarded from the circumstances he describes, such as "by candlelight", or being celebrated in private houses. Episcopal correspondence of the period frequently mentioned the "hedge parsons", described by one bishop as a "parcel of strolling curates, who for a crown, or at most a guinea, would marry anybody under a hedge". Another bishop, White Kennett of Peterborough, considered that these "itinerant curates or preachers … spread factions and disorders", possibly hoping that such expressions would encourage the government to step in and regulate their abuses. Dean Prideaux of Norwich held that the problem was largely caused by the abuses too often permitted in the issuing of licences. "If the rules and precautions required by the canons were duly executed and cbserved," he wrote, "it

was scarce possible that any clandestine marriage should ever happen."
Fifty years later Lord Chancellor Hardwicke concurred in this
judgment, remarking in *More v. More* about the same canons: "one
would think no body ever read them, neither the officers of the spiritual
courts nor clergymen, or else they would not act so diametrically
opposite to them".

Many examples of abuses in the issuing of licences are found in
letters written by Bishop William Lloyd of Norwich to Archbishop
Sancroft of Canterbury. On 29 November 1686, he wrote:

> ... we have had a famous clandestine marriage the 10th of this
> month, within the precincts of this church, one Hughs a petty
> canon of the church clandestinely married a young gentlewoman
> that lived with her aunt in this close. She might have four or five
> thousand to her portion, if she had married with the consent of her
> friends – what fortune she may be to Mr Hughs I cannot tell. The
> registrar Mr Wells gave out a blank licence to one Mr Willcox, the
> curate of Bingey, and the same Willcox filled up the blank and
> licence and married the parties in St Luke's Chapel within this
> Church. I shall shortly examine the matter, and give your Grace an
> account of my proceedings in it.

This he did, informing the archbishop that Willcox had been dismissed
from his curacy, Hughs and his wife excommunicated, and the registrar
suspended for six months. But the same letter had to report another
such marriage. "Mr Lucas came ... to complain that his daughter was
ruined by a clandestine marriage", he wrote, "she was married to his
coachman, by virtue of a licence granted by Mr Wells, the principal
registrar here ..." When first appointed to Norwich, Prideaux wrote
that Lloyd had endeavoured to "suppress these abuses and regulate
these licences", having found "a great clamour against clandestine
marriages". For a while "things were kept in good order",

> But they had not been long so, but the Master of the Faculties, and
> the Vicar-General to the Archbishop, took the advantage to send
> their licences into the Diocese; which the Bishop perceiving, and
> having no authority to control them herein, he thought it better,
> since he saw there was no remedy, to suffer the corruption to be
> still continued by his own officers, over whom he had some awe,
> than by those interlopers, with whom he had nothing to do; and
> therefore relaxed all his former orders, and left his officers to

proceed in the same course as they did before, and the mischiefs, which have since followed hereon, are too many to relate ...

This situation was to continue in most dioceses until the Marriage Act. In the city of Oxford, for example, where both the bishop of Oxford and his three archdeacons had their respective registries, 2,655 marriages were solemnized by licence in the church of St Mary Magdalen between 1692-1754, generally on the same day as the licence was issued. The church was almost opposite the bishop's registry office and nearly all the couples came from outside this parish, thus making their marriages clandestine. There were thirty-one surrogates licensed to grant marriage licences in the city of Worcester in 1752, while individual surrogates established St Nicholas's, Rochester, and Holy Trinity, at Stratford on Avon, as centres where marriages by licence could be performed. At Fledborough, Nottinghamshire, William Sweetapple, the incumbent, interpreted the surrogateship to which he was appointed in 1728 as a licence to marry all comers. Out of 490 couples married in his church between 1730-54 only fifteen could claim parochial status. The number of marriages at this church between 1712-30 was even less, merely eleven. Bayworth in Berkshire was another centre, according to Lyson's history of that county, and other centres were found at the Peak Forest Chapel and Dale Abbey, both in Derbyshire. The minister of the former is said to have suffered an annual loss in income of one hundred pounds as a result of the Marriage Act, as well as his title, "Judge in Spiritualities in the Peculiar Court of Peak Forest", which he claimed permitted him to issue his own marriage licences.

The situation in London is noted in another chapter, but Lawrence Stone has estimated that about half the income of the various ecclesiastical courts derived from the issuing of these licences.

If there were clergymen who made use of their office as surrogates to line their own pockets, there were other clergy who solemnized clandestine marriages with no such pretences. At the lowest level were some clergymen about whom Dean Prideaux wrote, namely those who solemnized such marriages in order "to gratify some gentleman of his parish ... who, he thinks, is able to protect him from the penalty, or else make him amends for what he suffers by it". An anonymous writer of 1692 who wrote *A Representation of the Prejudices which may arise from an intended Act concerning Marriages*, offers collaborative evidence of this practice. Many clergymen, he alleged, were forced to solemnize clandestine marriages "by mighty men ... to oblige them", adding, "there never was any peasant or mechanic in his parish, but will taken upon himself to be offended when the stubborn priest will not waive the rules he is to go by to oblige him". This must have been the case in many parishes, and many clergymen, either to please or not to offend, were prepared to waive some of the requirements of the marriage law.

There were other clerics, Prideaux noted, who solemnized marriages on a much larger scale than these local and individual affairs. These, he suggested, were mainly "indigent curates or unpreferred chaplains ... who having nothing to lose, on this account, are out of the reach of the penalty; and, therefore, if there are but one or two such in a county, usually the whole trade of clandestine marriage goes to them." One such parson was Samuel Gibson, who lived at Bures in Suffolk during the first part of the eighteenth century, who was said to be willing to "marry anyone without banns or licence". Another one of these "lawless clergy" or "hedge parsons" is thought to have based himself at Tetbury in Gloucestershire, where twenty per cent of the marriages solemnized there during the late seventeenth century were clandestine in form. It is assumed that their entries, along with even more unusual entries recording only the name of the groom, were entered into the parish register by an incumbent anxious to safeguard himself from possible prosecution under the penal clauses of the marriage law.

****

The first clandestine marriage centre known in London was at the Savoy. The evidence for this is contained in the case of Lord Cobham's grandson, a minor, who was married to his first cousin "by night" and without consent. The chaplain of the Savoy, who married them, Mr Bigge, was summoned before the archbishop of Canterbury at Lambeth, in June 1596:

> ... and confessed his abuse. He said he thought he might well do it, as his fellow chaplains, Mr Horwode and Mr Lyllye, had married without licence as many or more than he had. The Archbishop committed Bigge to the Gatehouse in part punishment until Lord Cobham's pleasure was known; meaning, it is supposed, at his next appearance by deprivation to displace him ... The Archbishop has taken good order by commission that no such disorderly marriages shall be offensively in the Savoy

performed.

This episode appears to have been more in the nature of an isolated series of incidents, but the chaplains of the Tower of London, a royal "peculiar" and thus exempt from episcopal visitation, claimed as early as the reign of Edward VI that they had the right to marry couples without banns being first called or licences previously obtained. The chaplains were assisted in their claims by the constables and lieutenants of the Tower. Several attempts by Archbishop Abbot in the early seventeenth century to end these practices were successfully resisted by the then Lieutenant, Sir William Wade. On one of these occasions Hayes, a curate at the Tower, was prosecuted by the Court of High Commission. It was then reported that Sir William:

> Sent thrice for his curate, threatening to take up one of their chaplains at their heels to serve at the Tower in the interim and so the curate was delivered.

He also argued that:

> If they of the Faculties might farm among other things the licences of marriages to laymen for several hundreds of pounds, he saw no reason that he might continue the privileges of marriages at the Tower, being for so many of the King's servants that take pains by night and day.

The result of this attempt to close this centre was that bonds of "£300 with two sureties in the same form that other ecclesiastical officers use" were taken in an attempt to regulate the practice. This suggests that the chaplains at the Tower claimed the right to issue their own licences of marriage. Through the neglect of a later governor in 1623 the marriages were temporarily ended, the senior chaplain claiming that he thereby lost an annual income of one hundred marks.

When Sir William Balfour as governor endeavoured to reassert these privileges, he discovered that Archbishop Laud was more powerful than his predecessor in the see of Canterbury, for Laud prevented their continuance, hinting that the Lieutenant's protests were not without self interest, as his share of the proceeds "was as dear to him as the privilege". The ending of these marriages formed one of the charges laid against Laud at his trial in 1644. In his defence Laud maintained that he opposed them for the sake of the subjects of

England, "many of whose sons and daughters were there undone, for there were no banns, no licence, nor any means of fore-knowledge to prevent it." He also noted that the chapel was called, significantly, "The King's Free Chapel", but doubted whether it had any claim to that title.

The Tower of London never regained these privileges, and with other arrangements made for marriage during the Commonwealth, the clandestine marriage trade was discontinued. It started afresh by the 1660s, and, significantly, one of the earlier centres, as Tony Benton notes, was St Katherine's Collegiate Church, not far from the Tower's walls. This church also claimed to be a privileged place exempt from visitation, and averaged 322 marriages a year in the late 1670s and 470 in the 1680s. Another centre which became established in London was St Pancras Church, where "there were several persons that attended here purely for marrying people, and it was a perfect scramble who should get to perform the office". This was a comment made in the parish register in the early 1660s, but such comments were also made on the London stage, indicating the notoriety these marriages occasioned. Lawrence Stone, in an examination of the plots of 241 comedies published between 1660-1714, states that 91 of them had a plot involving a clandestine marriage. St Pancras received its fair mention. In the play, *The Apparition or the Sham Wedding*, the remark is made:

> The Curate of Pancras is in a heat for Sir Tristram, he has waited, he says, two hours at his house, and has now followed him thither, he has two more couples to despatch tonight, and will not wait any longer.

William Congreve, in a more celebrated play, *The Way of the World*, puts these sentiments into the mouth of James, a manservant:

> 'Sir, there's such coupling at Pancras, that they stand behind one another, as t'were in a country dance. Ours was the last couple to lead up, and no hopes appearing of dispatch – besides the parson growing hoarse, we were afraid his lungs would have failed before it came to our turn – so we drove around to Duke's Place, and there they were notched in a trance.'
> Mirabell: 'You are sure they are married?'
> James: 'Married and bedded, Sir, I am witness.'

This state of affairs could not escape notice, and in 1660 Randolph Yearwood, the vicar of St Pancras, was suspended for three years for the solemnization of one clandestine marriage. As Congreve's play was not written until 1700, it is clear that this action did not end the activities of this centre.

As the bishop of London and his ecclesiastical officers (excluding, perhaps, those who issued marriage licenses) were generally able to prevent clandestine marriages from being performed in churches under their immediate jurisdiction, these marriages became concentrated upon two particular churches, the one mentioned above, St James's, Duke's Place, and Holy Trinity, Minories. Both these churches were within the city of London, and each claimed to be a privileged place, or, as they were more commonly termed, a "lawless" church, and thereby exempt from the jurisdiction of the bishop of London. This claim was a pretended one, for both churches were visited by various bishops on many separate occasions, but such knowledge did not prevent their ministers insisting that the Crown alone could visit them or from claiming the right to issue their own marriage licences.

Timothy Bracegirdle, curate of Holy Trinity, presumably taking advantage of the closure of the Tower as a matrimonial centre, commenced his own business in the 1640s. In 1641 Humphrey, bishop of London, was authorised to visit this church, described as a royal peculiar, in order to correct any abuses that may have arisen in the said chapel or in its vicinity, but it is not known if this visitation was occasioned by these clandestine marriages. By 1644 there was a notable increase in the number of marriages solemnized at this church. Fifteen marriages were recorded in that year up to the 9th of June, but between that date and the end of the year there were 115, and in 1645 there were 249, and a steady increase thereafter until such marriages were banned by the Commonwealth in favour of lay celebrations performed without the use of the Prayer Book service. Holy Trinity, Minories, soon revived its business after the Restoration as we note below.

William Harrison, rector of St James's, Duke's Place, from 1664-85, appears to have commenced his matrimonial activities in the late 1660s, exploiting the situation caused by the pretended privileges of his church. Although Archbishop Sancroft stated that such men were "greedy of filthy lucre", Harrison at least could claim that he had an extremely poor stipend, for there was no endowment attached to the living, and the "maintenance" of just over £62 raised from the 160 householders was indifferently paid, and sometimes not paid at all. In

1674-5, the Court of Aldermen, as patrons of the living, dismissed their incumbent for marrying "at all hours", but Harrison was shortly afterwards reinstated. However, St James's only became notorious as a clandestine marriage centre with the appointment of Adam Elliot as rector in 1685.

Adam Elliot was one of the most interesting men of his generation. Son of a Scottish clergyman, he took his degree at Gonville and Caius College, Cambridge, and was recommended by the King himself, via the good offices of the earl of Middleton, to the Lord Mayor and Aldermen of London, as "a loyal orthodox man", fit to serve as rector of St James. No court could turn down such a request noted in such terms as this: "His Majesty will take your compliance with his recommendations very kindly".

This royal recommendation was probably made because of Elliot's book, published in 1682, entitled *A Modest Vindication of Titus Oates, the Salamanca Doctor.* A correspondent of the Greenwich Hospital newsletters described it in this way: "amongst all the pamphlets I have read since the liberty of the press it may be that none hath given an eviler character of our Salamanca doctor than he hath done." Titus Oates, the instigator of the Popish Plot, had been a fellow student of Elliot's at Cambridge. Elliot remembered his arrival there "by the same token that the plague and he both visited the University the same year".

Elliot's pamphlet relates how, after much travelling in Europe, he was captured by Moorish pirates, sold as a slave to a person who understood that he was related to the duke of Norfolk, and when he heard the truth that deprived him of the projected ransom, treated Elliot so badly that he exerted himself to escape. This he did successfully in 1670. After several years spent in Dublin, Elliot was summoned to London to give evidence in a court case about a contested will. The unsuccessful party, Lord North, annoyed at Elliot's evidence, allied himself to Oates, who remembering some old grudges against Elliot, informed the King that Elliot was one of "'the most mischievous wicked men in the world, that he believed he had more malice in him than all the Jesuits who were hanged, nay, more says he, he is a circumcis'd Jesuit.' 'God bless us,' said His Majesty, 'what sort of Jesuit is that?' 'A Jesuit that is no Christian but a Turk,' replied the Salamanca devil." Although Oates obtained a warrant from his friend, Justice Waller, and had Elliot arrested at the home of the dowager Lady Grey, influential friends protected him, so that North backed out of the case, which then collapsed. Elliot returned to Ireland, openly stating that "if Oates had deposed with no more truth against the

Jesuits than he did against me, they died martyrs". In revenge Oates accused him of robbery, murder, forgery and debauchery, but in 1681 Elliot successfully obtained a verdict of slander against Oates which was the beginning of his eventual downfall. This, of course, is Elliot's story, and no doubt was suitably embellished in order to impress his readers. He died in 1700, when John Grasty was appointed to the living, but by this time the clandestine marriage trade at St James's had almost ceased its activities.

While the churchwardens of Trinity Minories might reply to the question asked in the 1664 episcopal visitation as to whether their minister solemnized marriages without banns or licence, that "we know not of anything to present", possibly accepting the right of their minister to issue his own licences, and gave an equally negative reply in 1677, they, with their parishioners, not only connived at this state of affairs, but encouraged their minister to engage in this business. This was because part of the profits arising from these marriages was appropriated for the use of the parish poor, so saving the parish an expense of one hundred pounds or so each year. Thus when John King was appointed to the living in 1693, the parish obtained an agreement form him to allow the sum of three shillings out of every marriage fee he received for the support of the poor. The agreement read:

> That Mr Jno King, minister of the said parish doth freely consent and agree for and towards the better support and maintenance of the poor of the said parish and for the better encouragement of the clerk in the diligent performance of his duty to allow the sum of three shillings out of every wedding he receives.
>
> Now it is hereby designed that no wedding dues shall be demanded or taken under five shillings even of the poorest sort, unless in such cases as Mr Jno King in his prudence shall think fit. Witness my hand this day and year above written
> JOHN KING

The parish was also prepared to pay the cost of any litigation which occurred as a result of "our privileges in marriages". This assistance was given when the incumbent was cited to appear before Doctors Commons (an ecclesiastical court), and in 1690 in order to oppose the passage through parliament of one of the innumerable bills designed to suppress clandestine marriage, which a special vestry of the parish considered would be "much to the loss and prejudice of the inhabitants and also of the poor of the parish" if enacted. In 1694, when the number of marriages had declined considerably because of the legislation of that year, and through competition from the Fleet, a special committee was appointed to support "the interest of the private weddings". This decided that the remedy lay in lowering the marriage fee, and it was agreed that any two marriages under the sum of six shillings were to be regarded as one for the purpose of calculating the parochial share of the fee. It has been estimated that King received an annual income of three hundred pounds from these marriages.

These centres had an enormous appeal, for while they possessed all the advantages of clandestine marriage, the marriages were solemnized in an orderly fashion within a consecrated place of worship by a person with a recognised ecclesiastical position. While several members of the fashionable classes found it convenient to be married at St James's, (such as Richard Coote, later created earl of Belloment, in 1680, the earl of Gainsborough, Sir Henry Bathurst and Sir Thomas Stanley in 1683) the majority of those married were probably seamen and craftsmen. In 1658, the only year in which such details were recorded for the bridegroom in the Trinity Minories register (perhaps indicating a resumption in these marriages during the closing years of the Commonwealth), 66 per cent of the men whose occupations are recorded came from these two categories. The poorer classes, represented by labourers and servants, are few in number, thus suggesting that these marriages catered for those who wanted a quick and convenient marriage rather than a cheap ceremony. In addition the clientele for these marriages came mainly from the artisan areas of the city, such as Stepney, Whitechapel, and St Giles' Holborn, although people from every part of the city and even beyond were attracted to these centres. In 1658, for example, 14.5 per cent of those married at Trinity Minories came from places in Kent and Essex, although in that same year just over one per cent of those married there could claim parochial status; a similar percentage is found in the St James's registers for 1696. The popularity of these marriages is illustrated by the contemporary dramatists. *The Pleasures of Matrimony* represents "mother" arguing, "I don't intend to marry my daughter in hugger-mugger, I'll have her married like my child, not among the rabble at the Minories." Her friend, Mrs Pringle-Prattle, agrees, stating:

> I like none of your stolen weddings ... for it may so happen that the parson may die before I may think of getting a Certificate, and then if my husband and I should fall out and he should deny me to be his wife in what a pickle must I be ... No, Madam, you act

prudently, make a public wedding, and then all will be safe, according to the proverb, Fast bind, fast find.

It was good advice, publicly aired, but generally neglected. The humorist Tom Brown almost added a postscript to it, "Thursday 24, six couple pair'd at Duke's Place near ten, repent next morning."

The Ecclesiastical Commissioners were quite correct in their assertion of 1686 that these marriages were so popular that "many thousands" had been married in these two churches. E. M. Tomlinson, in his history of the Minories, estimated that 32,000 marriages were celebrated there between 1644-95, while it has been calculated that over 40,000 marriages were celebrated at St James's between 1664-8 and 1676-92.

Apart from these two leading centres, there were other centres of minor importance at this time, including St Pancras, and the Fleet, whose popularity was yet to be realized. Lamb's Chapel, the chapel of the Clothworkers' Company in Hart Street, Cripplegate, was noted by Bishop Crompton of London as a centre for such marriages in his protest against Dr Payne's commission, and it was again noted as such in 1705. Another centre was at Ludgate Prison which apparently survived until 1710, little noticed and barely recorded, for many of the bills which advertised the various and mainly fraudulent schemes of matrimonial insurance which flourished in that year excluded couples from their benefits if they were so imprudent as to marry at the Fleet, Queen's Bench or Ludgate prisons. Lincoln's Inn chapel served a similar purpose between 1695-1709. A further centre was Sion Chapel in Hampstead, which managed to survive as a marriage centre into the 1720s, for its proprietors insisted that couples who wished to marry there should possess valid authority to do so. In an age of laxity with respect to marriage licences this was not difficult to obtain. One of the advertisements of this centre stated:

> Sion Chapel, at Hampstead, being a private and pleasant place, many people of the best fashion have been lately married there. Now, as a minister is obliged constantly to attend, this is to give notice, that all persons, upon bringing a licence, and who shall have a wedding dinner at the house or in the gardens, may be married in the said chapel without giving any fee or reward, and such as do not keep their wedding at the gardens, only five shillings will be demanded them of fees.

Other advertisements noted that a certificate of banns was as acceptable as a marriage licence.

****

The open rejection of the canons ecclesiastical and statute law by the clergy associated with these centres, and a situation in which "incredible mischiefs" were permitted, to use Archbishop Sancroft's phrase, could not be tolerated by either Church or State. Henry Compton, bishop of London in the late seventeenth century, for example, was deeply concerned to ensure that all marriages performed in his diocese were celebrated in a regular manner. He spent much time and energy in pursuing this concern, and when he was able to act he was severe in his judgment. Edward Hicheringil, rector of All Saints, Colchester, in his diocese, was required by Compton to make a public confession and recantation of his practice of solemnizing clandestine marriages, even though he required each couple to pay five shillings for a licence. Whether this was because he was not authorised to give licences, or the licences he was authorised to issue as a surrogate were used in an improper way, is not known. He was suspended for three years. He aggravated his offence not only by treating the Court of Arches with "insolent and unmannerly carriage and behaviour", exposing "it to the scorn of the rabble that attended ... there", but also by writing various pamphlets denying its authority, thus allowing "the factious and fanatical party to condemn the government of the Church ... and to persist in their errors and sedition, to the great disturbance of the peace of this Church and nation".

Although Compton was unable to effect much with regard to these privileged places, the concern was taken up by the Commissioners for Ecclesiastical Causes, a body appointed by James II. The establishment of this commission took place against the backcloth of James's attempt to restore Roman Catholicism to England, so that every action contemplated by it caused considerable fear to churchmen. This did not help to commend its work in this direction. In September 1686 the commissioners cited "Dr Hollingswalk of St Botolph, Aldgate, Mr Westand of Little Minories, and Mr Elliot of Duke's Place to give account by what authority they marry without licences, and how they are exempted from episcopal jurisdiction". On the 28th Elliot was ordered to forbear marrying any couples without a licence during the King's pleasure, and his claim to be a minister of a privileged place was accordingly dismissed.

To make their intention clearer, and to enforce their authority over a wider area than that covered by these three churches, the commissioners issued a public order in January 1687. This order was to be read in every church "immediately after the Nicene Creed". It caused a theological debate among the bishops as to whether the commission had authority to issue such an order. It was even said of Archbishop Sancroft, who "had been long desirous" that measures should be taken "to prevent so foul an irregularity" as clandestine marriage, that "in his practice [he] approved that which in his opinion [he] doubted". Yet this order did no more than simply reiterate the requirements of canon law. It stated that because of the "great mischiefs and inconveniences – even to the ruin of many families," all rectors, vicars, curates or other ministers whatsoever, were forbidden to celebrate marriages without banns being first published or a licence obtained, according to law, on pain of being suspended *ab officio et beneficio* [from office and benefice], and being further punished according to the ecclesiastical law. All those who so married would be proceeded against for contempt. The "privileged places" received a special mention in this order, as places where irregular marriages had been practised "of late years".

In spite of the monition against him and the public order, Adam Elliot and his colleagues were not to be intimidated, and continued with their practices. In a final attempt to prevent this, the three episcopal commissioners for the diocese of London, acting for Crompton who had been suspended from his duties by the Court of High Commission, ordered Elliot in February 1687 to be suspended *ab officio et beneficio* for three years and to abstain from his priestly function and office. In his place one John Pinchback was licensed as curate, but Elliot, after petitioning the commissioners, had his suspension relaxed in May, and was restored to his living.

His suspension had the desired effect of checking the number of marriages celebrated at these centres, for at Duke's Place, as a register stated, "there were no marriages from the tenth of May till the 29 day of May", while the incumbent of Trinity Minories also found it expedient to suspend operations. However, as soon as his suspension was lifted, Elliot resumed his matrimonial activities, whilst his colleague at the Minories in the following month began to marry couples at the rate of eight to ten a day. The commission, which was greatly overworked, probably had no time to check on these malpractices, although they were obviously noted in at least one quarter, for after the "Glorious Revolution" of 1689, during which the

Protestant succession to the throne of England was secured, a royal commission was granted to one Dr Payne in January 1691. Its preamble stated its cause and purpose:

> Whereas divers clandestine marriages are had and celebrated and other crimes and illegal practices daily committed in several exempt churches and chapels in and about our City of London, and we being willing ... to punish and prevent the same for the future

Dr Payne was required to visit

> All churches and chapels which are indisputably of our royal and exempt jurisdiction within our City of London and twelve miles of the same where the episcopal authority has no pretence and claim and where it hath but is contested to us as particularly in the parish churches and chapels of St James's Duke's Place, and Trinity in le Minories ... there to visit no longer ... than it shall appear by a legal determination or entire submission that they do belong to the episcopal jurisdiction ... which is no way designed to be ... hereby infringed but assisted in punishing all offences contrary to the canons.

In order to accomplish this task Payne was given the power of a visitor to enquire into these marriages, to punish the offenders by ecclesiastical censures, and to grant licences of marriage in those churches he visited "to seamen and other persons as is used in other places according to canons ecclesiastical".

Dr Payne, however, exceeded his commission and abused his trust, so that in 1695 Bishop Compton strongly protested against its continuation. He noted that as his commission had a virtually unlimited jurisdiction over various parishes in London it allowed clergy

> To collude with Dr P. and to set up pretences of exemption from the ordinaries. And Dr P. by virtue of this Commission may pretend to be their visitor, and abet their exemptions, and thereby draw benefits to himself by granting blank licences to marry &c. and to make the incumbents partakers of his gain.
>
> As in effect he has done. For the curates of the two churches above named [St James's and Trinity Minories] do refuse to submit to his authority and visitation and he takes no effectual

care to reform them but suffers them to marry clandestinely – for a person desiring a licence of him to marry in Duke's Place he replied he did not grant any licence to that church. But the Curate of Aldgate who before had owned and submitted to the jurisdiction of the Bishop of London does now by sinister collusion and agreement with Dr P. disown the jurisdiction of his diocesan, and to share part of the gains to be got by marriage licences to be granted to him by virtue of this Commission, does now own the jurisdiction of Dr P. and receives blank licences from him to marry any persons of any other parishes or dioceses whatsoever in his church. The end of this is merely to procure some part of the gain to himself, for otherwise no reason can be given why the Curate of Aldgate should choose rather to be under the jurisdiction of Dr P. than of his own diocesan.

Compton also claimed that the same applied to the curate of Lamb's Chapel.

To these protests Compton added another, namely, that this unrestricted power given to Dr Payne to grant licences "intrenched upon the episcopal authority and especially upon the prerogatives of the Archbishop of Canterbury". Indeed, he added, Payne was behaving "as if he had the power of a Vicar General to the King", especially as he was underselling the licences of the ordinaries. The archbishop also protested, stating that Payne "instead of reforming abuses, increased them", defrauded the King of the duties placed upon matrimony, and had undermined the authority of the bishop of London. The activities of both archbishop and bishop were instrumental, and Payne's commission was revoked in the same year, with the result that another attempt to close these centres failed. Dr Payne's son, by contrast, felt that the real reason for the withdrawal of this commission was not that there were any abuses in its working, but rather that a number of the bishops held that the privileges granted to his father by it were too great for any private person to hold.

****

Many bills were brought into parliament throughout this period in an attempt to end the problems associated with clandestine marriage. A bill of 1651 provided that minors who married without parental consent would forfeit most of their inheritance. Between 1670 and 1697 eight similar bills came before parliament. Each was termed a

"Clandestine Marriage Bill" and their tenor may be summed up by quoting the preamble to the 1689 bill:

> Whereas minors (having or expecting considerable portions or estates real or personal), are daily subject to be inveigled or forced away from their fathers and guardians, and thereupon do contract matrimony with persons unsuitable before they are of years capable to dispose of themselves with that discretion which is requisite, and notwithstanding the severities of former laws, yet there being no provision to annul such marriages, wicked persons presume they shall afterwards obtain the consent and reconciliation of friends, and are thereby encouraged to the said evil practices ... and whereas clandestine marriages are and have been found to be of very pernicious consequence, and have given occasion to many wicked practices and many disorders in families ...

The bills were designed to prevent these marriages by regarding them as legally null and void, so that no rights of property could accrue through them. Severe penalties were placed against those who so offended. Clergymen, "real or pretended", who married minors without parental consent could be condemned to death; those who officiated at clandestine marriages could be suspended from office and committed to the common gaol for three years; while those who issued licences to minors, knowing that they did not have parental consent, were liable to lose their office, chances of preferment, and be fined five hundred pounds. Any guardian who abused his trust would not only be liable to lose his guardianship but also a sum equivalent to one third of his ward's estate, and domestic servants who married or assisted in the marriages of their employer's children or pupils were to be imprisoned for three years. The age of consent was fixed by these bills as eighteen for males and sixteen for females.

The bills failed to pass, probably because of their severity and the fact that society was not ready for such a change in the law of marriage. This is borne out by the writer of a 1692 pamphlet, *A Representation of the Prejudices that may arise in time from an Intended Act concerning Marriages*. His argument that no secular authority had the right to void marriages, "other than by the law of Christ", was one which clearly appealed to tender clerical consciences, and clearly carried much weight.

In that same year Nathaniel Whetham, with others, offered

suggestions for the consideration of parliament designed to increase the revenue of the country. They proposed that a tax should be placed on every male married, upon every child baptised, and on every person buried, according to the wealth of their estate. They estimated that an annual revenue of £80,000 to £100,000 might be obtained from these taxes. This was an attractive proposal to a government fighting a costly war against France, and the result was that these proposals were embodied in an act of 1694, *An Act for granting to His Majesty certain Rates and Duties upon Marriages, Births and Burials, and upon Bachelors and Widowers, for a term of five years, for carrying on the War against France with vigour*. Apart from placing a tax upon every person married according to an established rate, as already noted in the previous chapter, clause LII took up the suggestion of the earlier bills which had been designed to prevent clandestine marriage, stating that "no person shall be married at any place pretending to be exempt from the visitation of the bishop of the diocese, without licence first had and obtained, except the banns shall be published and certified according to law". Every parson, vicar or curate marrying contrary to this regulation would forfeit £100 upon conviction, and for a second time would be suspended *ab officio et beneficio* for three years. This act remained in force until 1706, although the anticipated revenue, derived from such items as a tax of at least two shillings on birth or an annual tax of one shilling on bachelors, never came up to expectation, possibly because of widespread evasion, a matter which Whetham considered could be prevented by establishing a central register office. This particular proposal was not implemented until 1837!

An earlier act of 1693-4, entitled *An Act for granting Duties upon Vellum, Parchment and Paper for four years towards carrying on the War against France*, established a duty upon "every licence or certificate of marriage issued" of five shillings, and imposed a penalty of £500 on defaulters who failed to use the required "stampt paper". The penalty was reduced to £5 the next year. This act, reinforced by clause LII of the 1694 act, appeared sufficient to bring to an end the activities of the lawless churches as centres for clandestine matrimony, for it seems clear that the licences issued by their ministers were not regarded as valid under the terms of these acts.

The incumbents of these churches were not to be deterred, however, for they soon realised the loophole in this legislation. This was that the terms "parson, vicar or curate" as mentioned in the latter act did not cover every type of ecclesiastical office, and thus to avoid the penalties imposed upon them by these enactments and yet at the same time to continue their lucrative business, they permitted, as a subsequent act admitted in its preamble:

> Other ministers to marry great numbers of persons in their respective churches and chapels without publication of banns or licences of marriages first had and obtained; many of which ministers so substituted, employed, permitted and suffered to marry as aforesaid, have no benefices or settled habitations, and are poor and indigent, and cannot easily be discovered and convicted of the offences aforesaid ... by all which means the duties and impositions upon licences of marriage as aforesaid are greatly diminished and subtracted, and many other great inconveniences do arise.

The incumbents of these churches were probably encouraged too by the fact that the penalty provided of £100 was not extended to each offence they or others committed.

Consequently, a further act was passed in 1695. This extended the earlier clause LII to include all churches and chapels, exempt or non exempt, and also provided that the forfeit of £100 should apply for every offence committed. Any clergyman who employed a substitute, or suffered another to marry without banns or licence, would also be penalised in a like sum for each and every offence. In addition to these penalties a forfeit of £10 was placed on every man who was married without banns or licence, and every sexton or parish clerk who aided or promoted such marriages would forfeit £5 if convicted. The act also required that all incumbents or their curates should produce on demand to the commissioners the licences of all persons married in their churches, or the certificates declaring that their banns had been called, on pain of a further penalty of £5.

It is important to note that these acts did not affect the validity of any marriage solemnized contrary to their requirements, nor did they require the licences to adhere to the residential qualifications imposed by canon law. They were passed not because parliament wished to regulate the conduct of matrimony, but rather to safeguard the revenue devoted to the foreign policy of the country. The penalties given by these acts were not imposed primarily to punish the ecclesiastical offence committed, as to ensure payment of duty. After all, the government is said to have raised a loan of £650,000 offering as security the revenues these acts would produce.

Nevertheless, these acts sounded the death toll for the activities of these lawless churches, although their decay was more gradual than sudden. This may have been because any informer under the terms of this legislation was required to initiative a private prosecution, which was an expensive undertaking. The clerk at Trinity Minories was sufficiently cautious to insert after the register entry of each marriage performed after 2 May 1695 that it was celebrated either after a banns certificate had been produced, or a licence obtained. He did this for three years. Tony Benton notes that the same care was taken in other churches, naming in particular St Katherine by the Tower and St George Southwark. There is a suggestion that by way of compensation the incumbents of Trinity Minories and St James's were permitted to become surrogates by the bishop of London, possibly in order to obtain some degree of supervision over their activities. On the other hand, it may simply be that they organised some kind of understanding with the bishop's own registrar!

The number of marriages recorded in the registers of these two churches dropped substantially. At Trinity Minories the 1,060 marriages of 1692 fell to 477 in 1695, to 181 in 1700, and to an average of 25 from 1705 onwards. St James's faced a similar decrease. In 1690 there were 1,803 marriages, but only 123 in 1700.

Although the episcopal visitations of 1700, 1707 and 1715 reported that all was well with these lawless churches, there remained a suspicion that clandestine marriages were still being performed at them. In 1704, James Coulton, a well known Fleet marriage parson, probably to eliminate rival centres or to detract attention from his own activities, gave evidence that "at Lamb's Chapel and Duke's Place, London, the parson attending does marry without licence or certificate of banns and doesn't register which is a great loss to the Queen". He requested a commission for himself in order to inspect their registers. In 1720-1 a royal warrant was issued to John King, Master of the Charterhouse, to visit the two main lawless churches in order to stop the performance of clandestine marriages at these places and to restore them to the authority of the bishop of London. The wording of this grant is an exact reproduction of Dr Payne's earlier commission, so that no mention is made of the now well established Fleet marriages. Such a mistake in copying down the terms of a former precedent is probably the reason why nothing further is heard of this commission.

While these centres were in existence, they had a substantial effect on the number of marriages in the other London parishes, and in particular upon the surplice fees of their incumbents. Between 1680-6, St Giles' Cripplegate had an average number of 33 marriages per annum, and St Sepulchre's 24. In 1687, during the time of the intervention of the commissioners, St Giles' had 104 marriages and St Sepulchre's 70. Between 1688-95 when the clandestine marriage trade recommenced the average number of marriages at these two churches was 34 and 26 respectively, but between 1696-1700, when these clandestine marriages were in decline and before the Fleet had become well established, the average number increased to 140 and 73 respectively. In spite of the general provision, made in the various tables of parochial fees, that a woman who married outside her parish should still pay the same dues to its incumbent as if she had been married therein, probably impossible to enforce, the incumbent of St Giles' was clearly losing between £25 and £40 per annum in surplice fees because of the activities of these centres. It may well be that one of the sources of pressure against their existence came from the parochial clergy of London.

The Fleet Prison, London, in the 1780s, after its reconstruction

3
MARRIAGES IN THE FLEET PRISON, 1680-1713

The Fleet Prison, which occupied a site in Farringdon Street near to Ludgate Circus until its closure in 1842, was not only one of the oldest, but was also regarded as one of the most important and substantial of the English prisons. It was the prison for the courts of Chancery, Exchequer and Common Pleas, and also at one time for the Court of Star Chamber, as well as acting as a debtors' prison. As the office of warden (or keeper) was held in *grand serjeantry in fee simple*, that is, held by the grantee and his heirs of the king by virtue of a service performed, it was regarded as a private possession which could be sold, leased or mortgaged. Indeed, from 1588 onwards one warden in two had purchased his office. The office of warden was equally regarded as one of profit, for the prisoners were expected not only to provide for their own maintenance, but also to contribute to the costs of the prison administration and to allow the warden some financial recompense for his responsibility.

The result was that the prison became a commercial enterprise, and the wardens, anxious for a quick return on their "investment", permitted oppression and extortion on a vast scale. The consequence of this may be seen in the numerous complaints made against the prison authorities. These occasioned many enquiries into the state of the prison and its wardenship, particularly during the 1690s and the 1720s. After the last enquiry of 1729 the warden, Thomas Bambridge, who had purchased that office for £5,000, narrowly escaped a charge of murder, even though a parliamentary committee of enquiry resolved that he had permitted escapes, been guilty of "the most notorious breaches of his trust, great extortions, the highest crimes and misdemeanours in the execution of his office ... and destroyed prisoners for debt under his charge, treating them in the most barbarous and cruel manner, in high violation and contempt of the laws of the Kingdom". It estimated that the profits of the prison were £4,632 per annum.

As the Fleet was mainly a debt prison, and the law then allowed the creditor to proceed either against the debtor's estate or his person, but not both, there were many men within the prison who had substantial financial resources. Many deliberately accepted a lifetime's imprisonment in order to protect a family estate. The prison provided these men with such amenities as a tap room, a public kitchen and dining room called "Bartholomew's Fair", a coffee house and a chapel. In the courtyard facilities were provided for rackets and skittles, and several prisoners kept billiard tables in their rooms as a source of revenue. Individual chambers were available for those who could afford to pay for such privacy, which not only meant a weekly payment of half a crown as room rent, but also unspecified sums of money to other prisoners who were allocated to that room by the warden on a rota system. Many prisoners had to share rooms and beds, or even to sleep on the floor. In the 1790s it was estimated that the average cost of living in the Fleet Prison was twelve shillings per week, but this did not take into account the various fees charged on the entry and discharge of each prisoner.

The poorer debtors were required to live on the Common Side. This was kept in as poor a state as possible in order to encourage those who could afford something better to transfer to the more profitable Master's Side. The prisoners of the Common Side were able to share in various charitable bequests made to the prison, but they also had to take their turn at the begging grate which was set in the outside prison wall. Here they requested alms from passers by for the "poor prisoners".

The result of imprisonment for the so-called "honest" debtor could be disastrous. He saw his family suffer, he became aware that his imprisonment was often an act of vindictive spite on the part of his creditor, and soon he would probably share the common prison assumption that it was "just, equitable and reasonable … not to pay the creditor, but to keep his estate in gaol, to defend his own and his wife's and children's lives from perishing through want". The anonymous author of *A Speech without Doors*, published in 1731, continued: "he is soon deprived of all spirit, courage and industry, he falls into the way of living by his wits, and that sort of life is whetted by necessity". Of course, this was special pleading, for the majority of prisoners were able to take advantage of the various insolvency acts to obtain their release, but there was certainly a minority of which the above description would be true.

The prisoners did not lose contact with the outside world. Visitors were freely admitted into the prison to visit prisoners or to make use of its facilities. John Howard, the prison reformer, found butchers from the Fleet Market, then outside its walls, admitted into the prison house "as at another public house". In 1742 Warden Eyles wrote:

> All persons are at liberty to resort to the prisoners till ten at night, and as there are 200 prisoners within the walls the number of people who come there are sometimes 3,000 in a day and very often above 1,000 people come the winter time from the close of the evening till ten o'clock which makes it extremely difficult to guard against escapes.

At a later date the prison was regarded as the largest brothel in London.

The wardens of the Fleet persistently maintained that the office they held was distinct and separate from the prison house. While for the sake of convenience they chose to keep the prisoners committed to their charge by the courts at the Fleet Prison, there was no legal obligation on their part to do so, and they argued they could keep them wherever they wished provided they could produce them upon lawful demand. Continual complaints were made in the 1690s and early 1700s that the wardens permitted prisoners to travel far beyond the confines of the prison, some even suggesting that the geographical boundaries of the warden's charge took in the east and the west Indies. Warden Fox in the 1690s was known to have made a journey to Yorkshire "to look after his outlying deer", and around the same time complications arose when a Fleet prisoner, who had been permitted to visit his home town of Chepstow, was arrested there and confined in the town prison. The abuses this practice caused meant that the courts curtailed this privilege in the late 1700s, but two other privileges remained, and continued, until the prison was closed.

The *day rules* were an arrangement by which the Court of Common Pleas permitted prisoners to attend to their business in town or even beyond, provided they returned to the prison by nightfall. The privilege was confined to the days on which the court sat, and cost about five shillings a day in fees. A keeper was required to accompany the prisoner. As the warden was responsible for the debts of an escaped prisoner, all those who made use of these *day rules* were required to find securities which were always fixed in a sum greater than their debts.

Securities were also required of those who were permitted to live in the prison *rules*. This was an area outside the prison house which in the 1700s extended from the prison to the Fleet Ditch (later Farringdon

Street), thence to Ludgate Hill, along the north side of that hill until the Old Bailey was reached, both sides of that street until the entrance of Fleet Lane, and down that lane to its junction with the Fleet Ditch. All the various courts, alleyways and passages within that area were included. The origin of these *rules* is obscure, but it appears that it was first regulated by a rule of the Court of Common Pleas during the reign of James II, and affirmed by statute law in 1697. It was probably granted, or affirmed, because of the overcrowding of the prison house which caused considerable fears of pestilence through gaol fever. Its granting was thus an outcome of the non-penal nature of debt imprisonment, in that the chief emphasis lay in a prisoner's ability to find securities for his safe imprisonment. There were no fixed fees for the use of these *rules*; rather it was customary to make an initial bargain with the warden, a practice which often gave rise to charges of extortion. There were many suspicions that the *rulers* did not confine themselves to the *rules*, but wandered about wherever they pleased.

In 1729 over 382 of the prisoners had the benefit of these *rules*, forming 62.5 per cent of the total number of prisoners at the Fleet. This large number in the *rules*, together with the ordinary population of the area, meant that it was always overcrowded, and, as a result, house or room rents were always extremely high. The situation was aggravated by the number of people who entered into the "protection of the Fleet", often with the warden's connivance, in the expectation that their creditors would decline to prosecute them, assuming that they were already debt prisoners. Richard Savage, the playwright, was one of many who were advised by their friends to take lodgings in this area for that reason.

****

Marriages had been celebrated in the Fleet Prison long before it became a centre for clandestine marriage. The first recorded marriage there was in April 1611, when the registers of St Bride's Church recorded that Valentyne Lane and Mary Foxe were married "in the Flete". Another marriage of 1613 is known to have been solemnized in the prison chapel between George Lester, a prisoner, and the wealthy Mistress Babbington. This provided a comment by one Alderman Hicks that "the man will [be] able to live and maintain himself in prison, for hitherto he hath been in poor estate". There is no reason to believe that this marriage was irregular in any shape or form, and probably many other marriages were solemnized in the same chapel.

It was not until the 1680s or thereabouts that the Fleet Prison chapel became established as one of those lawless churches and chapels where clandestine marriages were performed for the convenience of customers and to the profit of their operators. Significantly, Payne's commission did not notice the Fleet, but its existence as a centre for these marriages was hinted at in the preamble to the 1695 act mentioned in the previous chapter. This noted that "divers ministers being in prison for debt or otherwise, do marry in the said prisons, many persons resorting thither for the purposes aforesaid, and in other places for lucre and gain to themselves." It was this legislation, by ensuring the closure of the other centres and the elimination of their competition, which drew attention to the Fleet as an alternative centre, and permitted it to achieve an almost total monopoly of the trade.

There were many reasons why the Fleet emerged as a centre for these marriages by the 1680s. The prison chapel had a good claim to be exempt from episcopal visitation because of the warden's insistence that the prison was his private property, and being derived from a crown grant, could only be visited by the crown. It has already been noted that there was unrestricted access to the prison house for all those who desired to enter, and several places of entertainment within which might appeal to a matrimonial party desirous of celebration. However, what was of major importance was that clergy were willing to enter the prison in order to officiate at these marriages.

It has long been thought that these marriages commenced at the Fleet because there were clergymen resident in the prison as debt prisoners. It was these men, the argument continues, unscrupulous due to their poverty and despair, who saw in the performance of these marriages a means not only for the better support of themselves and their families, but also a possible means of gaining sufficient capital to pay for their discharge, and so prevent the possibility, if they were beneficed, of forfeiting their living by their neglect of it. Charles Yorke, a son of Lord Hardwicke and the alleged author of *A Letter to the Public upon the Marriage Act*, written in 1753, provided a similar argument for those who were unbeneficed. He claimed that these men

> drew profit by performing marriages against the law, without danger of the punishment for there was no legal means of levying a fine for a man already in prison, and suspension from the exercise of ecclesiastical functions was a jest to him, who never had, nor could get, any cure ... wherein these functions might be exercised. The desperate condition of these men placed them

beyond the reach of such punishments as [the] law had prepared
for their offence.

It would be wrong to over-emphasise this argument, for there is no
documentary evidence to suggest that any of the Fleet parsons of this
early period were prisoners at the Fleet, though many, at a later date,
entered the prison on what were then described as "friendly actions" in
order to take advantage of this supposed immunity from ecclesiastical
and civil penalties.

Another factor which assisted the Fleet's emergence as a centre was
the indifference of the prison authorities to the activities of these
parsons. Throughout this period the prison was administered by deputy
wardens, some of whom were said to have been former prisoners
themselves. A better word than "indifference" might be encouragement, for the authorities would be well aware that this business would
increase the profits of the prison. The additional trade given to the tap
room and the other prison facilities by the matrimonial visitors would
mean that these places could command a higher rental. A
parliamentary commission of 1705 even alleged that some of the
prison officials, including the deputy warden, Grindall, were given a
share of the resulting fees. It is also significant in this context that two
of the later marriage house keepers were originally prison turnkeys,
namely Lilly and Ewell.

Neither did the prison chaplain stand idly by, for Robert Elborrow
officiated at some of these marriages and encouraged the others. Pepys,
a fellow schoolboy at St Paul's School, described him as "a silly
fellow". Finding him preaching at St Lawrence Poultry, where he was
curate, Pepys considered that this "simple rogue" preached "a very
good sermon, and in as right a parson-like manner, and in a good a
manner, as I have heard anybody; and the church was very full which
is a surprising consideration". This was in 1666, and 36 years later
Elborrow was described as "an ancient man, master of the chapel, and
marries but very few without banns and licence, but under a colour
doth allow his clerk to do as he pleases". For two Sunday services, at
one of which he preached, and a daily morning service, the chaplain
received a stipend of £40 from the warden, irrespective of the fact that
he was entitled to a fee of two shillings from each prisoner on entry,
and a further payment of four pence a week from each prisoner. The
warden claimed that a former chaplain had compounded these sums for
a fixed stipend as he had found it impossible to collect this money.

The actual origin of the Fleet as a centre is veiled in obscurity, for while one cannot completely exclude the possibility that there were some clergymen imprisoned there who commenced this trade in imitation of the other centres, it is more probable that clergymen who were not prisoners were permitted, encouraged or even recruited to use the prison for this purpose by either the chaplain or his clerk, Bartholomew Bassett. The early Fleet parsons had no official connection with the prison until after the legislation of 1693-5, with perhaps one exception, and one presumes they frequented the prison as visitors before this date. The only outward sign that this legislation affected the Fleet occurs in one of its registers which has been described by Tony Benton as the original register of the chapel. This register notes that from June 1696 onwards "the marriages at the Fleet Chapel, London, [were] by licence", and another note reads, "noting at the end of every line ... *Cant* stands for Canterbury and *Lon* for the Bishop of London". In 1697, one hundred and forty marriages are recorded in this register. Ten couples are noted as having been married with a certificate of banns, nine are by the licence of the bishop of London, and one hundred and ninety-nine by the licence of the archbishop of Canterbury. Such licences, if genuine, would have been obtained at the archbishop's faculty office at Doctors' Commons. Tony Benton discovered that of the twenty-three marriages contained in this register said to have been by the bishop of London's licence, five have been identified in the diocesan records. Three of them had been granted specifically for marriages at the Fleet Prison chapel, and two for marriages in city churches. Similarly, Benton checked the registers of the archbishop against ten of the Fleet entries which claimed to be by his licence. Five of them were found.

In spite of these precautions, the number of marriages fell considerably, although there was a slight initial gain caused by the virtual elimination of the other centres. The severe legislation of 1695 possibly frightened many potential customers, and may have led people to believe that the act had ended the Fleet trade. The number of marriages in one particular register of this period may be taken as a guide: in 1692 there were 174 marriages, 1693 201, 1694 285, 1695 538, 1696 445, 1697 140, 1698 74, and none in 1699. The marriages recovered by 1700, when an estimate based on the number of known register sequences suggests that at least 2,250 marriages took place. In 1702 it was reported that between 50 and 60 couples were married each week, and the 1705 commission stated that within five months 2,954 marriages had been celebrated at the Fleet. This may have been an exaggeration, although the register of King's marriage house alone records 1,162 marriages during 1709, and in 1710 altogether there was an estimated 3,600 marriages.

This recovery was undoubtedly due to the encouragement given to prospective clients by the absence of any effective attempt to end the centre or to prosecute those who took part in these marriages. It would have been discovered too that the Fleet marriages were much cheaper than the more conventional ones, as the parties were unofficially exempted from paying the fiscal demands placed on marriages and certificates. Furthermore, we may add that the 1695 act was counter-productive in any case, for by placing a fine upon the bridegroom and the clerk it effectively prevented those best qualified to give conclusive evidence of such transgressions from doing so. This was because the clerk would lose his lucrative position, and the bridegroom would call the attention of the ecclesiastical authorities to the fact that his was a clandestine marriage and so subject to ecclesiastical censure.

There even appears to have been some sort of an official recognition of the Fleet as a matrimonial centre, for in 1702 a letter to the Chancellor of the Bishop of London, the bishop's senior legal official, states that Bassett, the chapel clerk, "had sworn in 'Doctors' Commons' not to marry any without banns or licence unless it be such poor people as are recommended by the justices in case of a big belly".

The last requirement for the Fleet to emerge as a marriage centre was for the provision of clergymen ready to enter the prison or its *rules* on a voluntary basis, possibly by the use of friendly actions, and thereby gain the advantages alleged to be possessed by debt prisoners.

John Draper, who acted as a Fleet parson from 1689-1718, is shown in the books of the prison to have entered as a prisoner in May 1698, and Nehemiah Rogers, active as a Fleet parson from 1697, entered the Fleet in January 1700, but was able to proceed at large to his living at Ashington, Essex, until deprived of it in 1706. Jerome Alley is first noted as a prisoner in 1702, and James Coulton entered the prison in the same year, though he had been concerned in the marriages since 1690. Such clergy, by a judicious use of the *day rules* and the *rules*, or through a private understanding with the warden, could marry all over London and even beyond.

The prison chapel was normally used for the marriage ceremony. It was on the first floor of the main prison house. A certificate of marriage contained in one of the registers is typical of many certificates and register entries in recording that:

David Cambell and Susanna Flaxmond were married in the

Chapel of the Fleet, London, the 13th day of November 1701 according to the Rites and Ceremonies of the Church of England. Barth. Bassett, clerk.

Nevertheless, marriages did take place elsewhere in the prison, and one which was celebrated in a prison chamber in 1694 gave rise to a subsequent court case in 1705, *Morrais v. Morrais*. During its hearing a witness informed the court as to how she had enquired at the Fleet Prison for a Mrs Smith:

> Upon which the said Smith conducted the defendant through a dark place into a room up two or three steps, which was a darkish room and had two candle alight in it ... [here she saw] the said Phoebe and a gentleman in a very long coat and another man in a morning gown and cap, another person in the habit of a minister of the Church of England who the defendant took and believed to be a minister of the Church of England, and another pretty lusty man and the defendant's fellow witness Mrs Bird ... the defendant observed that the said minister was just beginning to solemnize a marriage, ... after the customs and manners of the Church of England, and the said man in the morning gown and cap gave the said Phoebe in marriage and the old lusty man officiated as clerk ... [the] marriage was solemnized between nine and ten o'clock in the morning ...

Phoebe later requested the court "not [to] look upon this case no worse on my side for being married in a prison ...".

Bartholomew Bassett was clerk of the prison chapel and he also served as the "registrar of marriages" from about 1692 until 1705. In that year he was described at Beau Fielding's trial as "a doddering man"; "if he spoke two words he could not speak a third." Robert Saunders, a prisoner, replaced him in 1706. Bassett obtained an income from fees paid him by the parsons for his services. Shellburn, one of the parsons, noted in an account that he had paid Bassett a shilling, and a further shilling for the "chapel", presumably for its hire. Bassett appears to have been a prisoner, for the prison books record in May 1698: "turned over in court and brought in an old prisoner that kept the cellar formerly, now clerk of the chapel, Bartholomew Bassett". This record suggests that he was brought in from living within the *rules*, possibly in order to renew his securities. The cellars of the prison contained the public kitchen and dining room, aptly called

"Bartholomew's Fair", which Bassett must have found useful and lucrative for the entertainment of the wedding party. In 1702 he is said to have paid a rental of £120 for this, but it was added, "he himself pays but £20 per annum for the clergy pay all the rest monthly, and if they do not pay they are threatened to be confined or outed". These activities were said to have given him an income of £200 per year "at least". It seems quite clear from this evidence that Bassett held both the "cellars" and the clerkship of the chapel at one and the same time.

Even though these marriages were a violation of the recent legislation, and a "running sore" upon the revenue expected from the taxes on marriages and the stamp duties, little was done to control or remedy them. No prosecutions were initiated, possibly because it was thought that Mr Shirley, the collector of these taxes, was bribed by the ministers and clerk not to enquire into their business, while the ecclesiastical authorities, apart from a token effort, remained quiet.

This token effort, a visitation of the prison and its clergy, took place in 1702 after a written complaint from a prisoner to Dr Newton, chancellor to the bishop of London. This is found in Appendix Four. Its scope was limited, for by ensuring that the clergy had proper credentials and that all the couples married possessed either a certificate of banns or a licence, it seemed designed more to regulate the situation than to end it, and as already suggested, it gave the Fleet marriages a quasi-official status. Its only result was that Jerome Alley, one of the ministers, fled, being unable to exhibit his letters of ordination as requested.

A committee of the House of Commons was appointed to investigate these marriages after a complaint had been received from Thomas Ashton, a Fleet prisoner. Possibly he was the same person who had complained to Dr Newton. The committee reported in 1705. It noted the existence of many abuses, apparently under the sanction of Grindall, the deputy warden of the prison. The clandestine nature of the marriages was fully established, and the registers produced for the committee were pronounced to be "sham books" rather than "the true and secret register kept there". A resolution was made that the "Queen had been defrauded of all, or the greatest part of the duties due by the several Acts", to the amount of about £1,000 annually. Yet its report was ordered to "lie on the table" and nothing was done to remedy the situation it depicted, even though it was noted that it was within the warden's power to prevent these marriages.

The concern of the ecclesiastical and civil authorities was finally expressed at the meeting of the Upper House of Convocation in 1710.

Convocation was – in one sense – the Church's parliament, and its Upper House was essentially the House of Bishops. The government, distressed by the loss of revenue, inserted into the Queen's licence to Convocation a request that it should regulate the issuing of marriage licences and take measures for the prevention of clandestine marriage. The Upper House accepted the recommendations made by a specially appointed committee, namely to establish new canons to safeguard the use and the issuing of marriage licences, and to promote an act of parliament which would prevent those clandestine marriages which could not easily "be brought within the oath of the ecclesiastical authority". Fines were suggested as a penalty for those who married in any church or chapel not mentioned in their marriage licence. It was proposed also that all those who were clandestinely married in prisons, and the clergy and clerks who assisted at these marriages, in addition to the ecclesiastical penalties, should be fined and committed as prisoners to the county gaol for one year, while any prison keeper who permitted such marriages in his prison was to be fined.

This was a practical suggestion, for if the Fleet clergy were to be imprisoned for their activities in the county gaol (which in their case was Newgate), and if the warden was to be intimidated by severe penalties from permitting the clergy to continue their activities within his prison, it might seem that the only place where clandestine marriages could flourish on a large scale and in a central area would no longer be available. In a similar way, the customers for these marriages, although undeterred by the prospect of a fine from the earlier legislation, might not be prepared to risk imprisonment for the sake of matrimony, although in view of the large numbers who resorted to the Fleet this penalty would have been almost impossible to enforce.

The legislation which followed in 1711 ignored Convocation's proposals for the regulation of licences and the penalties for the customers. It merely enacted that after 24 June 1712 all clergy who married couples in churches or chapels exempt or non-exempt without banns and licence would forfeit £100 and the cost of the suit against them. In addition the act took up Convocation's recommendation that any clerical offender who was a prisoner should be transferred to the county gaol, "there to remain charged in execution with the penalty inflicted by this Act, with all and every the causes of his former imprisonment". Any prison keeper who knowingly permitted a clandestine marriage to be solemnized in his prison would forfeit for every offence £100. These clauses were contained in a general revenue bill, sandwiched between arrangements for the licensing of hackney coaches and the relief of careless gamblers in public lotteries.

This legislation had little effect on the Fleet. This was for two reasons. First, because by the date of its enactment, few, if any, of the Fleet clergy were prisoners. Secondly, the clergy could only be proceeded against if they had been successfully prosecuted beforehand. This required a private prosecutor, but few were willing to undertake this as the costs of the action could only be recovered when a conviction had been secured. Consequently, the only damaging effect of this act was preventing any further marriages from taking place within the prison house. The prison authorities took great care to enforce this requirement. It was incorporated into the prison rules and the warden and his officers were ordered "to use their utmost vigilance" to prevent these marriages. A further expression of this concern is to be found in the numerous advertisements placed in the public papers. One, of September 1743, reads:

> Whereas the methods hitherto taken to prevent clandestine marriages at the Fleet have proved ineffectual, though legal notice hath been given by the Warden of the Fleet to such of his tenants in whose houses it is reputed such marriages have been suffered, to quit the possession thereof; therefore, and as such warning cannot have the desired effect, this public notice is given, that whoever shall make it appear to the Warden's satisfaction, that any of his prisoners shall at any time hereafter clandestinely marry, or be, in any manner however, concerned in any clandestine marriage, or suffer such marriages to be performed in his, her or their houses, or lodgings, such person or persons making discovery, shall receive a guinea reward from the turnkey of the said prison. William Manning, turnkey.

For some time, too, after the enactment of this legislation, the Fleet parsons exercised caution. Vyse, suspicious of a couple, declined to officiate at their wedding, passing them on to Draper. He, not so scrupulous, solemnized their marriage, and gave them a certificate subscribed in his name, but not in his hand, believing that this somehow exempted him from the penalties of the act. Furthermore, he placed the entry into a private register, his public register only including the entries of marriages which complied with the law. This information emerged in a court case mentioned by Lawrence Stone in his book *Uncertain Unions*, the bridegroom being Edward Griffin, later

Lord Griffin.

The real result of the act was that various developments, noticeable long before its enactment, were given an added impetus. One of these was the gradual movement of the marriages from the prison house into the *rules* and even beyond. In 1702, for example, Coulton was described as marrying couples in coffee houses and in his own house in Leather Lane, "in and about the Fleet Gate and all the Rules over not excepting any part of the city and suburbs ...". Rogers, it was alleged, "marries both within and without the chapel like his brother Coulton", as did Elborrow, one of whose marriages was at Gray's Inn Chapel, although recorded in a Fleet register. Byres, who lived at the *Sun and Falcon* in Blackfriars, also married there. Alley is known to have married a couple in his own house in Moorfields, and Bassett entered not only these outlying marriages in the Fleet registers but also issued Fleet marriage certificates for the couples concerned. One of the early registers, of 1708, thus states that "it contained the several marriages celebrated within the Rules of the Fleet and Chapel thereof". By 1710 at least two establishments in the *rules* had emerged as marriage houses, namely those run by Tuftin and King. The month before the act became operational, John Lilley, a turnkey at the Fleet Prison, opened a third house with its own "chapel" at the *Bull and Garter* alehouse adjoining the prison. During these developments Thomas Hodgkins was the clerk of the prison chapel. He liked to be known as an "attorney at law", although when occasion required he was equally happy to act as the minister. As the number of marriages in the prison chapel steadily dropped from the 308 in 1711 to the 72 of the following year, he too decided to move into the *rules*, establishing a marriage house in Fleet Lane in 1713 or 1714. Here he served as clerk and registrar until his death, when his widow Anne continued the business.

The clergy also moved into the *rules*, where they continued their already successful expedient of sheltering under the pretence of being Fleet prisoners in the expectation that this would hinder discovery and prosecution, as well as confusing the authorities responsible for the elimination of their business. This deception was commonly practised until the end of these marriages in 1754, although there was no foundation in fact for it. The State's inertia, and the problem of private prosecution already noted, could only assist the Fleet clergy, while the warden was powerless to prevent their activities as they were not his prisoners.

A natural sequence to these developments was the decay in the importance of the chapel clerk and the rise to prominence of the marriage house keeper. In the prison such men as Bassett and Hodgkins had exercised a stronghold over the Fleet clergy, for without their co-operation the parsons were unable to make use of the prison chapel or even to register their marriages in the semi-official *Fleet Register*. Indeed, it may have been due to the rigidity of Bassett or the weakness of Hodgkins that rival marriage houses were established in the *rules*. As none of the parsons had sufficient capital to obtain their own premises, or to give security for its rent, they became dependent upon these marriage houses. Some became the resident clergyman of a particular house, others freelanced for custom around the different marriage houses or the numerous taverns and private houses that eventually catered for these marriages.

One side effect, not wholly unexpected, was that the number of marriages at the Fleet temporarily declined. The estimated number of marriages for 1710 is 3,679 and for 1711 4,919, but this dropped in 1712 to 2,799 and in 1713 to 2,228. Some disruption must have been caused by their removal into the *rules*, and as a result of the legislation and the publicity it probably caused. But as soon as it was noticed that the marriages were continuing unchallenged, that they were still regarded as legally sound, and that no realistic penalties had been placed on those who were married there, the Fleet returned to its former popularity, so that the estimated number of marriages for 1720 is 4,021.

It might even be said that the Fleet marriages benefited from this legislation, for having been driven into the *rules*, its operators found that its area possessed facilities far greater than those provided by the prison. It was in a far more prominent area in which to seek business, and it was removed from the stigma of being within the walls of a prison. The problem of too many clergy using one chapel and being dominated by the tyranny of one clerk was overcome at last, though it was replaced by the problem of too many marriage houses and too few clergy to service them. In the last analysis this legislation proved to be so great a blessing to these Fleet marriages that it inaugurated the era of their greatest prosperity.

4
THE SCANDALOUS CLERGY OF THE FLEET

"He was a person who had incurred the displeasure of the bishop in whose diocese he was settled, and being unequal in power to his antagonist, had been driven to the Fleet, in consequence of his obstinate opposition, though he still found means to enjoy a considerable income by certain irregular practices in the way of his function."   Tobias Smollett: *Peregrine Pickle.*

Thomas Stackhouse, writing in 1722, claimed there existed an even worse abuse in the Church of his day than the non-residence and pluralism of many of its clergy. This was the state of its inferior clergy, few of whom would ever obtain livings of their own. These men were held in contempt because of their poverty and ignorance. In fact Stackhouse considered it was ridiculous for men to be ordained "as have less learning and knowledge than your Lordship would require in a secretary, or less honour and honesty than you hope to find in a steward". Their condition meant that they were forced to "keep mean and inferior company and to frequent such little places of refreshment, as comport with their fortune, rather than their office and vocation".

One such curate, demoralised by his poverty and despairing of preferment, was William Skelbeck. In a petition to Queen Anne he argued that the benefits of her Bounty (a church charity) "designed to extend to all, viz. to the destitute as well as to the poor", did not assist those:

> Whose misfortune and fault it is because the Church is overstocked and filled with calvinistical foreigners and domestic occasional tools, when as her own truly English and loyal sons are thrust out. [He requested that] … the destitute as well as the poor clergy may be taken care of, and that all non resident parsons or vicars … may no longer scandalously by lurking or by interest have the best curacies and lectures here [London] but be

immediately sent down to their proper cures in the country to make room for the destitute.

He requested for himself "that he may be thought worthy of a small office in the Corporation [of Queen Anne's Bounty] when settled".

Many of these destitute clergy, often unable to obtain small curacies, or forced out of them by the return, death or preferment of their incumbents, sometimes became, in the words of a contemporary bishop of Peterborough, "itinerant curates or preachers that ramble without licence or settled employ to spread faction and disorder". Norman Sykes, writing in his book *Church and State in England in the Eighteenth Century*, observes that "episcopal correspondence abounded in incidents of the discovery of curates whose rapid transference from diocese to diocese eluded the eye of archdeacons and bishops till scandal revealed their presence". A popular term for such men was "hedge parsons". A considerable number of these men settled in London, as might be expected, and some of their names and deeds are recorded in *A List of twenty-four Debauched Clergymen in London*. This was written as an anti-Jacobite document in 1698, and may be a little over-coloured, for it describes some of these men as "a pretended non-juror, keeps a seraglio of women"; "a great Jacobite and scandalously drunk"; "he begs with or without a gown"; "a cheating debauched fellow"; or leading "a very loose life"; while others formed a "great cabel of lewd divines" which met at the *Castle and Sun* tavern in Fleet Street.

It is from this class of clergy that the Fleet parsons emerged. Two of them, Coulton and Byres, were mentioned on this list, although two others on the list, Nicholson, described as living "by private marriages and such ways" near Finsbury "at the prison house", and Giles Wilcox, suspended from a Norfolk benefice for celebrating clandestine marriages, do not appear to have served at the Fleet.

Many of the Fleet parsons had started well. Several of them had been educated at one of the two universities. Nehemiah Rogers, son of a distinguished clergyman who had been a prebendary of Ely Cathedral and rector of St Botolph, Bishopsgate, took his degree at the Queen's College, Oxford, in 1678. Robert Cuthbert, son of a rector of East Hendred, received his degree from New Inn Hall, Oxford, in 1711. John Gaynam, son of "S. J. of Salopia, pleb.", matriculated at Christ Church in 1689, and although he never received his degree, described himself as "a student of Oxford" in one of his many publications. The number of Cambridge graduates included Samuel Backler, James

Coulton, John Draper, Anthony Hanson, Edward Marston, Thomas Ryder, and Daniel Wigmore. Peter Symson, who frequently declared himself as "educated at the University of Cambridge and late Chaplain to the Earl of Rothes", matriculated but never graduated, as did Mottram, though in his case the reason is known, as "he turned Papist and afterwards recanted".

A few of these clergy had held livings, the value of which in every case was extremely low. Interestingly two, possibly three, of the more prominent of the early clergy held livings in the rural deanery of Rochford, Essex, in the diocese of Rochester. Rogers was rector of Ashingdon from 1687 until his deprivation for marrying clandestinely in 1706. Its annual value of £44 was found so meagre that in 1696 he was permitted to serve in "the cure of Much Stanbridge near Rochford in Essex with an allowance of ten shillings a Sunday". James Coulton was rector of Stanbridge from 1680 until about 1704, when he was deprived for his "ill practices". This parish was valued at £42. Edward Roberts, vicar of Rayleigh and South Benfleet in the same deanery during the 1700s bears the name of a Fleet parson of that period.

John Draper held the livings of Stegsden and Steventon in the diocese of Norwich from 1677 until his deprivation in 1712. It appears this was because he had married his deceased wife's sister, contrary to canon law, and had refused to separate from her. A copy of the episcopal visitation for these parishes in 1707 is written in one of his Fleet registers. It points to a neglected parish with two Easter communicants in one church and eighteen in another. Over three hundred inhabitants out of a total of eight hundred were members of dissenting churches.

John Savage declared in a court case that he had been suspended from two small livings in Nottinghamshire in 1731 for marrying a couple clandestinely. His successful plea of poverty prevented a prosecution by the Stamp Office, although its threat "obliges him to abscond for fear of going to a gaol, be being very poor and having upon all occasions shown the utmost zeal for his Majesty's government". So reads his petition. Samuel Backler, rector of Bartlesden in Bedfordshire, in 1727, may have been a Fleet parson of that name. There is no record of his deprivation, a penalty which appears to have drawn many clergy to the Fleet.

Two alternatives to a curacy were available for those clergy who were unable to obtain a benefice, these being an appointment as a naval chaplain or promotion to a colonial living. Thomas Crawford, later a Fleet parson, wrote accordingly in a letter addressed to the bishop of

London in 1703, expressing the hope of such an appointment, and added that he placed "himself entirely to your Lordship's commands concerning his service either in the plantations or on board Her Majesty's fleet", the bishop having responsibility for both. Others who served at the Fleet followed his example. In 1678 James Coulton was chaplain of the *Antilop*; Daniel Wigmore is mentioned as a naval chaplain in 1727; Richard Mason, describing himself as "chaplain of the *Maidstone* man-of-war", married couples at the Fleet in 1745, while James Lando mentioned in his advertisement that he had served his country "gallantly" as chaplain of the *Falkland*. The ship's logbook for his period of service, 1744-6, reveals that it was mainly concerned with routine duties with little hint of danger of battle.

Edward Marston was one of the Fleet clergy who had held a colonial living, having been admitted into "the ministerial function in Carolina". In that year he published a book on simony and sacrilege in which he described himself as an "unworthy priest of the Church of England, sometime of Whitby in Yorkshire". Thirteen years later Marston issued another pamphlet in which he described his sufferings. He had been ejected, he claimed, by trickery from his living of St Philip, Charlestown, in South Carolina, and thereby lost a stipend of £200, a manse with seventeen acres of glebe, and two negro slaves. An itinerant ministry had followed in Port Royal Island and at Bermuda until he settled as minister of St Andrew's, Ashly River, only to be driven out by similar tactics. Other clergy who served in the colonies and whose names are identical to those of Fleet parsons are the already mentioned Thomas Crawford, who in 1703 was a minister in Pennsylvania; John Mottram, who was sent to Virginia in 1714, and John Becket who was in Virginia by 1727.

Those parsons who possessed neither livings, colonial or naval chaplaincies remained as curates and existed upon a nominal stipend and an uncertain tenure of office. John Wagstaffe, in order to be ordained, was prepared to go no higher than deacon's orders, his Letters Testimonial (a document required to be signed by three beneficed clergyman stating his fitness for ordination) having this clause added: "He will be bound with a surety never to go higher, and the thing he aims at is but £6 per annum, only to read prayers". John Stainton, of St Bees in Cumberland, was curate of South Stambridge in Essex in 1727, for which he received a stipend of £40 per annum from his incumbent with the proviso added, "if the surplice fees &c. fall short of, I hope in time to be able to make up". This letter also contained a reference to a "Mr Colton" who was requested to sign one of the documents required by Stainton for his ordination. This may have been James Coulton's son, for this was the parish of which Coulton had once been rector. Peter Symson, when asked at the trial of Robert Archer for bigamy in 1752, "Have you ever had a benefice?", replied, "Never in my life, I have had but little petty curacies twenty or thirty pounds per year. I don't do it for lucre or gain". Similarly, Gaynam, asked in another bigamy trial whether he was not "ashamed to scandalise his character", answered, "I do not choose it, but I am old and infirm and am not able to get any preferment". In 1736 he stated that he had been a schoolmaster and curate in Bow by Stratford twenty years previously. Many other curates followed his practice of supplementing an income by school mastering. John Floyd was granted a licence "to instruct boys in grammar at West Ham in Essex" in 1714, and Thomas Ryder opened a private boarding school in Manchester. Both these men were Fleet parsons.

Although the exceptions received great publicity, the majority of the Fleet clergy were lawfully ordained. A writer in *The Grub Street Journal* noted with surprise a person he saw near the Fleet, who with "flowered morning gown, a band, hat and wig" appeared to be so neat and properly dressed:

> That I took him for some worthy divine, but upon enquiry was surprised at being assured that he was one T.... C...... , a watchmaker, who goes about in minister's dress, personating a clergyman, and taking upon him the name of doctor, to the scandal of the sacred function.

Another person, brought to the Guildhall Court dressed in clergyman's habit and charged with begging, was described as:

> A notorious idle fellow, and a common cheat, having made use of that habit only to impose on the public, as able to perform the office of marrying several persons at the Fleet Prison, whereupon he was committed to Bridewell to hard labour.

The orders of Jerome Alley were probably assumed, for he fled rather than produce his papers of ordination during the prison visitation of 1702. A letter written by the bishop of Exeter to the archbishop of Canterbury in 1674 may refer to him. The bishop wrote that having discovered two persons with "counterfeit orders":

Last week one of them appeared, and after a little discourse, confessed the cheat and who was the artist that had made them, and received five pounds for his knavery. He was cunning enough to fly out of the diocese before I returned home. I heard he was gone to Somersetshire, whither I sent after him, but he is fled from thence, out of my reach, so that I thought it necessary to acquaint your Grace with it. His name is Jeremy Alley, who served a cure in Devonshire a year or two, and then left his place to this person, who I discovered last week, and made these orders of priesthood for him. I humbly desire your Grace's direction, what I shall do with this silly man, that is yet in my reach. I threatened to pursue him upon the statutes, but he is worth nothing.

Edward Ashwell's orders were also alleged to be forged. William Hodgson, vicar of Southam in Warwickshire, wrote to his brother on 21 June 1725 stating that in his absence from his parish Ashwell:

Got possession of our school and preached in several churches in this neighbourhood ... I take the liberty of informing you since he is at Kettering ... he is a most notorious rogue and imposter, ... having two wives alive at this present time, and he was very near marrying the third in this town, but the fear of a prosecution upon the discovery of the flaming and scandalous immoralities of his life forced him away from us. In a short time afterwards in a village not far from us he attempted to ravish a woman but was prevented by a soldier then in the house. I can assure you he is in no orders though the audacious villain preaches where he can get a pulpit. I have a whole packet of letters by men, all tending to the same character, which I think for variety all manner of enormous practices that can be charged upon the very scum of mankind, the accounts are from persons of integrity and known reputation. I prevented him preaching one day at Brauston, Mr Some's parish. It would be a very kind and Christian office to give some intimation among the clergy that they may not be imposed upon by him ...

It was frequently alleged that the Fleet parsons were invariably prisoners in the Fleet Prison. As we have noted, this was true of some of the earlier parsons who became prisoners, often through "friendly actions", as it was also true of a few of the later parsons, who either entered the prison as debt prisoners or as prisoners on civil charges connected with matrimonial offences. In the former category three may be noted, John Vyse, Henry Gower, and James Lando.

John Vyse's career has been well documented by Lawrence Stone in his book *Uncertain Unions*. A youthful indiscretion led to a clandestine marriage at Lichfield Cathedral and ruined a prospective university career. Eventually ordained in Cork, Ireland, he and his wife separated, and he moved to London and contracted a bigamous marriage at the Fleet. Arrested for debt in 1707 he removed himself to the Fleet Prison by the writ of *habeas corpus*, took advantage of its *rules*, and began to marry couples both in the prison chapel and in the *rules* outside. He was making a handsome living, when his first wife and her family caught up with him and threatened proceedings for bigamy. This was averted by the usual practice of giving her an allowance for her maintenance.

Henry Gower was another parson who made use of this writ of *habeas corpus* to enable him to transfer to the Fleet Prison from Hereford Gaol, where he was held for debt. This was established in a court case when Elizabeth Dent claimed "Dr" Gower had married her to Charles Bentley at the Fleet. Her claim was not upheld, in spite of much perjured evidence, as the marriage was alleged to have taken place three months before Gower was admitted as a prisoner at the Fleet.

James Lando entered the prison in November 1747, charged in debts of £60 and upward. He had the benefit of the *rules* until his discharge under an Insolvent Debtors' Act in the following September. In addition the names of John Tarrant, imprisoned in 1733, and Thomas Crawford, imprisoned from 1748-9, are identical to those of Fleet clergy.

A number of established Fleet parsons also became prisoners at the Fleet Prison on civil charges connected with matrimonial offences. James Wagstaffe was a prisoner from September 1727 until his death the following May. Daniel Wigmore entered the prison in February 1735 through his involvement in the case of *Hill v. Turner*, but was released in the following month by order of the Court of Chancery upon the payment of costs totalling one pound and thirteen shillings. Michael Barratt became a prisoner in October 1738 for his participation in the marriage of the infant Edes, while Edward Ashwell left the prison after a month's imprisonment in July 1737 through his involvement in the marriage of a ward of court. His plea that he was heartily sorry for his offence, had a sickly family, and was in poor health himself, appears to have hastened this discharge. These are the only instances known of Fleet clergy being prisoners in that prison after the 1712 legislation, and there is no evidence that any of them solemnized marriages during the period of their imprisonment.

The clergy invariably denied these allegations of being Fleet prisoners whenever they were made, particularly during the various trials occasioned by these marriages. Symson, asked in 1752 whether he was a prisoner in the Fleet replied rather lackadaisically, "I can't say I am"; Anne Hodgkins asked for details of James Starkey answered that he had lodged with her for nine years, but "he was not a prisoner", and Dare spoke of living in Fleet Lane, but "was not a prisoner". Many of the parsons are known to have lived outside the *rules*, for which offence their securities would have been forfeited had they been prisoners. Lando lived at a French pastry cook's in Church Street, Soho; Dare at Bell Court in Bow Churchyard; Floyd at Mint Street, Southwark, and Wyatt at Holborn Bridge. This allegation of the connection of the marriages with the prison was prominently refuted in a petition of the Fleet prisoners themselves in 1745-6, when they answered an objection made to their request that the *rules* should be extended in area. The objection was that if this extension was granted, then the Fleet marriages would be spread over a much wider area. The prisoners accordingly replied:

> The objector's can't pretend but that these immoralities are more owing to those who are no prisoners who come occasionally and voluntarily within the verge of the prison than to those whose constant residence is unfortunately confined to the limits of that prison, and whose circumstances can never supply them with that means of pursuing such scandalous immoralities.

Their argument continued:

> Certain artful persons and pliers (not prisoners), having for a long time past herded about the city gates of the Fleet Prison to catch such unthinking persons as come into that neighbourhood to be married and finding their account in it, have by succession carried on that infamous practice and still continue to do so with impunity ... [they] beg leave to assure your Lordships that not one of the parsons who marry uncanonically in or about the rules of the Fleet Prison or of the pretended clerks, who assist those parsons at such marriages or of the pliers for weddings that infest the streets as setters for these parsons and clerks, are prisoners, but on the

contrary those parsons, clerks and pliers live and marry at houses out of the rules, as well as in several of the rules not occupied by prisoners which evil neither the warden not the prisoners can prevent ...

It may be suggested, therefore, that the Fleet clergy became involved in this matrimonial trade by reasons of poverty, lack of preferment, and sometimes as a result of ecclesiastical discipline. They found this matrimonial business a useful way of exercising their function and one that offered a more attractive prospect in the way of remuneration than the clerical poverty of their contemporaries. Many of them were ashamed of their way of life. Gaynam, asked in court as to whether he was not ashamed to have officiated at a clandestine marriage, bowed his head, and repeated the tag of Ovid, *video meliora, deteriora sequor* [I see the better way, I follow the worse]. Symson, requested to inform the court why he had married a couple clandestinely, replied, "because somebody would have done it if I had not". Dare was also troubled, and advised himself to

Read part of the LII psalm and part of the 55th from 12 to 16 and lay your hand upon your heart and say that a highwayman is a very honest man [compared] to you.

Draper wrote a piece of doggerel verse about his "life of sin" which ends with the couplet, "thy vile companions are nursing thee in evil, and smoothly pave thy way to meet the devil". Walter Wyatt, perhaps even more troubled, wrote on the front and back covers of one of his pocketbooks the following memoranda:

Give to every man his due and learn the way of truth.
This advice cannot be taken by those that are concerned in the Fleet marriages, not so much as the priest can do the thing that is just and right there unless he designs to starve ... For by lying, bullying, and swearing to extort money from the silly and unwary people you advance your business ...
The fear of the Lord is the beginning of wisdom, but marrying in the Fleet is the beginning of eternal woe.
May God forgive me what is past and give me grace to forsake a wicked place where truth and virtue can't take place unless you are resolved to starve. If a clerk or plier tell a lie you must vouch it to be as true as the Gospel, and if disputed you must affirm with

an oath to the truth of a downright damnable falsehood.

Though we might regard such remarks with cynicism, it is clear that a number of the Fleet clergy made every effort to leave the place and find employment elsewhere. A petition written in Ashwell's hand and contained in one of his notebooks was addressed to Lord Winchelsea and the Lords Commissioners of the Admiralty. It declared that he had "an earnest desire of serving His Majesty to the utmost of his power", and having previously served as a naval chaplain, and being informed of several vacancies, begged one for himself. He noted in another one of his books a vacancy for a schoolmaster in Broad Street Charity School, London. James Lando, clearly a Fleet parson before 1744, managed to leave the Fleet in that year as a result of his appointment as a naval chaplain. Discharged in 1746, he appears next as a debt prisoner in the Fleet Prison between November 1747 and September 1748. It was only during the autumn of that year that the amount owed him for his naval service, £200, was paid to one Mrs Whitney, identified as a marriage house keeper. Lando continued as a Fleet parson until 1752, his bid permanently to leave the Fleet for a more congenial sphere of clerical service having proved unsuccessful.

In spite of this distaste for their function, the financial rewards could be substantial, and may have been the reason why consciences were easily appeased. As early as 1723 *The British Gazetteer* alleged that one parson made about £500 per annum from "divinity jobs". Unfortunately for us only two of the parsons gave sufficient details of their financial affairs in their notebooks to enable some estimate to be made of their income. These were Dare and Wyatt, both prominent Fleet clergy. In 1741-2 Dare noted the income he received as his share of the marriage fee, and this indicates that his total income for a period of twelve months and one day was £215. In 1743 his share of the marriage fees amounted to £256. Wyatt had an even better income, as may be seen from the weekly amounts he recorded from September to November 1748. In that September he received £45, in October £57, and in November £51. On this basis Wyatt was receiving an annual income of well over £500, an income which would place him in the top five per cent of clergy earners at that time! No wonder that Mark Herber discovered that when he died in 1750 he left a small estate in Oxfordshire.

This position only applied to the more successful. Some of the earlier parsons were kept by a marriage house keeper for a small salary, and many of the later ones searched for means of supplementing their meagre income. Wigmore attempted to sell liquor without a licence; Lando advertised that he "teacheth Latin and French &c. three times a week", and that he kept a collection of registers available for inspection. Furthermore, their notebooks often recorded their frequent debts to the marriage house keepers.

In spite of their condemnation of these marriages, the Fleet clergy not only permitted members of their own families to marry at the Fleet, but had little hesitation about solemnizing their own marriages by such a ceremony. Anthony Hanson, misleadingly described as "minister of the parish of St Sepulchre", married in 1730 Margaret Hooper of the same parish; William Meredith, "clergyman", married Maria Pickup of St James's parish in 1722, and *The Old Whig* newspaper for 14 April 1737 recorded the following:

> Yesterday, Parson Gaynam, near 80 years of age, very remarkable for having coupled 36,000 persons in the Liberty of the Fleet, was himself married in the same liberty to his servant maid, who has lived with him upwards of fourteen years.

It is hardly surprising that men whose general reputation was bad endeavoured to appear as distinguished as possible. The Fleet clergy dressed in the conventional clerical gowns and bands, and styled themselves "doctors". Not all succeeded in this impression, for Thomas Pennant recalled:

> A squalid profligate figure, clad in a tattered plaid night gown, with a fiery face, and ready to couple you for a dram of gin, or a roll of tobacco.

These remarks, although inaccurate about the cost of matrimony, were yet kinder than many other contemporary critics allowed. Rogers was termed "a person of ill character" who lived for "drinking, whoring and swearing"; Byres was described as "a profane fellow", and Gaynam, termed by Henry Fielding as "the never to be forgotten Dr Gaynam, operator in marriages", was frequently abused in spite of his assertion in his book published in 1722, *Cato's Principles of Self Preservation and Public Liberty*, that "to despise clergy is to dishonour the BEING who sent them". In 1735 the Grand Jury "represented to the court that Gaynam was a scandal to his function and requested that some method might be taken to suppress his iniquitous proceedings". The nicknames given to him were frequently mentioned in the proceedings of this court, namely "the wry necked parson" or the "bishop of hell". The latter name was given by W. H. Draper to another one of the parsons in his poem, *The Morning Walk*, of 1751, although it was in popular use for Gaynam who had died some years earlier. This poem described the drunkenness and debauchery so often associated with these parsons, "who pass in brawls, lewd jests and drink the days". *The Grub Street Journal* contains many references to the quarrelsome nature of these parsons and their love of swearing. In 1732 it reported that a Fleet parson had been convicted of "forty-three oaths", which it thought rather hard on him as this made "his wit and politeness penal". In December 1734 its editor inserted the following piece of doggerel:

> On Wednesday two Fleet parsons preferred against each other
> Bills of Indictments for assault, made by brother upon brother,
> But they both appearing aggressors and scholars alike famous,
> The jurors returned both their bills 'Ignoramus'.

Two years later the Journal published a letter which referred to Joshua Lilly, one of the more important of the marriage house keepers, whom the writer saw:

> Cursing, swearing and raving in the street in the time of divine service, with a mob of people about him, calling one of his fraternity (J. E.), a player for weddings, an informing rogue, for informing against one of their ministers for profane cursing and swearing, for which offence he paid three pounds odd money, the hearing of which pleased me very well, since I could find one in that notorious place which had some spark of grace left, as was manifested by the dislike he showed to the person that was guilty of the profanation of God's sacred name.

An entry in Ashwell's notebook for that same year is typical of many other incidents noted and recorded: "Gaynam mobbed struck and abused me, gave me a blow on the breast about two of the clock of the afternoon".

The moral standard of these men was low, and it was equally so within the field in which they specialised. Ashwell was accused of bigamy and rape; Alley is said to have possessed three wives; Vyse's "whore" is mentioned, and Mrs Blood, who was a player for marriages in 1729, is described as Dr Floyd's mistress. Nevertheless, charity of judgment should prevail, for it was necessity which brought these men to the Fleet and forced them to remain in a business probably odious to their higher instincts. Degraded by their circumstances and surroundings, they took from necessity the lowest standards of their companions and so sank even further from the dignity of their calling. Their position must be set alongside those of the "inferior" clergy of the period, of whose circumstances Thomas Stackhouse wrote so eloquently, and whose words were quoted at the beginning of this chapter. While the Fleet clergy were not blameless, the high hope of their calling was never realised by a Church dominated by vested interests rather than by pastoral concern.

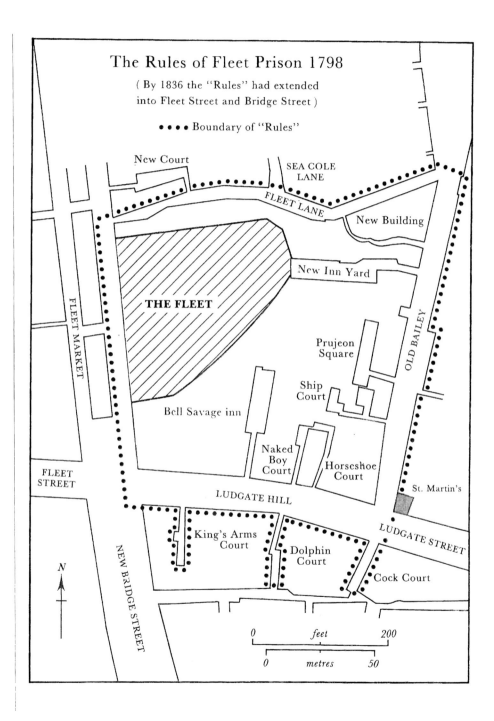

The Rules of Fleet Prison 1798

(By 1836 the "Rules" had extended
into Fleet Street and Bridge Street)

•••• Boundary of "Rules"

New Court

SEA COLE
LANE

FLEET LANE

New Building

New Inn Yard

THE FLEET

FLEET MARKET

Prujeon
Square

OLD BAILEY

Ship
Court

Bell Savage inn

Naked
Boy
Court

Horseshoe
Court

FLEET
STREET

LUDGATE HILL

St. Martin's

King's Arms
Court

Dolphin
Court

LUDGATE STREET

Cock Court

N

NEW BRIDGE STREET

| 0 | feet | 200 |

| 0 | metres | 50 |

5
THE MARRIAGE HOUSES AND THEIR KEEPERS

After the legislation of 1711 the marrying trade moved from the prison chapel into the *rules*. It has been noted already that even before this date such houses at Tuftin's and King's were catering for this trade in the *rules*, and that the parsons married couples all over London. Many of these marriages took place in such premises as taverns and alehouses. This is not surprising for it has been calculated that during this period one in every ten houses in London served as a brandy or gin shop, and in 1745 it was alleged that within the area of the *rules* alone there were between thirty and forty public houses. Many such houses in the *rules* were utilised for this marrying trade, although not all of them can be described as marriage houses. This description was reserved for those houses whose owner or keeper had a special relationship with a parson, or where the house by its furnishings and by its possession of a register could lay claim to such a title.

Either in anticipation of that legislation or as its result, other marriage houses opened in the *rules*, including those of Hodgkins and Lilly. By 1717 they had been joined by the *Turk's Head*, the *Three Tuns* in Fleet Lane, the *Swan*, the *King's Arms* and the *Crown* in the Old Bailey. As there was no statutory penalty imposed on the marriage house keepers, unless they acted as clerks, they were able to carry on their trade with impunity, and their situation was assisted by the poverty of the parsons which necessitated their dependence upon them. Nevertheless, the marriage trade was only incidental to their real business, for as most of the houses were either alehouses or taverns their main concern was the supply of refreshments to the wedding parties. As such Henry Gibson kept the *Elephant and Castle* in Fleet Lane, a prominent house, as a beer shop; Crossier kept the *Hoop and Bunch of Grapes* in Holborn Bridge as a place where wine and tobacco was sold; Burnford sold punch and brandy at his house, and John Lilly kept an alehouse as well as acting as a turnkey to the Fleet Prison. Some of the keepers, however, had a different relationship to the prison, being on the warden's list of prisoners. Samuel Pickering was keeper of the *Fighting Cocks* in Fleet Lane in 1725, though he was at the same time a prisoner in the Fleet. Thomas Bennett, the name of another marriage house keeper, was one of his creditors, along with John Evans, the name of a Fleet parson, and his own name, which probably indicates some sort of a friendly action. The same Thomas Bennett was also a debt prisoner from 1723 until 1728 at least. John Burnford of the *Noah's Ark* was a prisoner from 1733 and was still there in 1737, and George Gillet of the *Swan*, Fleet Market, was a prisoner from 1752. Other keepers were imprisoned for contempt of court, although their businesses were able to continue without interruption. The picture which emerges, therefore, is one of a small group of householders who, living in the *rules*, opened up their houses as marriage houses as a means of supplementing their income as trades people, and being able to continue their business even if they were imprisoned for debt at the Fleet Prison.

Many of these marriage house keepers had had some tangible connection with the marriage trade before becoming keepers. Matthias Wilson, for example, commenced his career as clerk to Lilly, but from 1727-35 he kept the *Hand and Pen and Golden Pot* in Fleet Ditch as a marriage house. Mrs Barratt, the widow of one of the parsons, inherited his registers, and established herself as a keeper at her home in Bride Lane, being in some form of partnership with Lilly. "Madam" Crooks was the widow of one James, and took over his business as a keeper around 1740, and in a similar way Mrs Anne Hodgkins had taken over her husband's business at the *Hand and Pen* in Fleet Lane, although she seems to have effactually managed it for several years prior to his death. William Wyatt was the brother of Walter, a prominent parson, while the son of at least one keeper followed his father into the trade. This was Wilson, keeper of the *Bates* coffee house, described as "young Wilson", who either succeeded his father or established his own house. Several of the parsons, notably Lando and Wyatt, also had their own marriage houses.

Burnford, who lived at the *Noah's Ark* in Half Moon Court off Ludgate Hill, represented that type of householder who made use of his opportunities by establishing his home, or brandy shop, as a marriage house. He was conspicuous for his claim to be "Clerk of the Fleet", although his reputation according to Parson Gaynam was that of a "rogue" who would cheat his customers. He certainly cheated the parsons. Ashwell's assertion that "God knows that I very dare to swear that he was in my debt even in that very small account" is typical of many comments found in their notebooks about him. Burnford died about 1747-8 after an illness of several years, during which the business at his once popular house seriously declined.

The Lilly brothers, John and Joshua, worked closely together. As both of them are termed "Lilly" it is sometimes impossible to distinguish between them. These two brothers had between them what probably amounted to the leading position among these keepers, running such establishments as the *Fountain*, Ludgate Hill, the *Bull and Garter* and the *Hand and Pen* by Fleet Bridge, and probably Mrs Barratt's house as well. Joshua, by claiming to have bribed the Lord Chancellor £1,000 for his self-inflicted office of "Clerk of the Fleet" (a matter which must have been a source of dispute between himself and Burnford), also acted as a general registrar, and so exerted a considerable influence over many of the minor marriage houses and clergy. In this capacity Joshua registered marriages at such places as the *Bell* alehouse; the *Swan* in Salisbury Court; The *Red Lion* at Bridewell; Rudd's at *Belle Sauvage* Yard, or the coffee house in Sword and Buckler Court off Ludgate Hill. The reputation of these brothers was infamous, for they shared all the worst characteristics of the Fleet marriage brokers. The parsons' accounts are full of Joshua's abuses: he forged their signatures to certificates of a rather dubious nature, allowed false certificates, and cheated the clergy, plyers and customers. Thus Ashwell, on the occasion of the marriage of William Moore of Deptford to Mary Bayley, wrote: "the woman wanted a certificate and gave 1s.6d. [and] by mistake half a guinea with the shilling and sixpence which he immediately brayed off before Burnford and myself". Another parson wrote in 1736:

> Josh Lilly swore two oaths, viz. damn my life blood, four oaths damn my blood, after that swore twelve oaths God damn my blood, he would not hurt any person and at the same time he had a warrant against Mr Ashwell and Mrs Frithes and would discharge them without going before a justice if they would pay for the warrant and discharge ... One hour after swore that he would not agree but would go before the justices; which was the desire of Mr Ashwell knowing that he had not offended ...

A further comment was made some years later:

> N.B., on Sunday November 6, 1740, at the hour of eight in my house Lilly declared that if he had not gone out of the country being fled for punishment (having cut off his hair to prevent being

known) that the indictment for marrying James Hurey to Miss
Henrietta Arnold he had been ruined but that he swore it off and
the attorney promised to defend him and it cost him only a treat of
ten shillings, had I stayed says the said Joshua Lilly where I was,
the Indictment would have stood good against me but my taking
the side of the prosecution ... I have got it safe off ...

The *Sessions Papers* for 1733 records Joshua's prosecution of two men
for theft from his shop. He was taken into custody as his evidence
appeared false and groundless, but he was later acquitted upon a
technicality of "wilful and corrupt perjury". All the worst excesses of
the marriage house keepers may be seen in this informer and perjurer,
for Joshua exploited his situation to the extreme limits, and by
permitting a whole series of abuses exposed himself and all those
involved with him to considerable risks.

It was not unnaturally these marriage houses had a market value and they
frequently changed hands. Walter Wyatt, a minister who possessed his
own marriage house, thus advertised under the sign of the royal arms:

> Mr Wyatt, Minister of the Fleet, is removed from the *Two Sawyers*
> the corner of Fleet Lane (with all his register books), to the *Hand
> and Pen* near Holborn Bridge, where marriages are solemnized
> without imposition.

A further advertisement reads:

> Mr Wyatt, Minister of the Fleet, gives this public notice, that his
> Chapel for Marriages, is between the Rose Inn and White Horse
> Inn near Holborn Bridge, two lamps at the door. N.B. take care
> you don't mistake by a *Hand and Pen* near the Bridge.

As Wyatt moved into other premises others took over his former
houses and retained them as marriage houses in competition against
him. This and other examples make it clear that once a house had
become established as a marriage house it rarely changed its function.
A list of the ownership of the various houses is given in Appendix
Three.

It was considered in 1755 that every second or third house in the
rules was used for the purposes of the marriage trade. Although the
trade tended to gravitate to the alehouses and brandy shops, all sorts of
premises were utilised, including coffee houses, private houses,

individual chambers, and even on one occasion a coffin maker's shop. In many of these places a private room was set aside for the ceremony, although the leading houses normally possessed a specific room for this purpose, often dignified by the term "chapel". At Burnford's it was called "the great room", but Lando, a parson who lived for a time at Half Moon Court, called his room "St John's Chapel", while another was termed "St Bride's New Chapel". John Lilly described his room at the *Bull and Garter* in 1717 as a chapel tolerated by the bishop of London, and Mottram used a room he called "The Lord Mayor's Chapel". This was furnished with chairs, cushions and "proper conveniences" according to a report in a 1719 pamphlet, *Reasons for Passing the Bill to Prevent Clandestine Marriage.*

In order to give some idea of the variety of premises used for these marriages, the names of the houses utilised in Fleet Lane as recorded in the registers and notebooks during the period 1725-45 are given below, together with the names of a number of the leading marriage houses in the locality. It should be noted that not all the houses in those streets where the *rules* were situated may actually have been within the limits of these *rules*, and some houses may well be recorded under several different names or descriptions. Others may have been situated in the numerous courts and alleyways which led from these streets.

Fleet Lane was never an attractive area, although it possessed more marriage houses than any other of the Fleet thoroughfares. The leading houses were few in number: the *Two Sawyers* on the corner of Fleet Lane once possessed by Wyatt and later by Smith; the *New Market House* of Roberts and later of Foster, and Harlings, a barber's shop. The other houses recorded as being used for these marriages are as follows: the *Anchor and Crown*, the *Angel* owned by Spicer, the *Angel and Crown*, the *Appletree*, *Baccus*, the *Barley Row*, the *Barley and Magpie*, the *Bear,* "Beddealls", the *Bell*, a bellow makers, the *Black Horse*, Mr Britton's, the *Bunch of Grapes*, Mrs Clerk's, "coffee house", "at a coal shop", Mr Collier's a barber, Mr Cousins', the *Crown*, Mr Curtises', the *Dolphin and Crown*, Jonathan Ferrells', the *Fighting Cocks*, Mrs Ford's, Mrs Fergis', Fridays', Mr Gordon's, the *Green Hatch*, the *Half Moon*, the *Hand and Pen and Two Sawyers*, Mr Herbin's, the *Highlander*, King a barber, Leverets', Mrs Moor's, Orlin another barber, Olland's, the *Red Lion and Ball*, Rigg's, Rose Court, the *Rose*, "next door to the Rose", the *Row Barge*, Mr Sawyer's, Robert Spincks a butcher, Madam Stante, the *Three Tuns*, Walkers a cake baker, "at your washerwoman's", John Withers's chamber over against Mr Hoskins, the *White Hart*, the *White Horse Inn*, *Wilkins*

Head, Wilk's, Williams', Wilsons' and Wood's.

The majority of the leading marriage houses were at Fleet Ditch, later renamed as the Fleet Market in the 1730s, after the "river" had been culverted. These houses included the *Wheatsheaf* of Sands, the *Rainbow* coffee house, the *King's Arms* owned by Harling in 1740, Wilson's *Hand and Pen and Golden Pot*, the *Hand and Pen* owned by Cox in 1730 and eleven years later by Mrs Sarah Bennett, Boyce's *Hoop and Bunch of Grapes*, and the *Swan*, Fleet Market, run by George Gillet, but previously owned by Bromhall. Ludgate Hill was a fashionable and more expensive area. The only important houses were in Half Moon Court which was on the northern side of the street. These were Burnford's house and Lando's chapel, both already mentioned. Other houses used occasionally in this area included the *British* coffee house, the *Ludgate* coffee house, and Rudd's house in *Belle Sauvage* Yard. The Old Bailey had few marriage houses, although the *Bell*, the *Baptist's Head* and the *Queen's Head* were used from time to time.

By the 1740s many of the leading marriage houses were to be found outside the immediate area of the *rules*. This may have been due to difficulties in securing accommodation or because of the strong competition between the various marriage houses. It was probably hoped that customers would be attracted to these houses before they entered the area of the *rules*, and that they would not be identified with the general but damaging title of a "Fleet house". These houses tended to concentrate, therefore, in the streets which led into the *rules*. Seacoal Lane, a street which led from Holborn into Fleet Lane, possessed Wyatt's important marriage house in 1746, and Turnagain Lane, which led into Fleet Market, had one prominent house, that of Wheeler's. In the Holborn area the *Hoop and Bunch of Grapes* of Crosier, and Wyatt's house at the *Hand and Pen*, Holborn Bridge, were both important, although Crosier declined to state in a trial that he had a "wedding all day, all the year through". Other houses used for marriages in this locality included the *Swan and Crown* of Mrs Butterworth at Holborn Bridge, the *Three Tuns* at Snow Hill, the *Swan* in St Sepulchre's churchyard, and the *Globe* and the *Crown* both in Hatton Gardens. Blackfriars had a number of marriage houses which catered for those coming from the Surrey side by water, as the Holborn area was concerned with those arriving from the north or east. The *White Swan* of Harrington in Salisbury Court was prominent, and other houses included the *Ball* in New Street, Blackfriars, and the *Dolphin* in Printing House Court. The houses in Fleet Street catered for those coming from the west, and possessed such marriage houses as the *King and Key*, the *Leg*, and the *Golden Lion* in Temple Bar. None of these houses was very prominent, with the possible exception of Mrs Barratt's house in Bride Lane.

These houses were in the immediate vicinity of the prison and its *rules*, but there were many other places around London where clandestine marriages took place and whose entries were inserted into the Fleet registers. In most cases the parson was summoned to the house, either for the greater convenience of the clients, or because the couple were repelled from having their marriage solemnized at the Fleet. Thus Christopher Owen of the parish of St Martin's in the Fields, a smith, and Susan Pains of St Giles in the Fields, were married in August 1728 at Mr Hanson's in Pridhorns Court in the Old Bailey, at four o'clock in the morning, "not caring to be married at the Fleet". This was a more local marriage, close to the *rules*, but others took place for the same reason all over London and even beyond. The parsons' notebooks are full of addresses and directions as to how to get there, together with instructions to call. One example may suffice:

> Mr Nathaniel Palmer, starchmaker, Dob Yard, Greenwich, on Thursday morning 13 July eleven am. To land at Gordon Stairs Greenwich to turn at the *Hand of Venison*, … straight on till come to the sign of *Wheatsheaf*, and the next door beyond the starch house.

Many of these marriages took place in private homes as well as at more public places. Charles Bowles, a Southwark merchant, married Dorothy Hunt of Worcestershire in 1719 at his own home; Josiah Hickery, an attorney at law, married Sarah Boulton of St Marylebone in 1740 at his chambers in Gray's Inn, and the Hon. John Bouke married Catherine Hamilton at the Temple Church in 1730, though the entry was recorded in a Fleet register. Other places recorded for Fleet registered marriages were Ironmonger's Hall, the Wood Street Compter or prison, the *Castle* Tavern in Paternoster, Scotland Yard, the *Fallstaffe* at Charing Cross, Drury Lane, "at an apothecaries" in Arundel Street off the Strand, St Clement Danes' watch house, the *Golden Anchor* in Shoreditch, Clerkenwell Bridewell, and Fanell's "bagnio" in Long Acre. Other marriages took place at Islington, St Marylebone, and Vauxhall; the last under circumstances described by Ashwell:

June 12th 1745: Challen Miller, gentleman, of the parish of

Borsham in Sussex, bachelor, and Elizabeth Parkham of the same spinster. N.B. a clergyman whose name was the Rev Mr Cheynell came to the *Fountain* tavern on Ludgate Hill, and wanted a minister to converse with, as then was pleased to say – When I came to him it was to go with him to the *Royal Oak* in Vauxhall, to marry a couple, viz Miller, which he said he would have done it himself, but was apprehensive he might offend some friends, he himself lived in that neighbourhood, but he would stand father and accordingly did do so.

These marriages were probably very similar to that of James Tindall, son of a clergyman, and Lilly Shenton of Ewell in Surrey, who were married at Greenwich Hospital Chapel, "by the direction of the doctor in the same manner as at the Fleet". One assumes they gained possession of a church and carried out the marriage without the knowledge or consent of the parochial authorities.

These places were all easily accessible from the Fleet, but the parsons could be called upon to attend marriage couples far further afield. Lilly was perfectly consistent with Fleet custom when he advertised that his parson was "ready to wait on any person in town or country". Such marriages took place at the *Royal Oak*, Twickenham; at Hemmingford Church in Huntingdonshire; at the sign of the *Swan* in the parish of Kingsclear in Hampshire; at "his own house in Plumstead, Kent", while William Bannaster, rector of Holy Trinity and St Mary in Guildford, married a Quaker, Susan Lucas, "at her house" in Guildford in 1740, with Dare as the officiating minister. Another clergyman, James Beadle, was married at his own church at Ashwanstead in Sussex in 1739, but the marriage was recorded in a Fleet register.

The fees for these "outlying" marriages was often considerable. Bassett, for example, received a fee of one hundred guineas when, under the pseudonym of Barry, he went in 1737 to Up Park in Sussex to marry Mary Eades to Charles Pearson, a marriage which caused a high society scandal. Dare received twenty guineas for what he described as one of his "longer excursions into the country". The circumstances of another marriage are related by Ashwell, in this uncompleted draft from his register of 1743:

Letter was sent by one J Jones East Horsley in Surrey curate to two parishes directed to one Mrs Nicholson to procure a parson from the Fleet or elsewhere to marry a couple (viz. the Revd Dr Hosly, Rector of Abinger, Prebend of ... to his maid). The case stands thus, the person that came to the said Mrs Nicholson was one Nelson, als. Mason a clergyman's son in that county whose father is lately dead with a letter to the said Mrs Nicholson. I lay the 12th instant at the sign of the *Swan* in Leatherhead five miles from East Horsely expecting to find Jones at Leatherhead. When I came he not being there I sent my horse with a letter to the said Mr Jones. He sent me word that he would come next morning between nine and ten, but did not but Mr Nelson who took me to Norton Hatch in order to consummate the marriage when Jones comes to me there for Jones fears of being known would not come there but ...

The text may be corrupt, but the sense is clear. Did Ashwell record this as an *aide memoire* in case of legal proceedings?

****

The majority of the leading marriage houses either kept a parson as a member of their establishment, or else they had some sort of an arrangement with one or several of the Fleet clergy. The former position predominated between 1710 and 1730, but from that date onwards it gradually gave way to the latter. A quotation from the *British Gazetteer* of 1723 described both of these arrangements. It reads: "several of the brandy shop men and victuallers keep clergymen in their houses at 20s. per week each, hit or miss, but its reported that one there will stoop to no such low conditions, but makes at least £500 per annum of divinity jobs after that manner". Most of the clergy of that period, however, were maintained by the marriage house keepers, so that John Lilly, who clearly kept his own parson, could advertise accordingly:

At the *Hand and Pen* next door to the china shop Fleet Bridge, London, will be performed the solemnization of matrimony by a gentleman regularly bred at one of our Universities and lawfully ordained according to the institutions of the Church of England.

A number of other examples may be given. The register of Tuftin's house suggests that Parson Bynes was attached to that house until his death in September 1711, when he was replaced by Brafield. Parson Vyse was attached to another marriage house whose identity is not known. John Lilly had Marston as his parson in 1713, but from 1714-

16 Mottram appears to have taken his place. In 1732, Mrs Hodgkins, a prominent keeper, testified at the trial of John Miller that James Starkey was "a minister that lodged with me nine years but was not a prisoner". He received a stipend amounting to about one third of the marriage fees. Richard Sindrey was attached to another marriage house in 1741 for he is termed "Mr Sindrey, minister at my house", in one of the registers, and Ashwell noted in 1740, "N.B., living next door to one Joshua Lilly and a person troublesome I agreed to marry none at home upon condition I married all that came to his house". Ashwell soon left and Tarrant was installed in his place by 1747.

Nevertheless, each example given is a conjecture, for Ashwell and several of the other parsons may simply have had an agreement with the marriage house keeper to be available as and when required. This probably included some arrangement about the parson's share of the fee. This varied considerably. At Barratt's house Ashwell received one shilling for every two given, but at the *Green Cannister* he found that he was allowed two thirds of the fee. Sometimes the parson received the residue of the fee after all the other expenses had been paid, for as Lando wrote, "gave a shilling to Sarah [the keeper of the house?], I gave John Boder three pence for clerking, the gentleman gave two shillings, so I got nine pence for my trouble". The fee was sometimes split between the parson and the keeper, but on other occasions it could be divided into three, the additional person involved being the clerk or registrar.

These agreements between parson and marriage house keeper did not prevent the parson from marrying elsewhere, nor did it prevent the keeper from making similar arrangements with other parsons. Ashwell, Floyd and Lando all appear to have had several arrangements with keepers and also at the same time to have maintained private chapels for weddings "of their own". Such arrangements probably meant that the first available parson would be summoned to the marriage house whenever customers arrived. Thus Ashwell was "fetched" by Dematt of the *Cock* tavern in Fleet Market to marry a couple, or "called" from the market to Wood's house in Fleet Lane. If the designated parson was not available, another would be summoned in his place. These arrangements were often of short duration and ended quickly. In 1738 Wigmore so offended Burnford that Burnford noted "made use of Wigmore no more", thus endorsing the verdict of another keeper made two years earlier at the marriage of Matthew Medcalfe, a weaver of Whitechapel, to Ann Hubbard: "honest Wigmore kept all the money, so farewell him". Burnford also found it expedient to break with

Gaynam in 1733, calling him a "rogue".

This arrangement between a parson and several marriage house keepers appears to have become the norm by the 1730s. This was because of the great increase in the popularity of the Fleet and in the number of marriage houses, most of which competed with one another for the services of the parsons, whose number remained fairly constant and never matched that of the leading marriage houses. The clergy were thus able to break out of the stranglehold placed upon them by the marriage house keepers and were able to make arrangements more acceptable to themselves. Various examples of this practice may be given. Dare in 1738 was mainly attached to Lilly's establishment, but he also married at such places as Mrs Barrett's, at his own home, and by 1741 he was marrying at Wyatt's, Vernon's and the *New Market House*. In September 1745 he resumed his relationship with Lilly, and this continued for some time, for in August 1746 out of the 58 marriages recorded in his notebook, 34 took place at Lilly's, 8 at the *Anchor and Crown*, 3 at Crook's, 2 at Crawford's and the remaining 11 at other places.

Of these freelancing parsons Gaynam was the most important: he was probably the parson alleged by the *British Gazetteer* to have made an annual income of £500. Certainly Gaynam had an extensive practice, in which he had many links with Lilly's house. Thus between 1736-7 he had agreements with Lilly, at whose house about 45 per cent of his marriages were solemnized, and with the *Rainbow* coffee house, where about 10 per cent of his marriages took place. In February 1736 there was also a connection with the *Noah's Ark* (25 per cent in that month), but by October this had been superseded by an agreement with the *Goat* (20 per cent), and in the following May this establishment and the previously unmentioned *Anchor* both played host to 10 per cent of Gaynam's marriages during that month.

Wyatt, in spite of his brother's position as a marriage house keeper, married at many other establishments. In June 1737 he married 99 couples, 20 at Wheeler's, 16 at Wilson's, 23 at Balls', 8 at the *Fighting Cocks*, 5 at Sands', the same at Harling's and one at Burnford's. A note in Wheeler's registers stated that "Walter Wyatt Minr. at the Fleet" came there on 26 April 1735, and from that date until 1740 he appears to have had a near monopoly of the marriages solemnized at that house. These represented about one fifth of his marriages each month. In 1740, he had a near monopoly at Boyce's, although occasionally Dare, Ryder and Ashwell took his place. By 1745 it appears he had some sort of association with Lilly, at whose house in November 31 of his 103 marriages during that month took place. From that date onwards until his death in 1750 Wyatt was associated more closely with his brother. These monthly figures exclude Wyatt's marriages "at home" and at his brother's house, for the notebooks and registers of these were kept separately from his marriages "abroad" and have not survived. That the number of these marriages was substantial is indicated by Wyatt's accounts which have survived in part for 1748. In the first seven days of that September he received £5 13s. for his marriages "at home", but only £4 5s. for those abroad, and during the period 8th to 14th of October the amounts were £12 17s. and £4 17s. respectively.

The activities of Edward Ashwell provide a fairly detailed picture of the way this system worked. From 1734 he was attached to at least three houses. There was an agreement with Mrs Barratt, for Ashwell himself took the fees from the clients, subtracted his fee, and then paid her the balance. On 28 December 1741 he paid her £3 4s.6d., on 7 January 1742 £3 2s.6d., and on 14 January £1 2s.9d.. There was also a similar relationship with Lilly, although Ashwell was far more cautious with him and noted the exact time of payment: "paid Mr Lilly Sept 14 half an hour after 12". This continued during 1738-44. Finally, Ashwell was linked with Burnford's house between 1739-45, and it appears the same financial arrangement took place here as at Barratt's. On 15 June 1743 Ashwell wrote that he "reckoned with Mr Burnford and paid £2 10s.", and in 1745 he noted, "remember I have paid Mr Burnford Saturday evening 16s.6d.". Ashwell also freelanced throughout these years, marrying couples in such houses as Crampton's, Boyce's and the *Shepherd and Goat*.

It is clear Ashwell was not satisfied with these arrangements. Always timid and cautious he was terrified by Lilly's practices, particularly those of forging his (Ashwell's) name to false certificates. What made the position worse was that in 1740, Lilly, "a person troublesome", forced him into an agreement that he would "marry none at home upon condition I married all that came to his house". As he lived next door to Lilly in *John Lilly's Rents* Ashwell was in a difficult situation, and was in Lilly's power both as a neighbour and, presumably, as a tenant of the family. Ashwell eventually evaded this agreement, although it appears to have been repeated around July 1743 when from that month until October Ashwell performed his clerical business almost exclusively at Lilly's house.

Still dissatisfied, his attempts to leave the Fleet foiled, Ashwell appears to have persuaded himself that it would be far more remunerative and safer for him to establish his own marriage house. He severed his connection with Lilly, and moved into a house in Bride Lane, although he still found it necessary to continue in business with several other marriage houses, especially Burnford's and the *Shepherd and Goat*, for the number of marriages at his own house never exceeded 30 per cent of his total.

His "business at home" commenced on 23 July 1745, when he noted after his entry of the marriage of Oliver D'land of "Bedlam Green" hamlet, weaver, and Jane Pennarly, that "one Woods living below Fleet Lane brought the above said couple at 12 of the clock at night to my own home in Bride Lane. It was the first I ever had there". Wood was cultivated, and brought more couples to this house, as did other plyers, so that by the beginning of August Ashwell could note, "the first marriage I had properly called my own wedding brought by Mr Borland". The entry suggests that Ashwell's initial start was assisted by another marriage house whose keeper may have acted as his clerk and registrar. He took particular note of the plyers who brought these couples to his house, entering their addresses into his notebooks. Their number included Mrs Crane, "a lodger in the neighbourhood", and "Richard Ballard, porter of the *Red Lion*". He also noted the addresses of other plyers who took weddings to rival establishments, presumably to advise them about the attractions of his own:

> Remember to call at 3 shads a waterman ... who came to Mr Burnfords with a wedding, good people.
> In St Saviour's Dock one Loveday lives who keeps the sign of the *Welsh Trooper* who brings weddings frequently to Mr Lillys.

He noted down the number of a coach which had brought a couple, and was surprised when John Lewis and his bride were married "at home and directed by no body." By September his marriage room had become, at least in his own terminology, a chapel, for on the 6th he recorded, "at home, they were conducted to my Chapel by John King, waterman". This plyer was sufficiently impressed, as he came during the next month with his own bride, Ann Bassett of Fulham, to be married in this chapel. In the conduct of his business Ashwell remained cautious. He required the permission of the mother before he would marry her daughter to a negro; he observed that a woman had not changed her name by marriage as the surname of her husband was identical to her maiden name, and he forced one Mr Vere, "that keeps a glass shop the corner of Salisbury Court", to vouch for the "safety" of a marriage.

Unfortunately for Ashwell, his attempt to establish his own marriage house failed, for not only did the number of his "own" marriages decrease, but his activities at the other houses declined. All this may have been aggravated by his illness for he died in the *rules* of the Fleet in January 1746, when, in an extravagant gesture, the obituary writer of the *General Advertiser* called him "the most noted operator in marriages since the death of the never to be forgotten Dr Gaynam".

It is hardly surprising that the Fleet marriages became, in Outhwaite's phrase, "a competitive institution". Nor is it surprising that such competition caused rivalry and friction between the various keepers and parsons. This had been so from the earliest days, but it seems to have become far more intense during the period 1730-40 when the situation was aggravated by the competition of the more fashionable May-Fair establishment of Dr Keith, and by the continual emergence of more and more marriage houses, at a time when the number of parsons was probably declining. The keepers themselves endeavoured to eliminate trade from their rivals' houses, especially by advertising in such a way as to cast doubts upon their reputation. Lilly advertised in this way:

> Marriages with a licence, certificate and a crown stamp, at a guinea, at the New Chapel next door to the china shop, near Fleet Bridge, London, by a regular born clergyman and not by a Fleet parson, as is insinuated in the public papers; and that the town may be freed from mistakes, no clergyman being a prisoner in the rules of the Fleet dare marry; and to obviate all doubt, the chapel is not in the verge of the Fleet, but kept by a gentleman who was lately on board one of His Majesty's men of war, and likewise has gloriously distinguished himself in defence of his King and country, and is above committing those little mean actions that some men impose on people, being determined to have everything conducted with the utmost decency and regularity, such as shall be always supported by law and equity.

This advertisement, veiled in hypocrisy, was aimed at Lando, who freely advertised his connection with the Royal Navy, and his own St John's Chapel, by suggesting that his chapel was elsewhere. Lando replied in kind, stating that he did not live next door to the china shop, and that he had "several times fairly advertised in the newspapers [that] the pretended chaplain of which place hath never dared to publish his name nor the ship's name, to which he pretends to have belonged".

There was also a considerable borrowing of the signs of successful marriage houses. Wyatt had so much trouble with the other houses trading under his sign, the *Hand and Pen*, he was forced to add to his advertisements the following postscript: "N.B., take care you don't mistake by a *Hand and Pen* near the Bridge." This same sign was used by Lilly, Burnford, Wilson and Wyatt, and there were at least two other houses of this name in the Fleet Market alone.

In such an atmosphere quarrels were frequent. One occurred, for example, when one Mr Jones informed a large company that:

> According to Mr Reynolds at the Lord Bartley Arms at Cranford Bridge ... Mr Crosier had broke several times and had cheated the courts and country of many thousands of pounds ... and for her she had seven bastards and could not prove her marriage for the seven children, which gave the country to conceive what sort of wretches they were.

Violence was often the result, and the parsons' notebooks frequently recorded such matters as "a litigious and quarrelsome thing between Burnford and Lilly", or, as John Evans wrote after he had been assaulted by Samuel Pickering, "he throttled me and most murdered me".

The marriage house keepers appear, by and large, to have been as unsavoury in character as the Fleet parsons.

"A Fleet Wedding, between a brisk young Sailor and his Landlady's Daughter at Referiff", 1747 (courtesy of The City of London, Guildhall Library)

6
THE MARRIAGES

By the third decade of the eighteenth century the marriages performed at the Fleet had become part of the common fabric of London life. People arrived there to be married as a matter of course. However, they were drawn to particular marriage houses by many different means. Some came as a response to advertisements placed in the newspapers, others were brought by their friends, but most probably came through the agency of the plyers. These were the people who touted for marriages in order to obtain a small gratuity from the parson or keeper for introducing or bringing prospective clients. The normal gratuity was sixpence, sometimes a shilling, but never more than one shilling and sixpence, for the amount varied according to the fee which the parson or keeper thought could be safely charged for the ceremony. Agreements appear to have been made between particular plyers and the keepers and parsons. Burnford, for example, had an agreement with Tom Brown, and was frequently annoyed when he took customers elsewhere, while Ashwell, when coach number 540 set down a wedding party at Joshua Lilly's noted, "never to drink with me".

It is possible to distinguish between three types of plyers. The most common and notorious type were those who exercised their function by gathering around the Fleet Prison or the Fleet Bridge, awaiting the arrival of customers on foot or by coach, greeting them with the cries, "Do you want a parson? Will you be married?" "'Tis pleasant to see certain fellows plying by Fleet Bridge", declared a sarcastic writer in the *Weekly Journal* of 26 June 1723, only to add, "to take poor sailors … into the noose of matrimony every day throughout the week". Parson Mottram, the same paper reported in its issue of 13 February 1717, had a coal-heaver "set to ply at the door to recommend all couples that had a mind to be married by him [Mottram], who would do it cheaper than anyone".

Many illustrations are given of the way in which these plyers operated. Thomas Pennant, writing about his youth, remembered:

In walking along the street, in my youth, on the side next to the prison, I have often been tempted by the question, "Sir, will you be pleased to walk in and be married?" Along this most lawless space was hung up the frequent sign of a male and female hand conjoined, with "Marriages performed within" written beneath. A dirty fellow invites you in. The parson was seen walking before his shop, a squalid profligate figure, clad in a tattered plaid night gown, with a fiery face and ready to couple you for a dram of gin or a roll of tobacco.

L'Abbé le Blanc was equally amazed to see a minister, "who had contrived in order to get a livelihood, to hang out a board from his window, with these words, "Here marriages are performed cheap". The plyer would have said something similar.

An engraving of a Fleet wedding "between a lavish young sailor and his landlady's daughter of Rederiff [Radcliffe]", has these verses written below it as a poetical description of its Fleet Market scene:

Scarce had the coach discharged its trusty fare,
But gaping crowds surround the amorous pair;
The busy plyers made a mighty stir!
And whispering cry, "D'ye want the parson, Sir?"
"Pray, step this way, just to the Pen in Hand,
The Doctor's ready there at your command";
"This way," (another cries), "Sir I declare
The true and ancient register is here!"
The alarmed parsons quickly hear the din!
And haste with smoothing words to invite 'em in;
In this confusion, jostled to and fro
Th' enamour'd couple know not where to go;
Till slow advancing from the coach's side,
The experienced matron came (an artful guide),
She led the way without regarding either,
And the first parson spliced 'em both together.

A correspondent to the *Grub Street Journal* of 1735 indicates that this was not an imaginary account. She described how her coach was stopped near Fleet Bridge:

One said, "Madam, you want a parson?" "Who are you?" says I, "I am the clerk and registrar of the Fleet" …. At which comes a second, desiring me to go along with him. Says he, "That fellow will carry you to a peddling alehouse"; says a third, "Go with me, he will carry you to a brandy shop." In the interim comes the Doctor. "Madam," says he, "I'll do your job for you presently."

The same writer went on to complain that people were stopped as they went to church on Sundays, and almost "had the clothes torn off their backs" by these plyers. Sir Tanfield Leman, a prisoner at the Fleet during the 1750s, considered such activity to be "not less common in these places than to be teased in Monmouth Street with 'Will you buy any clothes?'"

Some of these plyers may have obtained a sufficient income from their business to remain independent of any other occupation. Such names as Brown, Green, Mother Needham, Madam Roberts (described as mistress to a baronet), and another called "the old man", appear time and time again in the notebooks of Burnford and other marriage house keepers. As noted in the quotations above, the parsons, as well as the keepers, also plied for trade when occasion demanded, and such comments as "John Lilly plied hard for a wedding", or "picked him up under my window", are frequently found in the notebooks.

Coachmen, chairmen and watermen form a second category of plyers, who brought their customers to a particular house, with which they presumably had some sort of an agreement. One notes that many of these coachmen remained faithful to their particular "house" in spite of the wishes or instructions of their fares, so that in one of many cases "instead of going to Burnford's the coachman stopped at Marshall's". A third category of plyers was made up of those who might be called local agents for the marriages, bringing or directing their friends to particular marriage houses. Jonathan Todd, a waterman, was termed "a friendly advisor and director to the Fleet for marriages", as was "the man that keeps the *Rainbow* coffee house in Drury Lane over against Long Acre". John Dugard who "came with them, had been at the Fleet eleven times, and brought three couples to my house", was specifically noted, and Mr Ballantine was mentioned as having brought many couples to Mrs Hodgkins's house, where he sometimes gave the bride "away".

Necessary as these plyers were, they often added to the difficulties experienced by the parsons, for sometimes they were offensive, deliberately led people to the wrong house, or they would encourage their clients to resist the demands of parson and keeper by insisting upon reduced fees, as did the porter from the *Grey Hound* who brought a wedding to Burnford's. On other occasions they might suggest there was no need to be registered or to have a certificate, for which additional fees were charged, and, even worse, might persuade the couple to refuse to pay their fees.

****

All the parsons had a concern to make their ceremonies appear as legal and solemn as possible. The royal arms were printed on some of their certificates, and both Lilly and Burnford claimed the title "Clerk of the Fleet", the former alleging the Lord Chancellor had appointed him to this office. Lilly also clamed that his "chapel" was tolerated by the bishop of London and his certificates approved by the Lord Mayor. He described them as "My Lord Mayor's Certificates", while Mottram's certificates had the city arms displayed on them. The marriages generally took place in specifically furnished rooms, some even dignified by the name of "chapel", while the clergy inevitably bestowed upon themselves the accolade of "doctor".

For the same reason the parsons were careful not to be involved in any marriage which might give rise to enquiry or to legal proceedings. Marriages were refused for such reasons as the youth of the couple, their drunken state, or because Burnford had no wish "to be concerned in the family of Outtings". When John Fletcher of St Mary's, Oxford, came to Gaynam for his marriage, Gaynam refused to officiate "by reason of his being student at Oxford and knowing his father", a position which did not worry Parson Floyd who was quite happy to proceed with the ceremony. An account was often taken of such incidents so that the couple "should not come again hereafter and say that they was married and was not". Note was also taken of the names of couples whose families wished to prevent their marriage. Other customers were "strictly examined": one because the death of his first wife was none too sure, another because a person present at the ceremony said "she was sorry for being concerned which gave me no small uneasiness", a prospective bride because there was some doubt that she was "of the age of twenty", and in another case a young bridegroom was made to swear that he was not an apprentice. Their articles normally prohibited marriage. When Henry Marden, a chairman, and Mary Warner, both of St George's, Hanover Square, came to be married, "the said chairman was by me strictly examined whether he had a wife or no, he made answer he had been in my company with other gentlemen's servants but was never married himself". One parson even required a bond from the guardian of the bride to indemnify him should trouble arise, and when Lewis Talbot, a gentleman from Enfield, and Sarah Richardson, daughter of an attorney in Crane Street, came to be married, Ashwell insisted that her father should be summoned to give his verbal consent before he was prepared to perform the ceremony, even though "the company present ... protested it was safe ... and honest on the man's side". He later discovered that "it was the young gent. That [had] the fortune". Caution was also exercised in registration. Wyatt did not register a youth under age for that reason, and on another occasion he refused to give a marriage certificate until he had seen the burial certificate of a deceased partner.

The ceremony seemed to be conducted as quickly as possible. Double or triple marriages, when two or three couples were married at the same time, were not uncommon. Such weddings were often of soldiers or "shipmates". The service of the *Book of Common Prayer* was followed, although its wording could be cut down to the basic essentials. One witness at a bigamy trial testified: "the parson pulled a book out of his pocket and read a little bit of it ... I am sure he did not read half as much as was said to me at Pancras when I was married." In most cases the exchange of vows, the joining of hands, and the giving of a ring, together with the declaration of marriage, were the only parts of the service observed. One parson even devised a formula which omitted all reference to the Trinity. It stated, "with this ring I thee wed, with my body I thee worship, and with all my worldly goods I thee endow, from this time forth and for evermore, Amen, till death us do part according to law and thereto I give thee my troth". Ashwell on another occasion shortened the service in a different way. When some clients deeply offended him by their behaviour he took his revenge, noting in his register, "N.B. some material part omitted". On the other hand, in what was a parish affair, John Williams refused to say "with this ring I thee wed", but this omission did not prevent the Fleet registrar or the parish authorities from regarding him as legitimately married.

The parsons were also prepared to celebrate the Holy Communion at the service, as the rubric of the Prayer Book required, for the few who requested it. At one marriage "Dare gave her the sacrament", and a witness in a trial relating to a Fleet marriage described the ceremony and added, "he broke the biscuit over their head".

The ring was always used in the ceremony. Many marriage houses kept a stock of rings to enable customers to purchase one if they came without, while some of the parsons kept rings to lend a couple who neither brought a ring nor had the money to purchase one. We know this mainly because some of the customers were sufficiently dishonest not to return the ring. One particular entry concluded with the remark that they "attempted to run away with Mrs Crook's gold ring". On the other hand the ring could be given to the keeper as security for any outstanding sum of money owed by the couple. If the ring was reclaimed it was sometimes alleged that a brass ring had been substituted for one of gold. Alexander Douglas of Cripplegate made such an allegation, and so "raised a great mob about the house". On other occasions it was the keeper who suffered; "brass for gold", wrote one, "cheated me of a ring". When a ring was not claimed its value was sometimes shared between the clergyman and the keeper. From one such sale Burnford received eight shillings and ninepence from Parson Floyd.

The bride was sometimes "given away", occasionally by the marriage house keeper, the clerk or the plyer, if no friends could be persuaded to take this part. It was rare for an actual father to take this role, suggesting that few of the couples were accompanied by their parents. One casual visitor who had gone to a marriage house cum alehouse for a quiet drink was persuaded to give away the bride. In all probability the friends who accompanied the wedding couple acted as the witnesses, though only occasionally are their names recorded in the registers. In many cases the keeper acted as the witness, and as such gave evidence of the marriage if it was questioned in the law courts.

The function of the clerk who attended these marriages was not only to act as a witness to the ceremony or to give the bride away, but to write out the certificate and to register the marriage. The keeper often served as clerk, but the larger houses kept their own clerks. The names of some are known. There was "Black Ned" at Wheeler's, Rodd and Silk at Wyatt's, Evans at the *Bishops Head*, and Melton at the *Cock*. The clerk was paid for his services. At some of the houses he was paid a regular fee irrespective of the cost of a marriage, a shilling or so, but at other houses the sum he received depended upon the generosity of the clients. When Peter de St Remage was married, he gave the "gentlewomen of the house a shilling for officiating as clerk. I said it was usual to give something more; he frowned". Burnford's clerk received such sums as one and sixpence, half a crown, and so on, and Lilly's clerks received similar sums.

The Fleet clergy ignored the canonical requirement that all marriages should be performed between the hours of eight and twelve noon. Malcolm, a contemporary writer, observed that they left "the clocks at their offices ... still standing at the *canonical hour*, though perhaps the time of day be six or seven in the afternoon". The parsons were generally ready to conduct a service, even if they had to be called out of bed in the middle of the night to do so. Many marriages are recorded as having taken place late at night or early in the morning, such as that of Barrot Hutton, a clockmaker, of Christ Church, Newgate Street, to Sarah Moore, at one o'clock in the morning. Equally, marriages were conducted on each day of the year, even though the earlier canons of the Church forbade marriages during the penitential seasons. In 1702 it was said that the chief days were "Sundays, Thursdays and Saturdays, but every day more or less." Nor did the clergy always dress appropriately as the canons of the church required. Giving testimony in court in the case of *Warren v. Meadows*, John Vyse said he could not remember if he had been dressed in his priest's habit or his night gown.

The cost of the marriages varied considerably, for it mainly depended on the amount the parson or keeper considered the bridegroom could afford to pay. This situation was well known, and many couples attempted to evade what the parsons considered to be their just dues. Daniel Disell "said he was a gentleman's coachman, but afterwards told me so to marry him cheap", and another bridegroom tried a similar trick "in order to prevail with me to give my fees away". Some made a "bargain" with the keeper before the marriage took place, as did Valentine Carlisle who was married at the *King's Head* in 1740 and of whom it was recorded: "the bargain was made as Mr Boyce told me for 10s.6d. the night before". At least one couple went around the several houses to find the cheapest available price. Thus when Andrew Mills, a gentleman of the Temple, and Charlotte Garllairdy, of St Mildred Poultry, arrived to be married at Boyce's in September 1744, "one gentleman came first in a merry manner to make a bargain with the minister for the marriage, and immediately came the parties themselves disguising their dress by contrivances part buttoning up the coat because the rich waistcoat should not be seen ...". In the trial of Peter de St Remage for bigamy, Mrs Ann Hatfield testified that she had made an agreement for the marriage, "that was 13s.6d. and the prisoner came and consented to the agreement".

In the majority of marriages the fee was requested, and often first specified, during the actual ceremony, for as Dare recorded in one instance, the money "was laid down upon the book with the ring", as prescribed by the Prayer Book rubric. If, as in many cases, the fees had

not been previously agreed a situation would arise in which the couple
would quarrel or bargain with the parson over the cost. There were
some who grumbled, or made a great uproar, as did Benjamin
Shuckford who "paid nothing and kept us up all night", or John Crook
who "made a great uproar in the court and caused words between Mr
Fox and all the neighbours". William Hills of Bexley in Kent and
Elizabeth Weeks "had a great noise for four hours about the money",
and an unnamed person "who appeared by dress to be a gentleman of
fortune … would not pay but in a mean and scandalous manner, he
offered 5s. and went down stairs, and down the court, came back again
and paid 3s. for all … [and] went away without letting of their names".
Christopher Smith wished to be married for five shillings but
eventually gave way to Ashwell's demand for one guinea. Most
couples eventually paid the sums demanded, although as noted there
were exceptions: "a vile rude young fellow and little woman and
notorious fellow companion compell[ed] me to marry them", and the
same parson, Ashwell, having married Francis Williams at a barber's
shop for half a guinea, wrote, "after which it was extracted out of my
pocket and for fear of my life delivered". Another dispute was noted
with more satisfaction by the parson. He wrote of this marriage: "came
a man and a woman to be married at Mrs Lewis. Gave Mr Ashwell
2s.6d. he would have 5s. all, but they abused him and all persons went
to Bates, or Mr Davies and gave 6s.6d. and was married which was 9s.
when they might have done it cheaper". It appears that Ashwell kept
their fee, probably because he had already commenced the marriage
service.

There were other customers who underestimated the amount
required. Alexander Keith noted that many couples were married
"when they have but half a crown in their pockets and sixpence to buy
a pot of beer, and for which they have pawned some of their clothes".
Although some were turned away for want of sufficient money, others
were permitted to return to their own homes in order to fetch the
amount outstanding, or to bring it when they were in a position to do
so, having presumably been married with that proviso. Richard Sconce
and Mary Podmore, who though "they behaved very rudely", promised
"to come again and make the 5s. [they had given] 13s.6d." when his
prize money had been paid him. Not all returned. One note inserted
into a notebook reads: "June 10, came a man and a woman from St
Giles as he said left 2s. with Mr Ashwell went to fetch more money to
pay 7s.6d. and he married and have all things done but came no more".
Others managed to pawn or exchange some of the items in their

possession in lieu of their debt. The most usual item was the wedding ring, but amongst other objects offered were snuff boxes, watches, silver buckles, a handkerchief, a great coat, even a pint of wine and a "note in hand", which an indignant parson noted "never was paid". Michael Oliver, described as a "gentleman of St Katherines" appears to have paid "upon tick" for his marriage to Elizabeth Holloway.

Many couples are described in the registers as "half married". In most instances only their Christian names are given. The majority of these people were those, who, having disagreed about the price of a marriage when the fee was demanded along with the ring, left the premises "half married", or as other entries more delicately describe their condition, "married to the ring" or "half done". Their full names would only be disclosed with the other details required for registration after the marriage had taken place. This term was also used for those couples who left the premises in order to obtain money but failed to return, and in those numerous instances when the couple decided at some point in the ceremony that they had been "married enough", and had then departed. This occurred when William Dyce and Mary Ash, discovering that the parson wanted a further half a crown, accepted their plyer's advice that "they were married enough", and ran away, or when John Ballard "told the woman that was enough", though the registers emphasise they were not married. A few did return, so that when Robert Can married Margaret Days it was noted that they "had been half married some time ago". In order to cover themselves on these occasions, the parsons normally entered the details of these half marriages in their notebooks. One entry reads:

> February 3, memo: came two men and two women to have a couple married but one of the woman swore and damned Mr Dare because he would have d. and the clerk y. and took this account because they should not come and say they was married and not registered.

A similar entry concerns the alleged marriage between John Jones of Oaten Sutton in Bedfordshire and Mary Seward. The entry continues:

> They came to Woods in Fleet Lane about six o'clock in the morning. Mr Ashwell and self had been down the market, Wood called him and I went with him. There found the said man and woman. Offered Mr Ashwell 3s. to marry him, he would not so he swore very much and would have knocked him down but for me.

Was not married. Took this memo that they might not pretend they was married and not registered.

****

It is difficult to discover the exact cost of any marriage, for the cost might, or might not, include such items as the fees for the clerk, the registration of the marriage, or the certificate. Only one register quotes both the total figure and its composite parts: in a total fee of sixteen shillings two shillings were for the clerk and five shillings for the certificate; a total of eight shillings saw two shillings given to the clerk and two shillings and sixpence for the certificate, but a fee of five shillings produced but one shilling for the clerk although the cost of the certificate was still half a crown. Within this register the average total fee was four shillings and sixpence. Marriages without a certificate were much cheaper, Burnford charging half a crown to five shillings, and Floyd a similar figure. These were the cheapest marriages available. Fashionable clients paid far more, especially if they wished the marriage to be kept "secret". For this purpose prices such as three guineas, four guineas and even more were not unusual. The prices for the more ordinary marriages in Hodgkins's register for 1729 averaged between four and five shillings, the cheapest being two shillings and the dearest ten, while Burnford's charges varied between six shillings and thirteen shillings and sixpence, of which seven shillings and sixpence appears to have been a fairly standard charge. These costs included the fee for the clerk and the certificate. Lilly's prices were on the same scale. A few, elsewhere, were cheaper. In 1740 Owen charged half a crown for a marriage with the additional charge of one shilling for the clerk and half a crown for the certificate, while ten years later Deneveu's marriages at an unknown marriage house cost on average four shillings.

It has been suggested already that many of the marriage house keepers became connected with the marriage market more for the trade it would bring to their tavern or alehouse than for the matrimonial profits. It was perhaps inevitable that the customers and their guests should move from the "chapel" into another room for the "entertainment", or if this was impossible remove themselves to a house which provided such amenities. For most couples this "entertainment" did not go beyond the taking of alcoholic beverages, such as the three or four half pints of wine carried up to such a "party" by Mrs Crosier, and the eating of "bride cakes" which were sold at sixpence each at Burnford's and other establishments. A few went further than this, as witness the "handsomely entertained" comment recorded by a parson after the wedding of William Tew, while scenes of drinking, singing, dancing and general jollity are depicted in several prints and ballads of the period. The print of *The Sailor's Fleet Wedding Entertainment*, issued in 1747, had these verses printed below it:

> Jack, rich in prizes now the knot is tied,
> Sits pleased by her he thinks his maiden bride.
> But though a modest look by Molly's shown
> She only longs for what she oft has known.

> The bawd, now from her daughter's charge relieved,
> With pleasure smiles to think how he's deceived;
> Experienced in the trade, and void of shame,
> To her the man in crape imparts his flame.

> The lawyer grins, and Peg with wanton glance,
> Seems much delighted by Tom's antic dance.
> Kit kisses Kate, vows she shall be his wife;
> While cat and dog resemble nuptial strife.

> The Skimmington observes, mirth to provoke,
> Sam points the horns, with many a bawdy joke.
> For spouse's clothes the Baily's crew are seen,
> And change, Oh sad mishap! The jovial scene.

This is similar to a satirical ballad called *The Bunter's Wedding,* whose many verses describe the circumstances of the marriage, the entertainment, and the old London custom of the "marrow bones and cleavers", by which the butchers' apprentices would greet the bridal couple in a noisy fashion. Its text is as follows:

> Good people attend, I'll discover,
> A wedding that happened of late;
> I cannot tell why we should smother,
> The weddings of poor more than great.
> 'Twixt Ben of the Borough, so pretty,
> Who carries a basket, 'tis said,
> And dainty plump Kent Street fair Kitty,
> A coney wool-cutter by trade.

The guests were all quickly invited,
Ben order'd the dinner by noon;
And Kitty was highly delighted
They obeyed the glad summons so soon.
An ox cheek was ordered for dinner
With plenty of porter and gin.
Ben swore on the oath of a sinner,
Nothing should be wanting in him.

Joe the sandman and Bessie the bunter,
We hear from St Giles' did prance;
Dick the fiddler and Sally the mumper,
Brought Levi the Jew for to dance.
Tom the chanter he quickly was present,
And squinting Black Molly likewise;
With Billy the dustman quite pleasant,
And Nell with no nose and sore eyes.

Ned the drover was also invited,
Unto this gay wedding to come,
From Smithfield he came quite delighted
Before that the market was done;
And Fanny the pretty match-maker,
A sister to young Bunting Bess,
She wished the devil might take her
If she were not one of the guests.

Dolly the rag woman's daughter,
From Tyburn Road she did stride;
And Jenny the quilter came after
Whose nose it stood all of one side.
There was Roger the chimney sweeper,
No soot he would gather that day,
But because he would look the completer,
His soot bag and brush threw away.

There was bandy legged sheep's head Susan
We hear from Field Lane she did hie;
And draggle tailed Pat with no shoes on
Who pins and laces doth cry.
Ralph the grinder is set by his barrow,

As soon as he heard of the news,
And swore he would be there to-morrow,
Although he's no heels to his shoes.

Sam the grubber, he having had warning,
His wallet and broom down did lay,
And early attended next morning,
The bride for to-give away;
And Peggy the mop-yarn spinner,
Her cards and her wheel set aside,
And swore as she was a sinner,
She'd go and attire the bride.

Nan the tub woman out of Whitechapel,
Was also invited to go,
And, as she was 'kin to the couple,
She swore she the stocking would throw.
So having all gathered together,
As they appointed to meet,
And being all birds of a feather,
They presently flocked to the Fleet.

But when at Fleet Bridge they arrived,
The bridegroom was handing his bride;
The plyers they all to them dived,
"Do you want a parson?" they cry'd;
But as they down Fleet Lane did prance,
"What house shall we go to?" says Ben.
Then Kitty in raptures, made answer,
"Let's go to the Hand and the Pen."

Then into the house they did bundle,
The landlady showed them a room.
The landlord he roared out like thunder,
"The parson shall wait on you soon."
Then so eager he came for to fasten,
He staid not to fasten his hose;
A fat belted ruddy faced parson,
That brandy had painted his nose.

But before he the couple did fasten
He looked all around on the men;

"My fee's half a crown," says the parson,
"I freely will give it," says Ben.
Then Hymen he present and followed,
And the happy knot being tied,
The guests they whooped and hollowed,
All joys to the bridegroom and bride.

Like malt horses they all pranced,
The bride she looked not the same;
And thus through the city they danced.
But, when to the Borough they came,
The bride to look buxom endeavoured,
The bridegroom as brisk as an eel;
With the marrow bones and cleavers,
The butchers they rang them a peal.

And as they were homewards advancing,
A dancing, and singing of songs,
The rough music met them all prancing,
With frying pans, shovels and tongs,
Tin canisters, salt boxes plenty,
With trotter bones beat by the boys,
And they being hollow and empty,
They made a most racketing noise.

Bowls, gridirons, platters and ladles,
And pokers, tin kettles did bruise,
The noise, none to bear it was able,
The warming pans beat with old shoes;
Such a rattling, racketting uproar,
Had you but heard it, no doubt,
All hell was broke loose you'd have swore,
And the devils were running about.

The mob they all hollowed and shouted,
In the streets as they passed along,
The people to see how they counted,
Together in clusters did throng;
They made all the noise they was able,
And thus they were ushered in,
But e'er they all sat down to table,
They each had a glass of old gin.

Dinner being decently ended,
The table was cleared with speed,
And they to be merry intended,
So strait did to dancing proceed.
But Harry the night man so jolly,
With madness he almost cried,
And all the night sat melancholy,
For he had an eye for the bride.

Bob the bricklayer now being merry,
Tho' to foot it at first he was loath,
He told them he'd tip them Bob Perry,
But they swore they'd have Newgate broth.
Tom the chanter he tipt them a trilly,
That never before was in print;
While the dustman they call Sam Smutty,
Gnaw'd the head of Black Molly that did squint.

Jack the coal heaver thought himself slighted,
They carried the rig on so quiet,
And swore that as he was not invited,
He'd go and kick up a riot;
Then hectoring, bouncing and swearing,
So boldly he entered the house,
But when he saw Joey the sandman,
The cull was as still as a mouse.

Bess the bunter sang Murdock o'Blaney,
The chorus it made the house ring;
Nell with no nose cried you'll shame me,
If such bawdy songs you do sing.
Drunken Levi the Jew was abusive,
And would have got trimm'd as 'tis said,
Had not his pomatum been useful,
As Kitty the bride was a maid.

Joe the sandman he talked of the nailor;
Away the coal heaver did slink,
Quite faint hearted, worse than a tailor,
Lest Joey should give him a clink;
But being all drunk together,
Ben prayed they all night for to stay;

So coupl'd them in his long feathers,
And parted good friends the next day.

Although the entertainment in this instance took place in the east end
of London, the ballad is equally applicable for the Fleet festivities.

All too often the entertainment got out of hand and went on until the
early morning, so that the constable was forced to eject the party. This
occurred when a group "had the assurance to stay from about 7 to 11 at
night making a noise till the watch came", or when "some vile people
continued mobbing for three hours until 1 o'clock in the morning till
the constable came to disperse". It was even possible for the married
couple to remain at the marriage house for the night. Richard Stokes
and his wife did so, Mrs Balls having "brought them and had them
bedded" (presumably in the time-honoured way with mirth and
bawdiness), while Gaynam testified at the trial of Mary Somers that
she and her husband were married "at Mr White's at the *King's Arms*
Tavern and I drank tea with them the next morning. They lay there the
night".

The parsons did not give their exclusive attention to marriages, for
several also made a business of baptising people, for which they
charged a small fee in violation of canon law. These baptisms were
held in the prison chapel, private houses, or in the marriage houses.
Although some of those baptised were infants whose parents had
married at the Fleet, most of those baptised are described as adult
negroes or Indians. Their occupations, where given, are recorded as
servants. George Douglas, a black, was baptised on 14 February 1726,
and received a "printed certificate of the same". He was "servant to
Captain George Pumroy of Deptford, witnesses by the names of
Thomas York and James Graham", while on 17 June 1733 "was
baptised a certain black servant to Mr Crawford, surgeon, living in St
James, going under the name of Caesar, by the name of Thomas
Street". A number were baptised before being married to fellow
negroes, as was one Susannah in 1726, when it was recorded "a black
woman baptised Susannah and married at the same time or a few
minutes after to William Thomas, a black man". The reasons behind
these negro baptisms remain obscure. They might have been
occasioned by the desire for respectability and a "proper" name on the
part of the negro, or of Christian courtesy on the part of the "owner",
or there may have been a common belief that a slave was regarded as a
free person if they were baptised. This was certainly the case in Cape
Colony, where slaves remained unbaptised. Equally, the reason why

the Fleet was regarded as the place for these baptisms is not known, unless it was felt that the parsons would not require the permission of their owners before they would proceed with the baptism.

THE SAILORS FLEET WEDDING ENTERTAINMENT.

"The Sailor's Fleet Wedding Entertainment", 1747 (courtesy of The City of London Guildhall Library)

7
THE CUSTOMERS

Dr Gally, rector of St Andrew's, Holborn, and a noted opponent of the Fleet marriages, suggested in his book, *Some Considerations upon Clandestine Marriages*, that many of the couples who married at the Fleet would have been married by licence if that place had not been available. Accepting the fact that licences were freely available from the faculty office, it is still true that most of the customers of the Fleet would not have been acquainted with these procedures, or would not have been prepared to go to the trouble of obtaining a licence. The majority of those married came from the lower orders of society, and a considerable number of the bridegrooms were described in the registers as craftsmen or tradesmen. In some years more than half the bridegrooms married came into these categories: 52 per cent in 1700, 40 per cent in 1710, 46 per cent in 1720 and 50 per cent in 1740. Another large group comprised those who had no established place of settlement, such as travellers, peddlers of "no fixed address", and soldiers and sailors. Their number was always considerable. In 1700, 25 per cent of the men married came into this category, 32 per cent in 1710, 21 per cent in 1720, but only 13 per cent in both 1740 and 1750. Such figures are not surprising, for one of the striking characteristics of the London population in the 1720s, suggested Peter Linebaugh, was its high proportion of the young, the geographically mobile and the unmarried.

The number of sailors married at the Fleet was always outstanding. In 1710 one in four of the bridegrooms (684 in number) was so described. These men, their stay in London limited, with neither time nor opportunity to remain for their banns to be called, and having no money with which to purchase a licence even if they were aware of its existence, found that the only form of marriage available to them was that which the Fleet provided. Much of the contemporary material about the Fleet stresses this point. Malcolm, for example, remembered the plyers waiting at Fleet Bridge "to take poor sailors … into the noose of matrimony", while Captain Saunders in the debates on the

Marriage Act of 1753 declared that he would vote against the bill "for
the sake of the sailors". Alexander Keith well illustrated the progress
of a sailor's marriage when he noted "from experience" that:

> A young man, a mariner, comes ashore, receives his wages, is
> recommended by his friends and acquaintances to marry the
> daughter of a neighbour; comes acquainted with her one day, is
> married the next, and gets his wife with child, and is again on
> shipboard ... before the week is out, returns by the time his wife is
> brought to bed, gets her with child, then and there sets sail.

Keith also alleged that a landlord at Radcliffe told him that such
marriages were so numerous that it was a "common thing, when a fleet
comes in, to have two or three hundred marriages in a week's time
among the sailors". Many of these marriages, he added, were the result
of a "joke". His first claim may be illustrated by those registers of the
period 1710-12 that record the names of the ships on which the
bridegroom served. In 1710, 27 men from the *Boyne* were married at
the Fleet, 25 from the *Salisbury*, 20 from the *Defiance*, and 17 from the
Royal Anne. This ship provided 8 Fleet bridegrooms during the
following year, as did the *Lennox* with 13 men, and yet another 5 in
1712. The Admiralty *Bounty Papers* provide further evidence. These
records include petitions for the payment of compensation to the
widows of deceased seamen. Evidence of a marriage had to be
provided, and thus 10 out of the 36 marriage certificates presented in
1748 were Fleet ones, 5 out of 16 in 1749, and 8 out of 18 in 1752.
Furthermore, two of the three prints that relate to the Fleet marriages
depict the marriage of sailors. Interestingly enough, during the first
half of the eighteenth century about one quarter of those hanged at
Tyburn were discharged seamen.

    Although the majority of those married at the Fleet were of humble
birth, many members of the upper ranks of society were also married
there, or alternatively, obtained the services of a Fleet parson at their
own homes. Many men described themselves as "gentlemen": in 1720,
for example, one out of every 25 customers is so described, although
by 1750 their number had halved, possibly because of the competition
provided by the more fashionable business of Parson Keith at May-
Fair. Amongst what we might describe as "society" weddings at the
Fleet we may mention the marriages of Lady Catherine Annisley of
"Stoakes Poges" in Buckinghamshire who married William Phillips,
Esq. in 1718, Colonel William Piers, member of parliament for Wells,

who married Mary Ives at the Fleet in 1720, and "The Rt. Hon." Lady
Mary Benet of St Martin's in the Fields who married William Wilmer,
Esq. in the same year. Two sons of Owen Meyrick, a former high
sheriff of Merioneth, are also alleged to have been married at the Fleet
in a double wedding on 25 July 1732. Richard Meyrick was due to
marry Jane, the eldest daughter of Charles Cholmondeley of Vale
Royal, and Pierce to Lady Lucy Pitt, the only daughter of the earl of
Londonderry. None had their parents' consent. However, on the way to
the Fleet, the ladies proposed to change "husbands" and this was
agreed to the satisfaction of all.

Several clergymen were also married at the Fleet, including the poet
Churchill, a William Meredith of St James's parish who married Maria
Pickup in 1722, and Richard Mason of "Rayham" who married
Rebecca Herzell of High Wycombe. Several other marriages of interest
took place, among them that of "Don Dominous Bonanevictuar, Baron
Spitery, Abbot of St Mary in Peato, Notary Apostolick, Chaplain to the
King of the Two Scilla and Knight of the Order of St Zaluattor" of St
James's, Westminster, who in 1742 married Martha Alexandra "at his
house". One hopes she was not too disillusioned by this impostor.
When Andrew Wild was married to Mary Harold the clerk noted in his
register, "the bridegroom was the brother of the memorable Jonathan
Wild executed at Tyburn". There is evidence of two, possibly three,
Fleet prisoners having been married at the Fleet. One of them was
Thomas Fazakerly, "gentleman ... [who] was brought to me out of the
prison of the Fleet as being a prisoner by Mr Robuck the head
turnkey".

The personal characteristics of the customers were frequently
recorded, although the reason for this was not due to the idiosyncrasies
of the clerk or parson, but rather to the need to identify the couple
concerned should the validity of their marriage be questioned,
especially if they had refused to give their names or there was a
suspicion they had married under false names. Several were noted as
blind, one had only one leg, another was "effeminate in his voice", and
Ann who married Isaac and who refused to give her surname, "squints
very much with the right eye". When Elizabeth, a "gentlewoman"
married John Stunner, the clerk recorded: "when married had on a
flowered silk gown – after she was married she pulls off her flowered
gown and underneath she had a large full black silk gown on – went
away in the same the other was wrapt up". William and Sarah are
described in this way: "he dressed in a gold waistcoat like an officer,
she a beautiful young lady with two fine diamond rings and a black

high crown hat and very well dressed". Another entry reads: "the gentleman disfigured with the smallpox with gold lace hat and waistcoat trimmed with silver, Elizabeth his wife a middle sized woman, ... N.B. a young gentlewoman dressed in white present." Yet another entry states: "he a black swarthy man ... she a gentlewoman of thin complexion". "The prettiest woman I ever saw", and "plain Betty" are further comments, while one Robert "peel'd off his coat because it was black – said he would not be married in that coat for that reason". Instead he choose to be married in his waistcoat.

The ages of couples married are not generally recorded, unless there were exceptional circumstances, such as a substantial discrepancy between the ages of the couple, or because of their longevity, as when John Smith, a gentleman's servant, married Ann Page, "he 82, she 77, both fresh in perfect senses", in 1747. Francis Bureton, a brewer aged 80, married a woman aged 22, and Robert King, "about 18 years", married a bride aged 65. It was added that "they were brought in a coach and attended by four thumping whores out of Drury Lane as guests". Another more notorious marriage was reported in a contemporary paper:

> Not long since were married at the infamous Fleet a young broker near Moor-Fields of about 70 years old to his first wife's eldest daughter, a girl of 19, and it says she shows already tokens of his vigorous manhood. Let the present age or country produce a second, and equal, if they can. The bride and bridegroom were saluted by city and court music yesterday morning, which will be followed by a concert of all the neighbouring bedwarmers and frying pans. It is not expected our righteous ecclesiastical courts will take any notice of it, as there is no purse for commutation.

The marriages of negroes are not infrequent, but mixed marriages were unpopular, as when a black mariner, John Hermitage, was marred by Ashwell in 1745 to Hanna Wilkes. He recorded: "the woman was a neighbour's daughter, the sister raised a mob and said my maid was my whore".

All too frequently the customers were "rude", "quarrelsome", "wicked", "scandalous", "saucy", "troublesome", or "very abusive". Though the registers abound in such descriptions, Ashwell either seems to have been more sensitive than most of the parsons, or managed to attract more of this sort of people. He wrote of Hester Graham's mother that "she is one of the most abusive and scandalous women that I ever heard of". Thomas Thompson was "an ill mannerly soldier" and his bride "an old scolding woman". Christopher Smith "appeared like a gentleman but the actions quite the reverse". A guest at one of the weddings called "me and the minister all the rogues and villains as was possible to come out of her mouth", and Maria Deans informed Ashwell on Christmas Day, 1739, that "my gown ought to be stript off my back".

Other customers stole, swore, "made many words", "beat my sister", locked the door or took the key out of it, broke the coachman's glass, gave false descriptions of themselves, or compelled the parson to marry them, as did George Venables and Martha Lewis who "threatened my life if I would not comply to marry them." On another occasions the parson wrote: "Apprehending it to be a conspiracy I found myself obliged to marry them". Ashwell's condemnation was often aroused by those who came in a state of intoxication to the ceremony, as did Thomas Farr of Southwark who was "dead drunk", and by those who drank "in the time of divine service".

An indication of what may lie behind these words of parsonical rebuke may be found in Burnford's account of the marriage of Alexander Bunts of Deptford in 1742. He arrived with his friends, but became

> Very wicked and abusive and raised a mob ... beat my daughter Kitty, swore violently that if the parson or I ever dare to come out that they would have our hearts' blood, and a woman who was with them ... swore many times that she would come and bring her giant who should break every bone in our skins, or if we dare come to Deptford we should not be suffered to come away alive ... they locked the door and would not let Mr Ashwell nor me out a great while, struck Mr Ashwell, and Bunt struck me.

This was not an isolated incident, for the clergy and the keepers were frequently mobbed. At Thomas Garrot's marriage they were mobbed by a "gang of vile incendiaries". Often these mobbings continued until the watch or the constable was called to end the affray. One such incident occurred after the marriage "at night" of William Kelly and Elizabeth Lowther, when this "very vile creature ... mobbed [us] at home three hours – swore my wife had robbed her – the man was obliged to send for the watch and constable late of the night to take them away".

****

Couples came for these marriages at the Fleet from all over London
and beyond. Many possibly gave the place of their birth or legal
settlement rather than the parish of their domicile in London, as did
Margaret Smith, who although described as of Whitechapel is noted as
formerly belonging to "Brimble parish in Wiltshire". This may account
for those couples who apparently lived at great distances from the Fleet
being married there, as were Robert Rowland of "Lanwnooda in
Caernarvonshire and Grace Pugh of Lanystynwy of the same county"
who were married on 13 August 1721. When Beatrice Baker was
examined in 1769 under the settlement laws at Nantwich, Cheshire, she
revealed that she had been married to an Irishman, Richard Baker, at
the Fleet some 26 years earlier. He had never gained a settlement in
this country, and had died at sea some months earlier. It was accepted
that her settlement was at Tong, Shropshire, where she had been born
and brought up. Being a vagrant she was whipped out of Nantwich as a
disorderly person and sent on her way.

It is hardly surprising that a study of the parochial settlements of
those married at the Fleet in any given year show that the majority of
its clients came from the populous artisan areas of London, such as
Stepney, Whitechapel, Cripplegate, Clerkenwell, Aldgate, St Andrew
Holborn, St Giles in the Fields and the parishes around Westminster.
Tony Benton has suggested that a couple from Stepney were three
times more likely to be married at a clandestine marriage centre, such
as the Fleet, than in their own parish church. David Kent's study of the
parochial settlement papers of St Martin's in the Fields indicates that
59 per cent of those seeking a parochial settlement in that parish during
1750-1 had been married at the Fleet. An equivalent figure for Chelsea
was 90 out of 469 claimants.

In 1740, of the estimated number of marriages at the Fleet found in
the existing registers, 3.8 per cent (323) came from the three parishes
surrounding the prison, St Martin's Ludgate, St Sepulchre's and St
Bride's; 6.5 per cent (676) came from Stepney, 4.5 per cent (470) from
Cripplegate, 6.3 per cent (651) from St Giles in the Fields, 5.7 per cent
(592) from St Martin's in the Fields, and 5.2 per cent (557) from the
various parishes in Southwark.

The large number who came to the Fleet from the rural areas of
Middlesex, Surrey, Kent, Essex and Hertfordshire, speaks well of its
drawing power. The Hertfordshire Family History Society has
compiled an index of over 6,500 people from that county who married

at the Fleet. For many it must have been a hard day's journey, unless, once again, they were recording their places of settlement for the registration rather than their current domicile. In 1740, the Middlesex parishes outside the limits of the Bills of Mortality (which gave the weekly number of deaths in the city parishes), provided 7.2 per cent (783) of the total of that year, the Essex parishes 5 per cent (522), while 0.1 per cent (12) came from Wales and 0.06 per cent (7) from Scotland. In addition, every year saw a number married who were described as "foreigners". This category included such people as an Armenian in 1700, a Venetian mariner, a Portuguese merchant, and several Frenchmen, but only on one occasion was an interpreter required, when a couple from "Sweedland … could speak no English." Lando, in fact, advertised that his marriages could be performed in either French or English, but it is not known if this made any difference to his matrimonial trade or simply added to his reputation.

****

How many marriages took place at the Fleet? It is impossible to give an accurate figure, mainly because the registers are incomplete, and a vast number of entries are duplicated. What we do know is that the number was considerable. Mark Herber has recently estimated the number of entries in the existing Fleet registers as around 350,000, though this figure probably included a number of duplicated entries. This averages out for the period 1690-1753 as 5,555 marriages per annum, or a very conservative 4,000 if the duplicate entries are removed. In 1705 a committee of the House of Commons estimated the number of marriages at the Fleet to be between 20 to 30 on a day, and between 19 October 1704 to 12 February 1705 there were 2,954 marriages recorded there. An estimate based on the number of register sequences suggests that in 1710 there were 3,650 marriages, in 1720 over 4,000 and in 1740 about 6,600. At a time when it was estimated that the total number of marriages in England and Wales was about 47,500 per annum, the Fleet marriages would have accounted for about an eighth of the total or about fifteen per cent. Outhwaite suggests, however, that if we added the number of other clandestine marriages, especially those which took place after a licence had been issued, about a quarter of all marriages celebrated in any given year throughout England and Wales until March 1754 were clandestine in origin.

From notes given in his register Floyd calculated that he had married 2,821 couples, which averaged 470 a year, and in 1744 Dare married a total of 1,627 couples. Gaynam was alleged to have "coupled 36,000 people in the liberty of the Fleet", and he himself stated that he had married around 2,000 people between February 1734 and May 1735. The term "people" may have been a mistake for "couples" on the part of the reporter (it was stated at a trial), for his own registers indicate that in 1730 alone he had married 1,349 couples. In 1740 Wyatt had over 1,500 marriages recorded in his own registers, while his successor, Symson, married 1,128 couples from 25 June 1750 to 24 June the following year. E. A. Wrigley has estimated the population of London at this time to have been about 675,000. If the annual marriage rate was 10 couples per 1,000 population then there should have been about 6,750 marriages each year in the metropolis. The Fleet with its 6,600 marriages in 1740 indicates not only that it received the lion's share of the matrimonial trade, but is also further confirmation that many must have come to be married at the Fleet from the surrounding locality and further afield.

Two further questions also need to be asked: why did so many couples resort to the Fleet for their marriages, and why did these marriages become almost a social habit for the working classes of London?

The reasons for the Fleet's popularity were diverse. It was not so much the cheapness of the ceremony which encouraged people to marry there, for the average cost of a marriage, including the fee for registration and the charge for a certificate, was about seven shillings and sixpence, a sum not too dissimilar to the cost of a marriage at the city churches. In 1675, for example, a marriage by banns at St James's, Clerkenwell, cost eleven shillings, and three shillings more if it was by licence. The cost of a marriage at St Anne's, Blackfriars in 1703 was nine shillings, and thirty years later the vestry of St Botolph's, Bishopsgate, agreed that the charge for calling banns would be one shilling and sixpence, a marriage by banns six shillings and twopence, and twelve shillings if by licence, together with an additional one shilling and sixpence for registering the marriage and a further one shilling for the certificate. The initial charge included the fees for the incumbent, clerk and sexton. Francis Sadler in his popular book, *The Exactations and Impositions of Parish Fees Discovered*, which reached a third edition in 1742, argued that the scale of these fees was much resented by the populace, and suggested that they constituted an act of "defrauding the people under the pretence of law". Nevertheless, a canonical service at Bishopsgate only cost half a crown more than a shabby wedding at the Fleet, and gave, if required, a valid certificate duly stamped according to law. Those who married at the Fleet obviously saved the cost of the reading of the banns, the cost of the stamp duty on the certificate, but, more importantly, the expense of celebrating the marriage in the style and custom popular to the age. The late seventeenth century play, *The Pleasures of Matrimony*, described these as new clothes, the wedding dinner and "the fiddlers", and commented: "'tis a bad sign when a young man is forced to tap his portion to buy up his wedding gallantry ...". But the saving of these costs alone could hardly have drawn so many to the Fleet, often over considerable distances.

That the marriages could be had "without loss of time, hindrance and knowledge of friends" was probably a more decisive factor for their popularity, particularly when a couple were already cohabiting, or the bride was pregnant, or in the case of those whose time for marriage was limited, such as sailors. "Secret" marriages, however, were very few in relation to the total number, and these should not be overstressed in accounting for the Fleet's popularity. On the other hand it is probable that a number of couples came to the Fleet for their marriage in order to evade the social pressures which still existed in some parts of society against the free choice of a marriage partner. Jeremy Boulton has suggested another reason for the popularity of the Fleet marriages was that the less well-to-do Londoners wished to emulate the aristocratic fashion of private marriages.

It is well known that the calling of banns of marriage in the parish church or churches of the couple was bitterly resented throughout the early eighteenth century. Though this might have been a factor in the rural and suburban parishes, the incidence of church-going in the large urban parishes was such that only a small percentage of parishioners would have heard them read in any case. In an age of mobility it was quite easy to find lodgings or an accommodation address in another parish where the banns could be read without any one being the wiser about the identity of the couple. If Richard Gough, in his celebrated history of Myddle, Shropshire, could write about the "poor foolish girls" who though they could hardly afford a licence, still scorned "that ancient and commendable way of being asked in church", and Haldane, in the debates on the Marriage Act, could declare, "we know how adverse our people generally are to a proclamation of banns", one suspects it was a phenomenon confined to the rural areas. Although Mission commented earlier that "to proclaim banns is a thing nobody now cares to have done; very few are willing to have their affairs declared to all the world in a public place", he was writing within the context of the middle classes who wished to ape their betters and have a licence instead, thus ensuring greater privacy. Laurence Stone's comment that in an age when bundling, or courtship in bed, was widely practised, allowing some degree of sexual experimentation, a couple might feel diffident about having their banns read out in a church where former sexual partners might be present. Yet, once again, this would be truer of a rural than an urban context.

More to the point, however, the calling of banns meant that a preliminary contact had to be made with the local parish clerk or incumbent, and that time had to elapse for the banns to be read before the marriage could take place. Without the restriction of banns the marriages could be solemnized at once, as the writer of *A Letter to the Public* suggested, arguing further that one could "make an acquaintance with a female in an evening, to court her at night, and be married the next morning, which seems to me a reasonable measure of despatch, since it may be made up in less time than a suit of clothes". Alexander Keith with his maxim, "happy is the wooing that is not long a-doing", held that this was good for the country, and added that he had "often asked the married pair how long they had been acquainted; they would reply, some more, some less, but the generality did not exceed the acquaintance of a week, some only a day, half a day". For those who desired no delay in their marriage and no publicity about it the Fleet was ideal. If banns were disliked by the populace of London, it was not so much the asking in church that bothered them, but the delay these formalities caused to their plans.

These were some of the factors which influenced the growth and popularity of the Fleet. One other needs to be considered, and this derives from the suggestion that most of those who married at the Fleet had little contact with organised religion. Recent demographic research has indicated that many people, even in the early eighteenth century, still held the medieval view that spousals, or a solemn engagement, followed by a sexual relationship, constituted a valid marriage. This was accepted by English canon law with strong reservations, although the civil lawyers, for the sake of proof, rejected this notion in favour of a marriage before a clergyman. Furthermore, the Church had consistently taught over the centuries that a priest was needed together with some sort of an ecclesiastical ceremony for a marriage to be fully accepted. There was much confusion, therefore, in the popular mind, as to what constituted a valid marriage, and Lawrence Stone, in his *The Family, Sex and Marriage*, has concluded that a vast number believed that a clerical blessing alone was needed to legitimise an already existing or future union. Consequently, most people accepted that marriage was more a personal matter than a sacrament of the Church. The Church's inability to regulate the way marriage was solemnised by its officials did little to check this tendency. We may argue that those who had little contact with ecclesiastical edifices and formal religion found that the Fleet met the requirements of their deep-rooted views about what was right and what was wrong or what was fair or unfair, without the inconvenience and restrictions imposed by the ecclesiastical authorities.

It was for this reason, probably, coupled with that of convenience, rather than that of finance, that the Fleet became and remained the centre of matrimony for the lower classes of London, and to which they resorted as a matter of pure social habit, in spite of the dubious nature and reputation of this form of marriage. Regular marriage must have been a minority interest for Londoners, for, apart from the Fleet, there was another option available to those who wanted an equally convenient but more regular form of marriage. This required a couple to obtain, at some expense, a licence from the bishop of London's registry at Doctors' Commons, and this prestigious document could then be used for an almost instant marriage at one of the neighbouring churches. It has been stated that the number of licences issued by the bishop of London through his surrogates at this place trebled after the legislation of 1695. One of these churches, perhaps the most popular, was at St Benet's, Paul's Wharf, which stood opposite Doctors' Commons. Between 1708-31 an extremely large number of marriages were said to have been solemnized in this church, the majority by licence. The marriages were clandestine in so far as the name of the parish inserted for the couple was not their place of residence. In 1712 there were 302 marriages, and 569 in 1724. The number declined after the 1730s, probably because of the competition with the Fleet, so that there were 197 in 1746 and 124 in 1753, and after the Marriage Act an average of 15. Another one of these churches was St Gregory's by St Paul's, and Tony Benson has found that 95 per cent of the marriages solemnized there between 1599-1638 were by licence. The cost of these marriages was greater than that of the Fleet, and involved more complicated procedures. These two factors would not have commended this sort of marriage to that section of the community which was attracted to the Fleet. On the other hand, these more respectable forms of clandestine marriage might have been tolerated by the ecclesiastical authorities as a counterweight to what they would have regarded as the scandalous marriages of the Fleet.

A Fleet Wedding Certificate (courtesy of National Archives: ADM 106/3026)

8
REGISTRARS, REGISTERS AND CERTIFICATES

As English law would not support a marriage until proof of its
existence had been established, it was necessary for those concerned in
the Fleet marriages to provide for the registration of these marriages
and to give certificates of marriage to those who required them. The
prison chapel had always maintained its own register, official or
otherwise, and this practice was continued by most of the leading
marriage houses. Some of their keepers became established also as
register keepers, as the clergy whom they employed entered the
marriages they conducted elsewhere into their employer's register.
Oswald's register of 1710 is described as "an account of marriages
done by Clerk and returned to me to be registered", and entries in
another register state, "married by the doctor abroad but registered
here". Several of the smaller houses appear to have registered their
marriages in the register books of the more substantial houses, even
using their certificates of marriage. Hodgkin's register records
marriages at Bennett's and at the *Goat*, in addition to those at his own
marriage house. Burnford entered into his register marriages conducted
at such houses as Levy's at the *Green Cannister*, the *Leg* tavern in
Fleet Street, the *Hoop* tavern in Fleet Ditch, the British Coffee House,
and the *Fountain* of Ludgate Hill. Such circumstances must have
prompted his self appointed title as "the Clerk and Register Keeper of
the Marriages at the Fleet". The Lilly brothers acted in a similar
capacity, Joshua claiming the same office and advising Boyce and
Burnford that a "licence" presented to him by Charles Colebrall of St
James's for his marriage to Martha Hedges, which had been
invalidated "by being too late", was in fact the Lord Chancellor's
"pattern" for his office. He registered marriages from the *Bell*, Old
Bailey, Barratt's, the *Crown* in Fleet Street, the *Swan*, Salisbury Court,
and the *Red Lion*, Bridewell.

These register keepers often gave a name to their registers, which
they hoped would indicate their antiquity and authenticity. These
names included such titles as "The Chapel Register" of Lilly, "The

Fleet Register", "The Register Book of Fleet Marriages", "The Old and True Register", "The Original Register", "The St Bride's Parish Register", and "The True and Ancient Register".

The record of the marriage was generally written into a notebook, either by the parson himself or by the clerk of the house. These entries were later transcribed into a more formal and bound register, often by a person employed to do so. Mrs Bassett at Fielding's trial in 1706 stated that several people were hired "to write down the certificates in the register book", while Dare paid a person 1s.6d. per day and 1s.3d. per hundred entries "to post up" his register. The mistakes made in transcribing these registers were sometimes recorded. One entry reads: "in transcribing left out of the 9th Wartley and Smith as will appear by Mr Ashwell's book ...". Unfortunately, many other entries were badly transcribed as may be seen from comparing the notebook entries with the actual registers.

A number of these keepers and parsons maintained several registers at one and the same time. Mrs Bassett was asked at the same trial:

"Have you several registers at the same time?"
Mrs Bassett: "Yes, there are several ministers and therefore entries made in several books."
Court: "Do you keep two books for the registration of marriages, for one and the same year and time?"
Mrs Bassett: "There are several books and we enter sometimes in one and sometimes in another, by reason that there are several ministers and each hath his particular book."
Court: "How many books have you of that year?"
Mrs Bassett: "But two."

Parson Gaynam, asked a similar question at the trial of Mary Sommers for bigamy in 1736, replied:

"I have two register books and I have a ledger in which I enter them, and I can easily find out any. My books are paged and numbered."
Court: "Do you enter into these books from the little books?" [the notebooks]
Gaynam: "Yes, the entries into these books are always according to the entries in the little books.

At other trials Gaynam claimed that his registers were "as fair and legible as any church in England can produce," adding, "'Tis all in my own handwriting, and paged so that it cannot be altered, and all the marriages are put down alphabetically that I can readily find them."

These answers were a neat way of avoiding the real question, which concerned secret or "private" registers. Wyatt and several of the clergy maintained these "private" registers, as did Mrs Hodgkins, for a witness in one of the trials eventually agreed that an entry had been inserted into such a "private" book at her house, "because there would be trouble about the marriage". Gaynam varied this practice by inserting the word "private" against the entry of any couple that "desired it might not be known".

While the cost of registering a marriage was often included in the clerk's fee, it was sometimes charged separately, so that the entries of those who declined to pay were not recorded in the registers. "Did not pay to be registered" is a comment frequently found in the notebooks, and another entry, nearly erased, has this note alongside it: "paid for registering since the erasure". Miss Scrope, in evidence given in court, remembered that "the clergyman took a book into his hands, and demanded the fee for registering the marriage". His fee was too high, and as he refused to lower it, Creswell, her bridegroom, stated, "then it shall not be registered at all". The clergyman appealed to Miss Scrope, but she "not knowing the consequences, readily declared my indifference". Another instance is found in a notebook: "the woman very cross, and would not pay to be registered, should have paid but 1s. and had copy but now to pay two and for searching".

It is difficult to distinguish between those who declined to be registered and those who refused to pay the price demanded for the marriage, for in both cases only the couple's Christian names, required for the ceremony itself, would be recorded in the notebooks and, less frequently, in the registers. Nevertheless, it is clear that the number of those who declined to be registered was considerable, such as "a little man and she a great lusty woman disfigured with smallpox", who although "they were married would not have it registered", or "a very foolish old man with them would not let them stay to be registered or as much to tell the parish". George Meilden and Elizabeth Lawson "desired not to have it registered", while Henry Sweeting, a peruke maker, who was married at Wilson's to Eleanor Davies "was not to be registered there he being not of age".

"Would you trust a Fleet parson with keeping a register?" asked the earl of Hillsborough in the debates on the Marriage Act. He answered his own question by declaring "no one can suppose you would". For not only were the registers irregularly kept, they were often maintained that way for the express purpose of permitting entries to be fitted in at will, removed, or even forged entries inserted. This could be done with impunity, as the registers possessed no legal status whatsoever.

Antedating, that is, assigning an earlier date to a marriage than its actual date, was a constant preoccupation with the Fleet register keepers. Lilly seems to have made a speciality of this practice, which filled Ashwell with horror. Commenting about an antedate which he was "not to be acquainted with how long", Ashwell wrote, "I have a good mind to go and see the said Mrs Chapman that come with 'em to enquire what roguery Lilly has done". Many antedates are contained in the registers, and the Fleet became so well known for this practice that customers felt no inhibitions about requesting its application for themselves. Hence one Joseph, before he was married to Mary Bates, had agreed with the registrar about the antedate he required. A further couple "begged" to be antedated four months, another "would have it dated to 10 May 1736" rather than 1739, while Thomas Giles in December 1744 after he had been married "pulled his watch out and laughed and wanted antedate to October". These requests could be refused, and both Ashwell and Burnford did so, but their refusals appear to have been more the exception than the rule.

Many of the registers had space left in them for this purpose, and those registers, which were later transcribed, were able to incorporate these entries without any suspicion being aroused. One register even makes various references to this practice. The entries for August 1744 contain various notes, for example a note under an entry of the 4th states, "see July 1738"; for the 7th, "see 20 July 1743", the 14th, "see June 16", and the 16th "see April 18". An entry for the marriage of Barry Richards provides further evidence. He paid "for an antedate to March the 11th in the same year, which Lilly complied with and put 'em in his book accordingly there being a vacancy in the book suitable to the time". Another "vacancy" was described in this way: "this vacancy left for the person who came from Ives but had not money enough". This may have been a legitimate entry, but if that person failed to come, there was a space available for an antedate. Half a guinea was once offered for such a space in one of Floyd's registers. It was frequently alleged in court by counsel that some of the clergy kept two registers, "one with close lines and the other with open lines" for this purpose. The prosecuting counsel at Beau Fielding's trial thus argued, after stating that an entry was "where we may suppose there was a vacancy left to insert such a thing as this ... counterfeit entry", continued,

> But a mere book is produced, and not of the best credit neither; it
> is entered in the bottom of the leaf, but not in the middle; it is
> written with another coloured ink, and in another hand.

John Mottram was sufficiently indiscreet to date some of his marriages
several years before the date of his ordination.

The antedates given were usually for a period of months, but several
were given for much longer periods, such as five years, ten years, or
even eighteen years. Alexander White, a peruke maker of St
Katherine's and Phyllis Dick were "officially" married on 2 October
1739, but instructed the clerk that the marriage should be backdated to
1724. The cost could be high. Walter Bortwick offered five guineas for
an antedate of four years.

The most usual reason recorded for these antedates was in order to
legitimise an existing pregnancy, for most of the antedates given were
for a matter of months. Another reason was in order to regularise a
relationship of some standing. This occurred in 1742 when:

> Was married an acquaintance of Jos. and John Lillys, a noted
> gambler, viz. George Mattocks of Cripplegate and Catherine
> Smith. N.B. George had lived some years prior to the marriage
> and had several children and had thing done by Jos. accordingly.

Another couple supplied a further but related reason, they "wanted to
be antedated having a bastard before marriage". John Steward of
Stradlam in Kent and Mary Mason arrived at the Fleet in 1741 and
stated that "they had come to be married at my house February 6th 1730
but they differed and went away but now had a marriage settlement
made and dated February 6 1730, about an hour before married".

False entries were as easily inserted into the registers as antedates.
The entry of the marriage of Peter Hulett and Mary Ann Javiour in
1741 contains some additional words, namely, "forged by Dare". A
further note in a register states that John Crosier and Jane Ashew
wanted an "entry without marriage", which was offered them at
Smiths. Under another entry Mottram wrote a text in Latin which
translates that they were not married but obtained registration for fear
of their parents. In 1731 a witness at John Miller's trial for bigamy
stated:

I went with her to prove her marriage at Mrs Hodgkin's and Mrs Hodgkin's said, for half a guinea, she'd enter her name in the register, for a certificate would not do if the marriage was not registered. Her name was not in the book, and I saw Starkey, the parson, interline her name in the book five years backwards.

Anne Hodgkins, in spite of her denials, clearly made a business of these fraudulent practices, for she herself gave similar evidence at the trial of Ann Inott in 1733. It was then alleged that being unable to find the requisite entry, she had inserted a false one at a cost of 7s.6d., after Inott had "begged, prayed, and cried ... I am sure," argued Mrs Hodgkin's to the court, "you would have had some compassion for the poor creature". Mrs Hodgkins found the court less compassionate than she had claimed to be herself, for she was told:

> You ought to be prosecuted instead of the prisoner, and you, that for the lucre of three half crowns, would wickedly make a false entry and bring false evidence to charge a man with the cost of maintaining this woman and her two children, and now you come here to swear against her ...

She replied, "she didn't know there was any sin in it". Her sympathy was equally aroused for a "young woman that happened to be with child and was hunted by the parish officers, she said for half a guinea it might be entered backwards in the book, and it would screen her from the anger of her friends". Perhaps Mrs Hodgkins' compassion outweighed her discretion, for she was obviously a soft touch.

Entries were also forged in order to provide the evidence required for legal cases, as was suspected in the case of *Morais v. Morais* of 1705. Is this what Congreve meant when he wrote in the *Tatler* of 17 February 1711 about "a scoundrel that was grown rich and went and bought a coat of arms at the Heralds and a set of ancestors at Fleet Ditch"?

If false entries were inserted into the registers, good entries could also be removed. Andre Busquet and his wife were married at the Fleet in 1735. Five years later his wife came "to desire the said marriage to be destroyed". Richard Beckingsay was in the same predicament. He "came to me signifying that he was lawfully married to Ann Richards but living unhappy desired the marriage to be destroyed, which I refused". Ashwell records the following "memorandum" on 13 May 1730:

Being Whitsunday ... two gentlemen came into my house and asked for me, my wife called me downstairs. They had a quarter of brandy [and] asked me to drink. My wife and children and myself was going to the fields but the gentlemen coming in I desired my wife to go with the children. The gentlemen asked where they was going, I said to the fields, my wife being unwilling to go without me being our wedding day twelve years before. The children began to cry so that one of the gentlemen put his hand into his pocket and gave the youngest a shilling for a coach for her mother and desired me to make a strong bowl of punch which I did when [they] began to talk, it was for me to erase out of the registers the marriage of Winesdale and Wicham. I would not consent, but remembering I had seen it in August ...

Floyd recorded a similar refusal, when a Mrs Wells in 1729 requested him:

To erase the marriage out of the book, for that the husband had beat her and abused her in a barbarous manner and she had much rather be esteemed his whore that she might have proper recourse at law against him. I made her believe I did so for which I had half a guinea, and she at the same time delivered me the certificate, no person present, according to her desire.

In the case of *Muilman v. Muilman* it was alleged that Muilman made a number of unsuccessful attempts to tamper with or to destroy a register. It was a complicated case, for in order to prove the authenticity of this register it was necessary to find evidence of the registrar's handwriting on other documents, and to produce his death certificate.

The register books yielded another source of profit, this being the fees paid to their owners by persons who desired to search through them for particular entries. These fees varied from one to four shillings. Not surprisingly, many of the entries required were not to be found, so that in one instance at least, after a fruitless search, the couple decided to make the best of a bad job, and "were married afterwards as not being married before". In this way the register books obtained a certain monetary value, and were frequently sold, mainly to those already connected with the Fleet marriages. Mrs Barratt possessed the registers of her late husband's marriages and also looked after Cox's collection of registers until her death, when both sets of registers were sold.

Lando advertised not only his services as a parson, but also his extensive collection of registers which he claimed were "from the year 1700, to be searched without imposition".

The late Beric Lloyd identified one register, and others have identified further registers, as forgeries. The marriages they contain were said to have occurred in the 1670s, but in fact they are copies of marriages which took place, in some instances, sixty years later. The reason may have been to suggest to people that the Fleet marriages commenced at an earlier date than they actually did, thus encouraging more people to search the registers than would otherwise be the case.

Certificates of marriage were generally sold to the couples married at a charge which averaged 2s.6d. Floyd stipulated, however, "no certificates for less than three shillings", and was not pleased when his "particular acquaintance promised a certificate for a shilling at my room". The cost was determined, as usual, by the supposed rank of the parties, for Thomas Hield was not permitted to have "one under nine shillings. They thought she [his wife] had been an heiress and wanted a good deal of money". As these certificates could always be obtained at a later date many declined them when offered them on their wedding day, so that the about one in three entries in the notebooks of Burnford's and Wilson's marriage houses have the letters N.C. (no certificate) written alongside them. Many, like David Feltham, repented of their omission, and "came since and had one".

The earlier certificates were hand written, but by 1710 most appear to have been printed. Although several of the parsons used their own, as did Mottram and Floyd, most used a common stock form. This had space for the name of the couple, the parishes to which they belonged, the name of the parson and / or the registrar, and the date of the marriage. There was a great reluctance to mention the name of the Fleet on these certificates, and this was especially true of those parsons who issued their own certificates. Instead the name of the parish in which the marriage was solemnized was given, such as "married at the *Anchor and Crown* in the parish of St 'Pulchers, London". To make the certificate seem more convincing the royal arms might be placed on it, as was the practice of Lilly and Burnford.

These certificates were mainly on paper, though parchment ones were available at a more substantial cost. Ashwell, finding that a couple, James Huay and Elizabeth Jackson were "abusive to all the house", gave them a parchment copy to get rid of them, though he added to their entry "to pay 10s.2d. for certificate or 4s.8d. for a fair copy, what I gave them being very dirty".

However impressive these certificates may have been, they possessed no legal validity, for they were not issued by a legal authority, nor were they stamped with the five shilling stamp duty imposed on marriage certificates, although Parson Mottram gave:

> His certificates ... with the city arms printed on them, and ignorant people were imposed on, in being made to believe that was the King's stamp.

Of course, stamped certificates could be had, though in most cases customers who desired one were required to provide their own stamped paper, while they were charged an additional fee for the filling up of the certificate, which was, for obvious reasons, handwritten. "Five shillings stamp, half a crown filling up", is not an infrequent entry.

The abuses permitted and accepted in the issuing of these certificates were similar to those already described regarding the registers, but they were on a far wider scale, possibly because the certificates were easier to abuse and less likely to be noticed than a register entry. It frequently happened, therefore, that while the entry in the register was correct, the information given on the certificate was altered or made incomplete on purpose, for example, by the omission of the date of marriage or the parochial details of the couple concerned. Antedating was likewise practiced. The reasons given for this antedating were much the same as those for the antedating of the register entries: the woman was pregnant, to please parents, out of pity for the girl "being with child a month after married", or because the couple had lived together beforehand. Floyd even noted that "William Bozely had in 1726 a certificate dated 1722 but the marriage on the upper date", while it was not unknown for the person married to change the date on the certificate, as one did who was married in 1742, but who "made her paper 1732 her own self". For some reason this aroused the anger of the parson. In fact, the granting of these certificates was carried out in an extremely casual manner. Dare, for example, gave a certificate to a couple only "said to be married by Ashwell" two years earlier. Other certificates were issued on the oath of a bride, or of other persons, that a marriage had taken place beforehand for which a record could not be found.

It was almost inevitable that it became a standard practice for the defence of any person charged with bigamy in which a Fleet marriage was concerned, to insinuate that the keepers gave certificates without any marriage having taken place. Witnesses were often produced to testify that they had recently obtained certificates under such circumstances, as did William Morris in 1731. He told the court: "here is a certificate I had from the Fleet last Tuesday; this is a certificate of my being married to one I never saw in my life". He added, "they'll give certificates to anybody". These charges were not untrue. "This was a certificate ... granted without a marriage", wrote Floyd in 1726, and in the previous year he had charged a fee of 5s. for what he had described as "no mar. but a cer. granted". Lilly did the same, for when in 1742 a couple came to be married at his house:

> The man pretended he would marry the woman by which pretence he got money to pay for marrying and to buy a ring but left the woman by herself and never returned upon which J Lilly takes the woman from the *Bull and Garter* to his own house and gave her a certificate as if she had been married to the man.

John Rogers, a gentleman of St Margaret's, Westminster, and Elizabeth Hussey, came to be married in 1729. Their register entry, written by a scandalised Fleet parson, added: "Mrs Hussey [is] a Quaker and she could not comply with the ceremonies of our church, and would take the man to bed with her on the credit of a Fleet certificate".

There were many requests for these "sham" certificates. Most appear to have been favourably answered, even when it was known that they would be used to pervert the course of justice. This occurred, for example, when Mary Milboorn's "spor", William Edwards, "dying suddenly she came to the Two Sawyers for a sham certificate," or when Jonathan Ellis and Jane Davis were left a house in Aylesbury Market Place and needed "a sham certificate of the nuptials". In another case a woman attempted to claim an Admiralty pension by such an expedient, her husband being a mariner "deceased". She received her certificate even though the comment is written: "she wants a certificate whom I believe not married". However, the repercussions of obtaining a false certificate in order to obtain a "reward" were sufficient to cause Edmund Dangerfield to be tried for bigamy. Let him tell his own story. A lady, Arabella Fast, offered him something that was in his own interest:

> "There is," says she, "a minister who often lies with me, if you say you are my husband, we may get some money out of him." I thought there would be no harm in me to say the words, than for

him to do the deed.

The plan was laid, and he entered the room at a prearranged time, and

> Found Arabella and he a bed. "Hey," says I, "how came you to be abed with my spouse …. ?" "Sir," says he, "I only lay with her to keep my back warm." "O Sir," says I, "if she had kept your back warm you have kept her belly warm." However the gentleman lay with her all night and in the morning he asked for a certificate of our marriage. "I must make you a present," says he, "if you can produce a certificate." I knew not what to say, guilty conscience needs no accuser. "Sir," says Arabella, "we were married at the Fleet," and says she to me, "for a crown I can get a certificate from thence" and I gave a crown and in half an hour she brings me a certificate.

Unfortunately, Dangerfield was already married.

The parsons in their desire for legality even issued their own "licences of marriage". Several entries in one book are marked as "married by licence", or "licence having been first obtained". Such matters were even mentioned on the certificate, one reading: "Joined in the bond of Matrimony by the Rules and Ceremonies of the Church of England by Licence granted and dated the 28th of November". While there is the chance that some of these licences were issued from Doctors' Commons, there is sufficient evidence to suggest that the parsons issued their own. When questioned in court about them the parsons either denied that they issued licences, or else they acknowledged that the assertion recorded on the certificates that the marriage had been "by licence granted" was false. There may be some evidence that licences which had expired were reused at the Fleet, for one register gives two dates, viz. "Jan 12 edict: confirmed Mar 26" or "Jan 22. Ap 7". The first date may be the date of the licence, and the second that of the actual marriage. The cost in one example was one guinea. A number of certificates of banns are recorded in the registers. Thus Benjamin Deedman and Elinor Foster had a certificate that their banns had been called, and not been challenged, at their parish church of Kingston upon Thames, even though they were married at the Fleet.

The result of these practices meant that the courts frequently suspected the testimony of any Fleet parson. "You are on your oath," said counsel to Parson Gaynam, "I ask you whether you never enter marriages in that book, when there's no marriage at all?" Although

Gaynam might reply, "I never did in all my life", the suspicion remained. Similarly, as will be clarified in a later chapter, the existence of these abuses caused the non-acceptance of the Fleet registers and certificates in the courts of law, for, as Gally pointed out, the proof of any such marriage was precarious, for the registers might be in private hands, and could be easily forged, while the persons who kept them were not legal officers and were not responsible to the public for their safe keeping. Gally argued further that the experience of the courts had been that, whenever a case depended on the validity of a Fleet marriage, then the entries of such a marriage were:

> as in the case of Miss Scrope ... ready to be produced or concealed as a marriage is to be proved or disproved, which management is at the command of the person that pays best ....

He continued:

> There never was a trial concerning a clandestine marriage, but what was attended with many oaths on both sides. In which case there must be perjury. There are persons prepared for this purpose at the Fleet. They can prove or disprove a marriage, as they are paid for it, by making erasements of marriages which have been solemnized. Which erasements and entries cannot be deemed forgeries in law, because their books are only private books.

Even though the number of these abuses might be few, their existence meant that the proof of every marriage performed at the Fleet was rendered suspect, and immense difficulties were placed in the way of establishing the validity of any given marriage because of the non-recognition by the courts of the Fleet registers and certificates. When people realised this it led to much concern about, and eventually opposition to, these Fleet marriages, a matter enhanced by the other abuses to which attention is drawn in the following chapter.

9
BIGAMY AND SEDUCTION:
THE SEAMY SIDE OF THE FLEET

Although the incidence of matrimonial abuse was low in proportion to the number of couples married at the Fleet, they were so significant, were practised so openly, and attracted such great attention, that their effect was to make public opinion deeply suspicious of, and hostile to, the Fleet marriages. It became clear to many, especially the propertied classes, that it was easy to obtain fraudulent certificates, perjured testimony, even impersonation, in relation to these marriages, for quite modest sums. The cost to the injured parties could be substantial, not only in legal fees, but in the uncertainty of their position and even of their inheritance. The situation was intensified by the knowledge that the law regarded these clandestine marriages as valid, however irregular, or even criminal, their origin may have been.

The Fleet marriages, with their lack of any prior examination or enquiry, as provided by the calling of banns, were a direct inducement to the practice of bigamy. Nearly all the annual editions of the *London Sessions Papers* from the 1720s to the 1750s report cases concerning bigamous unions contracted at the Fleet. It has been estimated that half of all the bigamy trials at the Old Bailey that stipulated the place of marriage concerned a Fleet marriage. In one particular case, that of *Taylor v. Taylor* of 1756, the Court had to decide which of three women was the widow of Taylor. He had contracted three marriages, two, if not three, at the Fleet. These bigamy cases were often difficult to prove, for witnesses and prosecutors frequently failed to appear, the proof required for the court to convict was frequently lacking, and many judges declined to accept a Fleet register as providing valid evidence of a marriage.

The excuses made by the accused to answer for their conduct shed much light on other abuses and irregularities allowed at the Fleet. Many claimed, as noted in the previous chapter, that any person could obtain a Fleet certificate without undergoing a ceremony of marriage, while others alleged that they were so intoxicated at the time of their marriage that they were not aware of its significance. Accordingly, Robert Wilson testified:

When I was a little out of the way, a little in liquor and they got me to an alehouse, but whether I was married or not I cannot tell; indeed she told me we were married, and we lived together afterwards.

Wilson conveniently doubted whether the necessary words of the ceremony had been said, and he claimed, as did many, that his first wife had deserted him and that he had no means of knowing whether she was alive or not. Although the statutory penalty for bigamy was death, he received the lesser but usual punishment of being "burnt in the hand".

Ruth Woodward was accused of a similar offence in the same year, 1736. Her indictment read that having been married to William Woodward in 1730, she went through another form of marriage with Robert Holmes in 1735. This marriage took place at the *Hand and Pen*, a barber's shop, and was performed before a Fleet parson who was commonly called "the Bishop of Hell". Ruth, however, declined to remember these details on the grounds that she "was so much in liquor that I remember nothing about it". She was lucky to be acquitted for the judge made it clear to the jury that "drunkenness is no excuse in law for any crime". John Burton offered another excuse. His first wife "had poxt him in the wedding week and then ran away with his goods". Elizabeth Harman married again after her first husband "took away my clothes and left me destitute without anything in the world". Mart Picart, alias Gandon, offered an even more substantial excuse. This was sufficiently interesting for the account of her case to be incorporated into a book of the more notable Old Bailey trials, *Select Trials for the years 1720-24*. Her second husband, Philip Bouchain, a French sailor, gave evidence as follows:

Me was married to dis voman dat is de trute, upon de twenty-four of dis mont, sis heures after de noon, a l'enseigne de Hand and de Pen in de Fleet Lane, me gave tree shilling and tree quartern of sheneva to de parsoong. But me was vary mush elevate vid de liquor, and dis and dat and d'oder, so dat me no could tell vat I do ven de ting vas done. But me no go to de bed vid mine vise at all.

He claimed that this was because a relation of his wife entered the entertainment room, and informed him that his wife was married to another person. She then gave evidence:

He none husband for me. Vat signify de parsoong and de ring and all de Saremoree? Vy dat no make a der husband. Dare be no husband no vife till da go to bed togader. But Monsieur Bonchain he do no vid me in de bed, he do nothing in de varld – nothing but de saremonee – vy dat be no husband.

She was acquitted, as there was no proof that the marriage had been consummated.

Not all could claim such innocent excuses. When Walter Rawlins was married in 1744 he confessed after the ceremony that "he had a wife living". This gave the parson "reason to believe she [his second wife] married under a colour she being well dressed and he an Irishman". Nor did the Fleet clergy always decline to officiate at a marriage even when they were aware that the first partner was alive. John Norden married Elizabeth Smith in 1721, though it was noted in the register that "he has another wife", while on another occasion the parson noted that "the woman, I heard, had a husband alive at the same time, they would not tell their names". The *Whitehall Evening Post* in its issue of 24 July 1739 provides another example:

On Tuesday last a woman indifferently dressed came to the sign of the Bull and Garter, next door to the Fleet Prison, and was there married to a soldier; in the afternoon she came again, and would have been married to a butcher but that parson who had married her in the morning refused to marry her again, which put her to the trouble of going a few doors further, to another parson, who had no scruples.

This is similar to an apocryphal story that was printed in an unknown newspaper in the same year:

Last week, a merry widow, near Bethnal Green, having a pretty many admirers, not to be over cruel, she equally dispensed her favours between two, who were the highest in her esteem. The one, a butcher, meeting the good woman, took the advantage of the other's absence, and pleaded his cause so successfully, that they tucked up their tails, trudged to the Fleet, and were tacked together. Home they both jogged to their several habitations, the bridegroom to his, the bride to hers. Soon after came another of her admirers, an honest weaver, who upon hearing of the melancholy news, had no more life in him for some time than one of the beams in his loom; but recovering himself a little from the surprise, he was seized with a sudden delirium, swore his loom should be his gibbet, and he'd hang himself pendant at the end of his garters, if he also was not tacked to this comfortable rib: the good widow, considering that the butcher had not bedded with her, and desirous of preventing murder, consented, and away she jogged to be coupled to the weaver. On their return home, to bed they went, and the butcher coming to see his dear spouse, found her in bed with the weaver; upon which a quarrel ensured, and the butcher being the best man, she left the weaver and went to the butcher, being willing to please them both, as well as she could.

Another dramatic incident occurred three years later which was also recorded by a newspaper correspondent:

On Tuesday last, two persons, one of Skinner Street, and the other of Webb's Square, Spittlefields, exchanged wives, to whom they had been married upward of twelve years, and the same day, to the content of both parties, the marriages were consummated at the Fleet. Each husband gave his wife away to the other, and in the evening had an entertainment together.

It hardly matters whether these stories were true or not. People clearly believed they were, and could point to the evidence presented at many bigamy trials as confirmatory evidence.

The consequences of a bigamous union could be severe. In *Creswell v. Creswell* an heiress, Mrs Warneford, had married Creswell in good faith. However, Miss Scrope claimed she had married Creswell at the Fleet at a time previous to this particular marriage. The Warneford marriage was declared null and void, and the children of it were thereby rendered illegitimate. As Dr Gally remarked, there could be no confidence that a marriage might not be bigamous, since one partner might well have contracted a previous marriage at the Fleet.

Even more notorious than these bigamy cases was the use made of the Fleet by those who wished to seduce into marriage for their own purposes heirs, heiresses or wealthy women. Alexander Keith held that the number of "whores" who managed to better themselves in this way was considerable. Gally argued that the Fleet had been made into a "market for those persons who had fortunes", while Daniel Defoe considered it was hardly safe for such people to walk abroad. A gentleman, he wrote, "might have the satisfaction of hanging a thief that stole an old horse from him, but could have no justice against a rogue for stealing his daughter". Not unnaturally these marriages gave rise to great concern, for though these practices were offences against the statute law, they were still regarded as valid marriages by the Church. The only effectual remedy was to execute the offender, as happened to Sir John Johnston for his share in the abduction of Mrs Wharton in 1690, and to Hagan Swendsen for his involvement in the marriage of Mrs Rawlinson in 1702, when having taken her up on a "fob action" for debt he pretended that the only way of escape was by marrying him. This ultimate deterrent with its extremely practical solution to the problem of "until death us do part" fell into disuse, possible because of its severity.

In the *Tricks of the Town*, an early eighteenth century satirical pamphlet, this illustration is given of a setter, that is, a person who facilitated these seductions:

> His ordinary occupation is to attend the motion of young heirs to draw and trepan them into mean and unequal matches, and so impose upon them *jilts* and *whores*, under the character of heiresses and *virtuosa's*, and this he does with so much dexterity and so many subtle arts and crafty stratagems, that 'tis almost impossible, if you should be once so unfortunate to fall into his management, to escape out of it again, without being undone, for the remainder of your life.

There were well-defined ways in which the setter or the seducer could accomplish his task. He might persuade the victim of his honest intentions, as happened to Miss Scrope when she married at the Fleet her "most bitter enemy," or if that failed he might even go to the extent of kidnapping the person. A description of such an incident is contained in the *Grub Street Journal* of 1735. This related how a woman accepted a lift in a coach, which then stopped on Ludgate Hill on the pretence of picking up the owner's sister. The woman was induced to enter a house, where she found herself in a room:

> A tawny fellow in a black coat and black wig appeared. "Madam, you are come in good time, the doctor was just-a-going." The doctor?" says she, horribly frightened, fearing it was a mad house:

"What has the doctor to do with me?" "To marry you to that gentleman; the doctor has waited for you these three hours, and will be paid by you or the gentleman before you go." "That gentleman," said she, recovering herself, "is worthy of a better fortune than mine," and begged hard to be gone. But Dr Wryneck swore she should be married, or if she would not, he would still have his fee, and register the marriage from that night. The lady, finding she could not escape without money or a pledge, told them she liked the gentleman so well, that she would certainly meet him tomorrow night, and gave them a ring as a pledge; which, says she, was my mother's gift on her deathbed enjoining that if ever I married, it should be my wedding ring. By which cunning contrivance she was delivered from the black doctor and his tawny crew.

She was probably lucky to escape by merely providing a ring as a pledge for the doctor. Such precedents were followed by Jonathan Brooks, who married an heiress in 1749 at an uninhabited house in Fenchurch Street, and by Isaac Brand, who decoyed a thirteen-year-old heiress to the Mint from Westminster. He was fined £2,000 and committed to Newgate until the fine was paid. Mrs Ann Leigh, the *Original Weekly Journal* of 26 September 1719 reported, who was worth £200 per annum with £6,000 ready cash, "was decoyed away from her friends in Buckinghamshire and married at the Fleet against her consent. She was used so barbarously she now lies speechless".

A further case reached the columns of the *Gentleman's Magazine* for June 1748. It concerned Henry Williams, a naval officer, and Thomas Jenkins, an officer in the artillery, who were tried for conspiring

To force away a young lady in Tavistock Street, and to compel her to marry the said Williams, and for a riot in forcibly entering the house where she lived with a hired mob, in order to get possession of her person and her fortune, on pretence that she was married to the said Williams; after a trial of seven hours, the defendants were found guilty, and a Fleet parson produced to prove the marriage, having most grossly prevaricated in his testimony, was at the request of the jury committed to the Marshalsea, to be prosecuted for wilful perjury.

Defoe's description of an heiress forced into a marriage, and later ravished, at pistol point, appears to have been a literary invention. There is no evidence that this ever occurred.

Other seducers relied upon deluding the selected victim into believing that the marriage was a right and proper one between two persons of equal rank and fortune. Several entries in the registers testify to such circumstances. In 1744, for example, Ashwell noted at the marriage of Nathaniel Gilbert and Mary Lupton:

> There were five or six in the company. One amongst them ... seemed by his dress and behaviour &c to be an Irishman, he pretended to be some grand officer in the army ... he told me that the woman that was to be married that it was a poor girl agoing to be married to a common soldier but when I came to marry them I found myself imposed upon, and having a mistrust of some Irish roguery I took upon me to ask what the gentleman's name was ... answer was made to me, what was that to me, God damn me if I did not immediately marry them he would use me ill; in short apprehending it to be a conspiracy I found myself obliged to marry them in terrorem.

Another method used to decoy people into an unequal marriage was to rush their victims into matrimony before they had had time to deliberate upon their conduct or seek the advice of their friends and family. It could be done in this way:

> A girl that deigns to be the wife of a man, who would blush to own her for his mistress, works him up to such a pitch by her dangerous caresses, that she makes him declare, before witnesses provided for that purpose, that he takes her to be his wedded wife. Nay, it frequently happens that he has no other interest in giving his consent but to carry on a joke, but to her all joking in this subject becomes serious, the I WILL is taken literally ... [and she] takes care to have a chaplain ready.

Indeed, continued L'Abbé le Blanc, the English laws:

> Authorise the wiles which the most profligate harlot can invent, in order to seduce a young man of family: they favour vice and render indissoluble the shameful knot ... One cannot be too much upon his guard in England against this sort of woman: they have a wonderful address in laying snares for youth, and in some measure

wiping off the scandal of their lives, which had separated them from society, by a marriage which restores them to it.

One such device, he observed, was to make "the person drunk, whom they intend to hook in". Leman, in his *Matrimony Analysed*, wrote about the youth

> Inflamed with lust and liquor, incentives to both being readily furnished in the same places, [who] might there at all seasons, and at all hours, seal his final ruin.

This type of seduction occurred, for example, in 1735, when a youth by the name of Hill was persuaded to drink himself into a state of intoxication at an alehouse near the Fleet Prison. He was then drawn into a marriage with a woman "in mean circumstances and of bad character". The son of Ralph Peters, town clerk of Liverpool, intended for Holy Orders, was deluded by a servant maid into a Fleet marriage while he was at Westminster School. Later, his life ruined, he managed to be ordained in Ireland, and, having been told his "wife" had died, married his first love. But the rumour was untrue, and he accordingly fled with this second wife to a chaplaincy in the American colonies.

Sir John Leigh, a helpless and drunken old man, was yet another victim who was forced into a marriage with the daughter of his apothecary. A letter of Horace Walpole to his friend George Montagu of 1748 provides a further illustration. It concerned a beau about town, nicknamed "Handsome Tracy", who endeavoured to make the daughter of a Craven Street butterwoman his mistress. She, aware of his designs, decided to go further, and persuading her mother to borrow money to purchase "a leg of mutton" invited him to dinner, and

> Kept him drinking till twelve at night, when with a chosen committee the faithful pair waited on the minister of the May-Fair. The doctor was in bed, and swore he would not get up to marry the king, but that he had a brother over the way who perhaps would, and who did. The mother borrowed a pair of sheets, and so they consummated at her house, and the next day they went to their own palaces.

The parson who married them was probably Peter Symson, a Fleet parson who also assisted at the May-Fair establishment.

Unequal marriages did not always require the assistance of

seduction or alcohol in order to be effectual. The author of *A Trip through the Town*, published in 1735, wrote:

> If a slut be tolerable handsome or has any share of cunning, the apprentice or her master's son is enticed away and ruined by her. Thus many good families are impoverished and disgraced by these pert husseys, who taking the advantage of simplicity, and unruly desires, draw many needless youths, nay, some of good estates, into their snares; and of this we have innumerable instances.

The anonymous author of the satirical book *Tricks of the Town* refused to allow himself to be swayed by the anger of parents who saw these marriages as a threat to their family ambitions. He argued that the parent ought to take some share of responsibilities for these misalliances, for often these marriages were an outcome of "Miss" having been brought up with the servants. He explained his theory in this way:

> They will corrupt her ... ballads and love songs are daily presented to her, and vouched for truth: One tells "how a footman died for love of a young lady and how she was haunted by his ghost, and died for grief." Another, "how the coachman or butler ran away with his young mistress, and how he took to hedging and ditching, and she to knitting and spinning, and lived vast happy, and in great plenty." And a third, "how the young squire, master's eldest son, fell in love with the chambermaid, and privately married her at the Fleet; and how his cruel father turned them both out of doors, and how they went and took an inn, and got money as fast as hops; 'till at last the old gentleman died suddenly without a will, and then his son got possession of all and kept a coach, and made his wife, from a chambermaid, a great lady, who bore him twins for twelve years together, who all lived to be justices of the peace, &c.

There are numerous references to these unequal marriages in the contemporary papers. In 1731 the Master of the Rolls committed a Fleet parson to the Fleet Prison for marrying an Etonian schoolboy of seventeen years "to a servant maid". Three years later another paper reported:

> Last Saturday night, Mr D... late valet de chambre to a certain

noble lord near Soho Square went away, as was suspected, with
his lordship's niece, a young lady not yet of age, and co-heiress to
a very large estate. It seems they took a hackney coach soon after
they got out of doors, and upon strict enquiry, the coachman was
found out, who declared that he took a gentleman and lady up at
such a place, and set them down at the Fleet, and by the
description he gave it appeared to be the two lovers, who may
therefore be supposed to have been married and bedded that night.
A warrant was immediately obtained for apprehending the
supposed bridegroom, and he was accordingly taken in bed with
his lady, at a house in Queen Street, near Guildhall, on Wednesday
morning last, and immediately carried to the Poultry Compter, and
the lady was carried off by her friends. In the afternoon he was
examined, and afterwards recommitted to the same prison. So that
it seems he is to suffer for endeavouring to get himself a rich wife,
which is a practice followed by all the young gentlemen of quality
in England, but the difference is that this young fellow has
married, or endeavoured to marry, an heiress without the consent
of her friends, whereas the other generally marry or endeavour to
marry heiresses without their own consent.

Tobias Smollett, in his *Continuation of the Complete History of
England*, published in 1760, had this to say about the Fleet marriages:

The practice of solemnizing clandestine marriages, so prejudicial
to the peace of families, and so often productive of misery to the
parties themselves thus united, was an evil that prevailed to such a
degree, as claimed the attention of the legislature. The sons and
daughters of great and opulent families, before they had acquired
knowledge and experience, or attained to the years of discretion,
were every day seduced in their affections, and inveigled into
matches big with infamy and ruin, and these were greatly
facilitated by the opportunities that occurred of being united
instantaneously by the ceremony of marriage, in the transport of
passion, before the destined victim had time to cool or deliberate
on the subject.

Smollett went on to speak of the Fleet clergy, "a band of profligate
miscreants, the refuse of the clergy ... the outcasts of human society
...", as the operators of these marriages, and added these words to his
comments:

The ease with which this ecclesiastical sanction was obtained, and the vicious disposition of these wretches, open to the practices of fraud and corruption, were productive of polygamy, indigence, conjugal infidelity, prostitution, and every curse that could embitter the married state.

It is important to note the emphasis Smollett placed upon these "unequal" marriages. He was simply reflecting the spirit of the society in which he moved, which allowed a woman "only to refuse or accept what is offered" via her family's dynastic alliances. This "understanding" is characterised by a letter written by Lord Mountgarret to his eldest son, who was hoping to marry the daughter of an impoverished gentleman. "I am informed," he wrote, "that you are so miserably blinded as to incline to marry, and so with one wretched act to undo both the gentlewoman and yourself, and ... to dash all my designs which concerns myself and my house". The claims of obedience, family duty, and sometimes the threat of financial withdrawal, were normally sufficient to ensure that parental wishes were respected. The Fleet marriages, however, witnessed that other considerations might enter into the choice of a partner, and so these marriages received the condemnation of Smollett and those for whom he was writing. However, the Fleet parsons could be obliging to anxious parents, as one extract from a notebook makes clear: "I took their names and seven shillings to prevent their marriage". A further entry reads: "if any man comes to marry Deborah Monday send to John Alexander, attorney, in Finch Lane, Cornhill", and yet another, "Valentine Rumney to be stopped".

****

"Sham marriages", marriages in name only, used by one partner to obtain some favour from the other, frequently took place at the Fleet. Among these were those marriages in which the intention of one partner was to obtain as much money as he or she could from the other before absconding from the scene, or to gratify sexual lust. John James Jexon who married Mary Newell in 1723 thus "desired nothing but a little w....g and leaving the woman in the lurch". A further variety of sham marriages were those in which a woman married a woman. Wyatt's clerk noted that John Smith, "gentleman", and Elizabeth Huthall whom "he" married in 1737 were both women, adding, "if ye person by the name of John Smith be a man, he is a little short fair thin man not above five feet". After the marriage of Henry Sawyer and Elizabeth Seavar in 1754 the parson commented: "I almost could prove them both women though one dressed as a man thin pale face and wrinkled chin". In the case of John Farrar suspicion became fact, for he "was discovered after the ceremony was over to be in person a woman".

The most common of these "sham" marriages were those in which a woman in debt professed a willingness to marry any man in order to be released from her financial obligations, for the husband possessed a legal liability for the debts contracted by his wife before their marriage. Leman noted that a woman who had "contracted large debts to support her extravagance" was able, by this device, to "elude the honest demands and escape the just resentment of her defrauded creditors". A French visitor to London, Caesar de Saussule, alleged that many Fleet prisoners were quite willing, for a few pounds, to be married under a fictitious name to oblige such a bride. Then, he continued:

> The newly married bride departs and never sees her husband again. When the creditors come to be paid, she produces her marriage certificate; she cannot be arrested, having a husband, neither can they make him responsible for his wife's debts, he being a prisoner already.

Dr Gally was of the same opinion, writing:

> It is well known to be a common practice at the Fleet; and that there are men provided there who have each of them, within the compass of a year, married several women for this wicked purpose.

He pointed out that the cost of disproving the marriage could well be greater than the amount of the debt owed.

Gally was quite correct, there were men available for this purpose at the Fleet. One of them was Josiah Welch, a cordwainer. He married at least three women at the Fleet in fourteen months, using a different name on each occasion. The registers stated of him, "he marries in common". On 11 December 1727 he married Mary Spreadborough under the name of Walter James for a fee of 4s.; on the 23rd of the same month he married Mary Richards for a fee of 5s., using the name Richard Armstrong; and in July, under his own name, he was married to Elizabeth Catchey, who had been

> Brought by Mr Robert Hargrove who paid me two guineas to be married, to provide a husband for madam and defray all things, viz. Doctor 7s.6d., bridegroom 6s., the rest to myself. For a further account of Mr Welch viz. May 8 1727, Dec 11 and 23, 1727.

In another example of 1734 a Mr Commings gave half a guinea to a marriage house keeper to "find a bridegroom and defray all expenses", the husband being one Samuel Steward, a chocolate maker, who received a reward of half a crown. The same price was paid to George Mackarily, a soldier, "for his trouble", after a further request. A further and earlier example occurs in the life of Deborah Churchill, "executed at Tyburn December 17, [1708] for murder", which is to be found in the *Newgate Calendar*. The account of her marriage in this account reads as follows:

> Going to a public house in Holborn, she saw a soldier, and asked him if he would marry her. The man immediately answered in the affirmative, on which they went in a coach to the Fleet, where the nuptial knot was instantly tied. Mrs Churchill, whose maiden-name is unknown, obtained a certificate of her marriage, enticed her husband to drink till he was quite inebriated, and then gave him the slip, happy in this contrivance to screen herself from debt.

The parsons could be sensitive about these marriages, for when Thomas Games arrived with a Lucy Hern, "I examined them strictly, seeing a dirty fellow with a long beard, and was afraid it was done as a screen for debt". Such arrangements did not always work. Jane Hunter, when charged with debt, happily presented evidence that she was married to one Matterson, but:

> It being proved that Matterson had a wife then living, and that the defendant gave him half a crown to marry her, to screen her from paying her debts, the jury found for the plaintiff.

Walter Welch found himself in similar circumstances. His "bride" married him because she had a bond for £100 against her "and all her goods seized on it". He was charged with bigamy as a result of this "marriage" even though he alleged it was no more than a drunken frolic, and argued that the clerk [to the court?] had told him that "if I would give him five pounds I should hear no more of it". One is led to wonder whether *Walter* was another one of Josiah Welch's pseudonyms?

A popular belief of the time, but one without legal foundation, was that if the wife was married in her shift, her husband would be relieved of her pre-nuptial debts. Although this custom was well established in England only one such incident is recorded at a Fleet wedding, when Ann Daw, widow, married John Collier of Hossell, Surrey. The registrar wrote down what he had observed: "the woman ran across Ludgate Hill in her shift".

A further form of "sham" marriage practised at the Fleet was that in which a supposed partner was impersonated by another. John Vyse was involved in one of these marriages during 1709. It was allegedly between William Warren and Ann Meadows, but it appears that the groom was impersonated by another, and that Ann's motive was to force the real William Warren to support her and the child whom he had fathered. Warren declared there had been no marriage, and that "it was a trick and a treat", but declined to pay the £100 she demanded, this being her real concern. Forced into a corner she took the matter to court, but, unable to prove the marriage, lost her actions in the consistory court and in the Court of the Arches on appeal.

Another case was recorded by the *Grub Street Journal* of 1732:

On Tuesday one Oates, a plyer for a clerk to weddings at the Bull and Garter by the Fleet Gate was bound over to appear at the next sessions, for hiring one John Funnell, a poor boy, for half a guinea, that sells fruit on Fleet Bridge, to personate one John Todd, and to marry a woman in his name, which he accordingly did, and the better to accomplish this piece of villainy the said Oates provided a blind parson for that purpose.

The editor commented that "it would have been more difficult to have provided one that could see". In a similar way, Jennett Hunter, who was "dressed very fine, and looked like a common woman, wanted a man to personate". She found one who married her in the name of William Jones, who was described in the register as a vintner of Covent Garden.

The reason for this impersonation, as in the case of William Warren, was that the woman concerned hoped to gain a financial reward by it, often in the nature of some form of maintenance. It was "hush-hush" money, although the man might be entirely innocent. Such women often paraded themselves as the reputed wives of the men they claimed as their husbands, and even instituted legal proceedings in order to obtain their alleged rights. The only relief available for the victim was to institute a jacitation suit against the claimant. This meant that he had to disclaim the marriage, rather than make the claimant prove it. Many considered that this arrangement was contrary to the course of justice. This may be illustrated by the sad story of Francis Place's father, whose autobiography is a treasure trove for the social history of eighteenth century London. A woman instituted a suit against Place's father, claiming him as her husband because of an alleged precontract at the Fleet forty years earlier. Place was advised by the parochial authorities to make a small weekly allowance to the woman, but this he refused to do, claiming "to have nothing to do with her". After proceedings he was excommunicated, and sent his son to hear the sentence read in their parish church, but no further action was taken. However, his son added that the real consequence was that he "saved 4s.6d. a week at the expense of a thousand pounds" spent upon his defence. Entering into debt, he procured a friendly action, and removed himself into the *rules* of the Fleet.

Another device used by these women was once again to ply a man with drink until he was intoxicated, and then while he was unaware of what was happening, persuade him to say the promises of matrimony in the presence of a parson and witnesses. This occurred, for example, in the case of Richard Leaver, who testified at his trial for bigamy that:

> I don't owe that woman for my wife. I was fuddled over night, and next morning, I found myself in bed with a strange woman. "Who are you?" says I. "O my dear," says she, "we were married last night at the Fleet."

His wife stated at this trial, "I don't want him hanged, I only want him to maintain me". The possibility of a bread ticket for life was probably the only reason for her action.

There were occasions when a "wife" appeared after the death of a "husband" in order to claim his estate. This occurred when Hannah Green, calling herself Luff, attempted to claim the estate of James Luff, a deceased and bachelor brewer, basing her case upon the evidence of a Fleet parson and of an entry in a Fleet register. The court declined to accept this evidence as the books were irregularly kept. *The Political State of Great Britain*, in its edition of 1732, commented on this decision by hoping it would "put a stop to that scandalous custom of people going to the Fleet to be married". It did not, and next year the case of *Phillips v. Delafield* occupied the public mind. In it the validity or otherwise of a number of marriages depended upon an alleged precontract made at the Fleet some years earlier. The case displayed the same elements of duplicity and greed as did many similar cases. Dudley Ryder commented on these practices during the debates on the Marriage Act. He said:

> Sometimes a clandestine marriage is set up after a man's death, which was never heard of in his lifetime, and by an incontestable proof, which may by ways and means be obtained, his whole effects are carried away from his relations by the children of a woman he never acknowledged as his wife.

A fair number of the women who chose to marry at the Fleet did so in order to ensure that a child already conceived was legitimately born. It need be noted, however, that a study of Clerkenwell marriages at the Fleet, by the Cambridge Group for the History of Population, has suggested that the desire to hide pregnancy was not a significant factor in these marriages. Nevertheless, the terms "big belly" and "with child" are extremely common in the registers. There was nothing exceptional about this, for it is now known that a substantial proportion of the first born children of eighteenth-century marriages were conceived before wedlock. The popular mind often saw a church marriage or an ecclesiastical ceremony as the public or religious seal on an already existing union. The *Grub Street Journal* of 1735 in reporting the following did so within this general and accepted framework of popular belief:

> Yesterday morning an odd affair happened in the liberties of the Fleet, when a young man and woman, country people and very well dressed, came to be married; but before the minister had half performed the ceremony, the woman was delivered of a daughter. This poor girl, literally born in wedlock, seems to be more than half a bastard.

Unmarried couples were often encouraged to be married at the Fleet if the female partner was pregnant. James Noyce thus stated in evidence at Mary Jane Bennett's trial for bigamy in 1734:

> I saw the prisoner married at the Elephant and Castle in Fleet Lane to my cousin Thomas Bishop. But the thing was managed very oddly, for upon the 13 March last, she served a warrant upon him,

and swore a bastard child to him before the justice, and the justice advised them to make it up. She said she was a widow and so they agreed to be married that day, and I and the constable went with them to Fleet Lane and saw it done ...

Another similar marriage was reported by the *Post Boy* in 1730:

> Yesterday a cooper in St John Street was seized and carried before Justice Robe, being charged with a r--- upon a certain young woman. The man, considering the danger he was in, compounded the affair, by sending for a clergyman from the Fleet, who married them at a tavern in Smithfield, to the great joy of all parties.

Many "parish affairs" are recorded in the registers. These were the marriages of the parents or expectant parents of a child that the parochial authorities insisted upon in order to relieve their poor rates of any additional liabilities. Frequently, the parochial officers attended the ceremony to ensure due observance of their orders. By contrast, the bridegroom often attended with great reluctance. Robert Parker, a labourer of Yoel in Surrey, who was married to Hannah Norton in 1744, was "vile behaved", and with some reason, as "the officers of the parish took the fellow up by warrant to force him to marry her". John Witham on another such occasion was so "vile behaved" that "he would not say, with this ring I thee wed". He was still regarded as married even with such an omission from the service. One such marriage in 1721 was described as being "by virtue of a warrant from the Lord Mayor of London."

In many of these parochial affairs, the alleged father could not be found, or even identified, in spite of the oath taken by all midwives during this period that they would not assist an unmarried mother in childbirth until she had revealed the name of the child's "father". Some parochial authorities, concerned with a rising poor rate, endeavoured to throw the burden of maintenance of an unmarried mother and child onto another parish. The *Daily Post* of 11 July 1741 provides an illustration of this practice:

> On Saturday last, the churchwardens of a certain parish in the City, to remove a load from their own shoulders, gave forty shillings and paid the expense of a Fleet marriage to a miserable blind youth, known by the name of Ambrose Tally, who plays on the violin at Moorfields, in order to make a settlement on the wife

and future family in Shoreditch parish. To secure their point they sent a parish officer to see the ceremony performed. One cannot but admire the ungenerous proceedings of this city parish, as well as their unjustifiable abetting and encouraging an irregularity so much and so justly complained of as the Fleet matches. Invited and uninvited were a great number of poor wretches, in order to spend the bride's parish fortune.

Another example relates to the parish of St Bride's, whose officers may well have initiated this process as the Fleet Prison was within its boundaries. In 1719 John Sellwood married Elizabeth Gramer at the Fleet. This marriage was "by warrant" and was attended by Mr Harris, the churchwarden of St Bride's parish. He duly returned in the churchwardens' accounts that Sellwood was paid two guineas "for marrying Elizabeth Gramer at the Fleet, she being big with child", after a parochial officer had been paid 6s. for a fruitless journey to Enfield "to take up a fellow for getting Gramer with child".

Secret marriages were one of the great curses of eighteenth century society. They were almost impossible to prove and establish in law, and it was easy for one partner to repudiate the marriage. Many marriages were described as "secret" or "private" in the registers. Some were those in which the partners deliberately refused to give any further information about themselves beyond their Christian names, or were married in false names, as were "John King, as he called himself, the wife said his name was White and Mary Chambers as she was pleased to say, wanted to hide their names". In another instance Mark Herber records that the name of one bridegroom was given as "True and Loyall". In other marriages the couple paid for, or were granted, some amount of secrecy. To facilitate this need, "private" or "secret" registers were kept by some of the parsons and keepers, one writing: "have put a secret wedding in my private book of memorandum on this day". At the trial of Mary Summers, Gaynam was asked as to why the word "private" was inserted after a marriage entry. He replied, "the gentleman desired it might not be known". This system was practised by most of the parsons. A number of reasons were given for this need of secrecy. Jane Sparrow had "a jointure during the time she continued widow", the bridegroom was still an apprentice, or, as in the case of Caroline Carpenter, it was to be kept secret "till March next she being a minor". This was probably the most common reason.

One particular "secret" marriage that resulted in a court case, *Phillips v Cresse*, of 1738, is related by Lawrence Stone. Thomas

Phillips found himself in a difficult position. His girlfriend, Eleanor Cresse, was pregnant, but being an apprentice he was on the horns of a dilemma. If he married her he would forfeit his apprenticeship and find it difficult to obtain employment at his trade in the city, but if he did not, and her family proceeded against him for bastardy, he would lose both apprenticeship and reputation. Unable to obtain a licence for a marriage, being under age, he resorted to the Fleet, where he married Eleanor, but gave a false address for the registration that was also placed on the certificate. The marriage was to be kept secret until his apprenticeship was ended. Eventually her mother took pity on the couple, sheltered them in her home, but altered the certificate in her own hand. Later Phillips denied the marriage, but it was upheld in the Court of Common Pleas as valid. He, however, issued a suit for jacitation of marriage in the London Consistory Court, and this court, refusing to accept the validity of an altered marriage certificate, accepted his plea and ordered the Cresses to desist from their claim that Eleanor was married to him.

These secret marriages, often in defiance of parental consent and even of reason, together with all the other abuses and practices permitted or tolerated at the Fleet, and their sometimes tragic outcomes, threatened the whole fabric and security of family life. Marriages haphazardously entered into were just as lightly left, leaving wife and children to depend precariously on parochial charity. Marriages once regarded as a joke, or a drunken delusion, became serious when they affected a later marriage by precontract, or became the basis of bigamy proceedings. Women who could obtain "sham marriages" were able to cause not only a serious perversion of justice, but could also endanger marriages of many years' standing which had been regarded as legal and valid unions throughout that period of time. Many people found themselves bound fast by the law of the land in unequal marriages, undesired, devoid of any affection, productive of nothing save deep unhappiness and profound misery. These abuses, together with those connected with the keeping of the registers and the issuing of the certificates, so closely related to each other, could only lead to a climate of opinion that looked for a way to end these clandestine marriages once and for all.

The Revd Mr Keith, the May-Fair Parson

10
MARRIAGES AT THE MINT AND IN MAY-FAIR

The Fleet Prison was not the only centre for clandestine marriage in London that survived the legislation of 1694-5. One such centre was at the King's [or Queen's] Bench Prison, in Southwark. This debt prison possessed similar amenities and privileges as the Fleet, particularly in the existence of its own *rules*. The only contemporary reference to its earlier marriages is contained in the *Post Boy* of 13-16 October 1711. This stated:

'Tis expected that a bill to prevent clandestine marriage, under a severe corporal penalty, will be brought in very early next session of Parliament. For which 'tis said too just occasion has been given by a discovery lately made that laymen have been suffered to marry at the Queen's Bench; and that John Sarjeant, who now acts again as clerk, has forged certificates of pretended marriages, for which he keeps register books, with large blanks almost in every page, whereby very mischievous frauds are practicable. For preventing whereof, the late chaplain laboured hard with the most proper person to command the said books out of the clerk's custody, and not prevailing, resigned his office, which he has discharged among the prisoners, both in the house and in the rules, about five years, charitably, having never received one farthing of the fees thereto annexed.

The legislation of 1711 had the same effect on the King's Bench Prison as it had on the Fleet, and may have been occasioned by the above discovery. As a result, the marriages ceased to be celebrated within the prison house, and instead withdrew into the *rules*. In 1719 these marriages in the *rules* were singled out with those of the Fleet as constituting a serious abuse necessitating parliamentary action. The marriages were performed at such places as Mr Coles' house in Brandyleg Walk, the *Compasses* "in an aley over against the King's Bench", Mr Bubb's at the *Coach and Horses*, Blackamoor Street, the

Coach and Horse Shoe "in the Borough", and the *Two Necked Swan* in Shaw's Court. The marriage of Richard Hearne of Billingham in Essex and Mary Porter took place in 1735 "at the lodge of the Common Side of the King's Bench", but this was an isolated and unusual incident. The marriages at this centre, served by such Fleet clergy as Floyd, Barrett and Gaynam, died out by the late 1730s.

At about the same time as the start of these marriages in the *rules,* another centre arose at the Mint, Southwark. Due to its former position as a royal mint, its proximity to the King's Bench and Marshalsea Prisons, and because it had been an undivided estate for several centuries, it had acquired some prescriptive rights as a liberty or "sanctuary" for debtors. Although its pretended claim to be a privileged place had been abolished by an act of 1698, the area regained its former reputation, partly because of the lawlessness of its inhabitants, who held the place by force, and aroused much fear in the local authorities by their number and violence, and partly because of the uncertainty of justice in Southwark, for both the city of London and the county of Surrey were in open dispute about its administration. This was not remedied until an act of 1722 which ended these assumed privileges and ordered its lawless inhabitants to be driven away by force. That these marriages were forced to centralise in such a locality, in an enclosed area difficult of access, suggests that the prison authorities at King's Bench managed to prevent its *rules* from becoming a centre for clandestine marriage.

Between the 1710s and the 1730s the Mint centre achieved a small amount of popularity. The clergy who married there were the Fleet clergy, and they seem to have regarded the Mint as a sort of outlying curacy, marrying at both centres rather than concentrating on one. Their number included Walker, Hanson, Gaynam, Mottram, Floyd, and Barratt. The last three all resided for a time at the Mint: Mottram at the *Two Fighting Cocks* in Kent Street, while Floyd rented the back room of the house next to the *Swan* in Mint Street during 1727. Floyd later maintained a register at the *Goat and Crown* in Mint Gate into which he entered all his marriages, including those he married at the Fleet and elsewhere. Many of his entries conclude with such words as these: "married at the *Harrow* in Duke's Street, but registered over against the *Goat and Crown*". Nevertheless, he appears to have issued Fleet certificates for these Mint marriages, as Richard Losson and Ann Baker, married at the Mint, refused to allow him to "raze out the word Fleet in the certificate because [they] thought it not proper". On the other hand, Floyd was prepared to register a Mint marriage in a Fleet register, and so registered the marriage of John King and Elizabeth at the *Two Sawyers* in Fleet Lane, having already given them "a Fleet direction and writ the certificate".

The marriages at the Mint took place at a variety of establishments, such as Mr Johnson's of Blue Bell Alley, the *Royal Oak* in Lombard Street, the *Bulls Head and Plough* in Black Horse Alley, Mr Halifax's in Mint Street at the sign of *Tumble Down Dick*, at Mr Proudham's (a brandy shop), the *Half Moon* tavern, and the *Harrow and Lamb* which possessed its own "chapel".

Floyd had a substantial trade at the Mint until his death in 1730. Barratt followed him. Under him the centre greatly declined. His average fee was 4s.6d., which included the fees for the clerk and the registration. Towards the end of his life he was marrying no more than seven to ten couples each month, and his "Mint" income of about £32 per annum only reached that figure because of his activities in performing baptisms, conducting funerals and selling certificates.

After Barratt's death the Mint centre ceased to operate, although many of its marriage house keepers maintained a connection with the Fleet by acting as "friendly directors" or plyers to its marriage houses, in particular to Burnford's establishment. In 1738 a couple came from the *Half Moon* tavern in the Borough accompanied by the porter of that inn, and in subsequent years other couples were brought from that place by its lodger, tapster or hostler. The *Greyhound* Inn, the *Cat and Wheel*, the *Ship* Inn, the *Talbot* Inn, and the *Crown* Inn were other establishments from which marriages were sent to Burnford. On Burnford's death in 1748 this connection appears to have come to an end.

****

Apart from the Fleet and the Mint the other great centre of clandestine marriage in London was that established and maintained by Alexander Keith at May-Fair. Little is known of his earlier history. When Dr Trebeck denounced his matrimonial business Keith alleged that he had been admitted to priest's orders in the Church of England by the bishop of Norwich, acting on *letters dimissory* from the bishop of London, and added that before he had been nominated as incumbent of May-Fair Chapel he had been preacher at the Rolls Chapel. He was unable to substantiate this evidence.

Keith had been appointed incumbent of May-Fair Chapel sometime before 1728. This was a proprietary chapel in Curzon Street: it had been established as a commercial enterprise, and it was later rebuilt to match the improved and fashionable neighbourhood. Thomas Pennant had several comments to make about these proprietary chapels, writing:

> In this enlightened age it was quickly discovered that "godliness was profitable to many". The projector, the architect, the mason, the carpenter and the plasterer united their powers. A chapel was erected, well-pewed, well-warmed, dedicated, un-endowed, un-consecrated. A captivating preacher is provided, the pews are filled, and the good undertakers amply repaid by the pious undertaking.

It is possible that Keith established his business of clandestine marriages in an effort to supplement his income and so improve his security. Unlike the incumbent of a parochial cure he neither possessed the security of the parson's freehold, nor did he have the stability of an income derived from land, tithes or endowments. His main income came from the pew rents, of which the major share went to the proprietors, who had the power to dismiss him. His prosperity and living thus depended upon the number of people he could attract to the chapel by his preaching.

Keith commenced his matrimonial business almost as soon as he entered into office at May-Fair Chapel, in spite of the fact that as the minister of a proprietary chapel he was prohibited from officiating at such ceremonies, the fees of which rightly belonged to the incumbent of the parish in which the chapel was situated. Indeed, since the celebrated case of St John, Bedford Row, a proprietory chapel, in 1721, when the infamous Dr Sacheverell claimed, as incumbent of the parish, the right of nominating the preacher to this chapel, it had become the normal practice for the parochial incumbent to be consulted about any appointment to such a chapel, and to give his permission for its "preacher" to officiate in his parish. Nevertheless, a state of tension always remained, as these chapels normally creamed off the richer parishioners, a fact much resented by the parochial clergy. In 1730 Keith married 442 couples, but after 1732 the number of marriages decreased until in 1737 there were only eleven in number. While in part this could be explained by the recognition that the registers might be incomplete, it is more likely that the rector of St George's, Hanover Square, in whose parish the chapel lay, successfully forced Keith to stop this business, save for a few isolated instances.

By 1741 Keith recommenced his business upon the earlier scale of activity. It may be that he thought that after the lapse of years his earlier prohibition would have been forgotten, or that in this enterprise was encouraged by the proprietors of his chapel, who possibly had a percentage of his takings.

Dr Trebeck, rector of St George's, was not a man to forget prohibitions and, considering Keith's activities to be a threat to both his matrimonial rights and to his surplice fees, took proceedings against him. Trebeck's loss of fees was probably substantial. From 1738-53 the average number of marriages at St George's was 46, but from 1756-59, when the parties to any marriage were required to marry at their parish church, the average number was 213. Trebeck found the fatal flaw in Keith's position, for instead of indicting him for celebrating marriages in a proprietary chapel, which would have resulted in a mild censure and a prohibition from doing so in future, he indicted him in the court of Doctors' Commons during February 1742 for "preaching and performing divine service in the parish of St George's Hanover Square without the leave or the licence of the Bishop of London". Without such a licence Keith would not be permitted to officiate and could be deprived of his office, so that if Trebeck could substantiate his case he would be rid of the marriage centre and its principal offender at one at the same time.

He underestimated Keith. Not only did he refuse to appear before the court, he also declined to cease from officiating at May-Fair Chapel without an episcopal licence, or to pay the costs of the suit as the court demanded. It may have been deliberate. When Keith finally appeared it was to hear the sentence of excommunication passed on him on 27 October. Angry and bitter, Keith returned to his own chapel, and there in a solemn ceremony he retaliated by excommunicating Dr Gibson, the bishop of London, Dr Andrews, judge of the court, and Dr Trebeck. As Keith had still failed to make satisfaction by January 1743 a *significavit* was issued for his apprehension, but he was not arrested until 25 April 1743, on which date the entries in his register cease until May 1744. Keith was taken first to Newgate, but in May he transferred himself by use of the writ *habeas corpus* to the Fleet. He later wintered at the King's Bench Prison, making use of the same writ for his entry there and his return to the Fleet in April 1744, when his name was again entered into the prison books as charged with contempt against "the form of the statute made to prevent clandestine marriages" (probably the legislation of 1694-6), and with debts to the King (presumably for evasion of stamp duty) and to others.

As soon as he returned to the Fleet Prison, Keith laid his plans. Although deprived of his chaplaincy, and in spite of the lack of an episcopal licence, he obtained the use of a house opposite his former chapel, found assistance from a number of the Fleet clergy, and immediately advertised his business in this way:

> To prevent mistakes, the little new chapel in May-Fair, near Hyde Park Corner, is in the corner house opposite to the city side of the great Chapel and nothing within ten yards of it, and the minister and clerk live in the same corner house where the little chapel is, and the licence on a crown stamp, minister and clerk's fee, together with the certificate, amount to one guinea, as heretofore, and any hour till four in the afternoon … And that it may be better known there is a porch at the door like a country church porch.

He never took part in the Fleet marriages.

Keith maintained throughout an active part in these May-Fair marriages, for his clerk, Drummond, brought to him at the prison all the "licences" used in the ceremonies for his endorsement. This is borne out by evidence given by Drummond at the bigamy trial of Thomas Brown in 1747:

> Question: "Who is the parson of that chapel?"
> Drummond: "Mr Keith."
> Question: "What is that book in your hand?"
> Drummond: "The register book."
> Question: "Who is the person that keeps the register?"
> Drummond: "Mr Keith himself."
> Question: "Is there any form of prayer used there?"
> Drummond: "No prayers, but marriages."
> Question: "Does Mr Keith officiate in that chapel?"
> Drummond: "He has a person to officiate for him; and Mr Walker marries, and I carry the licences to Mr Keith and he registers them."
> Question: "Were those entries made by Mr Keith? Did you see them entered?"
> Drummond: "I carry the licences to him every night."
> Question: "Was the ceremony performed according to the rubric of the Church of England."
> Drummond: "Yes, sir, as far as I know."

One of Keith's so-called licences is contained in the British Library. Handwritten on parchment and stamped with a five shilling stamp, it reads as follows:

November 6, 1751. Whereas Nathaniel Sturch and Mary Edwards of St Andrews Holborn Being desirous to enter into the holy state of matrimony without publication of banns have solemnly declared that they are of the age of twenty-one years and upwards and that there is no lawful impediment by precontract by any other marriage by being nearly related by blood or marriage or any other ways whatsoever and that they are not under the care of the Court of Chancery, I have consented that they be married at the New Chapel on May-Fair.

.... [signature omitted]
Ordinary to the said chapel.

These licences served as a credible dupe to the innocent, for they had no legal validity as they had not been issued by a duly appointed surrogate. Nevertheless, they emphasise that Keith took great care to ensure that his marriages were as reverent and impressive as possible. As a result Lando paid him the compliment of advertising that his own Fleet marriages were as "decently solemnized" as those of May-Fair. Neither is it a coincidence that the May-Fair establishment became the fashionable centre for clandestine marriage.

The number of these notable marriages is considerable. The most impressive one was that between the duke of Hamilton and Miss Elizabeth Gunning, a rich heiress, in 1752. Horace Walpole wrote of this marriage to his friend Sir Horace Mann:

The event which has made the most noise since my last is the extensive wedding of the youngest of the two Gunnings ... Two nights being left afterwards being left alone with her ... he [the duke] found himself so impatient that he sent for a parson. The doctor refused to perform the ceremony without licence or ring. The Duke swore that he would send for the Archbishop: and at last they were married with a ring of the bed curtain at half an hour past twelve at midnight, at May Fair Chapel.

It was probably a May-Fair parson who married, unaware of their identities, Henry Fox to Georgina Carolina, the eldest daughter of the second duke of Richmond, at the home of Hanbury Williams. They were the parents of Charles James Fox, and their marriage became a topic of general conversation and scandal. Others who married at May-Fair included Lord George Bentinck, the infamous Sir James Dashwood, Bart., the countess of Oxford, the earl of Kensington, and the artist Thomas Gainsborough.

It was not from these people alone that Keith, in the words of Horace Walpole, gained from his chapel "a very bishopric for revenue". Keith was shrewd enough to realise that a fixed fee of one guinea, which included the parson's and the clerk's fees, the cost of the ceremony, licence and certificate, was far preferable to a position in which a separate charge was made for each item, and when the cost of the marriage itself was so uncertain that it frequently became a matter of dispute. Many working class couples came to May-Fair, and Keith freely admitted that while he had married many thousands of couples, few of them were from the fashionable ranks of society; indeed, he added, many hundreds of them were unable to read or to write. For this activity Keith received an unusual commendation from Horace Walpole, who praised him "for performing that charitable function for a trifling sum, which the poor successors of the Apostles are seldom humble enough to perform out of duty".

Throughout the years of his imprisonment Keith used every possible means to draw publicity to his marriages and to his own plight. He even utilised the death of his wife for this purpose. She died in 1749, and he inserted this notice in the *Daily Advertiser* of 23 January 1750:

> We are informed that Mrs Keith's corpse was removed from her husband's home in May Fair, the middle of October last, to an apothecary's in South Audley Street, where she lies in a room hung with mourning, and is to continue here until Mr Keith can attend her funeral. The way to Mr Keith's chapel is through Piccadilly ...

In the previous year his son had died, and the *Craftsman* reported that:

> Keith had his corpse carried on a bier by two men from the Fleet to Covent Garden Chapel. In their progress they made several halts and crowds of people assembled to read the inscription which referred to the father's persecution ...

The prosperity of Keith's business caused at least one of the Fleet parsons, Walter Wyatt, to set himself up in competition at the *Sun* tavern in May-Fair. The *General Advertiser* of 27 August 1748 reported as follows:

> W—yt told one in May Fair that he intended to set up in opposition to Mr Keith and sent goods to furnish the house, and maintain him [a deputy or curate] and the men who ply some days at the Fleet and at other times in May Fair ... But not to speak of the men, if he himself was not a Fleet parson, he could never stand in Piccadilly and run after coaches and foot people in so shameful a manner and tell them Mr Keith's house is shut up, and there is no chapel but theirs; and to other people he says, their Fleet chapel is Mr Keith's chapel.

As a result of this competition Keith was forced to advertise:

> It has been artfully insinuated that Mr Keith's Chapel in May Fair is removed lower down; this is to satisfy the public that the chapel set up in the Sun tavern one pair of steps is not Mr Keith's, but Mr Keith's continues where it was before.

After some months Wyatt returned to the Fleet, his experiment an apparent failure.

In 1750 there were rumours of an intended bill to suppress the May-Fair marriages. Keith, always ready to seize any opportunity to advertise his business, made use of this rumour in advertising, claiming that:

> Several persons belonging to churches and chapels, together with many others, supposing the marriages to be detrimental to their interest, have made it their business to rave and clamour, but in such a manner, as not to deserve an answer, because every thing they have said tends only to expose their own ignorance and malice, in the opinion of people of good sense and understanding. The way to May Fair Chapel is through Piccadilly ...

The Marriage Act of 1753 spelt the end for all the centres of clandestine marriage, although they were enormously popular until the last day on which they were permitted to exist. In 1752 the average number of marriages at May-Fair was 122 per month, but in January 1754 there were 153 marriages, in February 238, and in March 333.

This number included the 61 marriages of 24 March, and the 19 on the following day, being the day the Marriage Act came into force. The *Gentleman's Magazine* thus noted that "two men have been constantly and closely employed in filling up licences for that purpose."

At first Keith considered that the bill was "a most happy event for supplying him with an independency in a few months". and according to Horace Walpole, who had a soft spot for eccentrics of all kinds, proclaimed, "God d—n the bishops, they will hinder the marrying. Well let 'em, but I'll be revenged, I'll buy up two or three acres of ground and by G-d, I'll under bury them all". Keith soon changed his tone as the months progressed and the certainty of the bill's passing became clear. In an attempt to sway public opinion he published a pamphlet, *Observations on the Act for Preventing Clandestine Marriages*. In this work, mixed up with much fanciful comment, he incorporated some account of his experience as a marrying parson. The first page opens with the declaration that "this Act was fashioned with a pure design of obstructing the glorious method I had taken of serving my country." After this slight outbreak of persecution mania, Keith continued:

> I have the vanity to think that he [the king] has not a subject in the realm who has done him and his country more real service than I have done ... in a way ... which has daily and hourly added to the number of his loyal subjects.

The editor of the *Connoisseur* made capital of Keith's position and this publication. He claimed to have received a scheme

> From my good friend, Mr Keith, whose chapel the late Marriage Act has rendered useless on its original principles. The reverend gentleman ... proposed shortly to open his chapel on a new and fashionable plan [by] setting up as repository for all young males and females to be disposed of in marriage ... The Doctor makes no doubt but that his chapel will turn out even more to his advantage on this new plan, than on its first institution, provided that he can secure the scheme to himself and reap the benefits of it without the interlopers from the Fleet. To prevent the scheme being pirated he intends petitioning the Parliament, that as he has been so great a sufferer in the Marriage Act, the sole right of opening a repository of this sort may be vested in him, and that his place of residence in May-Fair may still continue the grand mart

for marriages.

By this time Keith was a tragic figure. Deprived of his source of income, incarcerated in the Fleet Prison and unable or unwilling to leave it, he was soon reduced to such "a deplorable state of misery" that he was forced to appeal to the charity of his friends. His last advertisement read:

By the late Marriage Act, the Rev. Mr Keith, from a great degree of affluence, is reduced to such a deplorable state of misery in the Fleet Prison, as is much better to be conceived than related, having scarce anything than bread and water to subsist on. It is to be hoped that he will be deemed truly undeserving of such a fate, when the public are assured, that not foreseeing such an unhappy stroke of fortune as the late Act, he yearly expanded almost his whole income, (which amounted to several hundreds of pounds per annum), in relieving families of wretched objects of compassion. This can be attested by several persons of the strictest character and reputation, as well as by numbers who experienced his bounty. Mr Keith's present calamitous situation renders him perhaps as great an object of charity himself, all circumstances considered, as ever in his better days partook of his own assistance, or that of others equally compassionate; and is indeed sufficient to awaken humanity in the most uncharitable. Any gentleman or lady may be satisfied of the above, by applying to Mr Brooke, engraver, facing Water Lane, Fleet Street, by whom donations from the public will be received for the use of Mr Keith.

Keith died in the Fleet Prison on 13 December 1758.

An illustration drawn from Hogarth's "The funeral of Moll Hackabout"
in his series "A Harlot's Progress".
It is alleged that the parson depicted in this picture is Dr Gaynam, one
of the leading Fleet marriage clergy.

11
CONCERN AND ACTION

It has been suggested already that the many abuses connected with the Fleet marriages and their registration caused not only public comment and concern, but also doubt about the validity of any given marriage. In this chapter we consider the development of this concern and the application of this doubt in the law courts. Before we do this, however, it is necessary to examine the measures taken by Church and State in an attempt to control these abuses. There was also a similar concern expressed about the abuses in the issuing of licences by the ecclesiastical authorities. Lord Hardwicke stated, for example, about the proctors of Doctors' Commons, that they solicited "persons to take out licences, just in the same manner as the runners to Fleet parsons do". Yet the main comments and concerns were reserved for the Fleet marriages. They were more noticeable, and the abuses practised there came more frequently before the courts and, as such, into the public arena.

The existence of these marriages posed a delicate problem to the Church authorities, for however irregular their performance may have been, they were forced by ecclesiastical law to recognise them as valid. Thus the measures that could be taken to regulate these marriages were limited in extent. The offending clergy, if they held a benefice, could be deprived of it, or they could be suspended from exercising their ministerial function. The consistory court, for example, suspended Mottram for three years in 1716 after a conviction for solemnizing marriages in the liberty of the Fleet, although this suspension made no difference to his matrimonial activities. If such a ruling was contravened the offender could be sentenced to a process of excommunication and subsequent imprisonment, but it was always difficult to obtain proof of such offences. All those who had been present at a clandestine marriage were regarded in canon law as *ipso facto* excommunicate, but this was impossible to apply in practice save at Doctors' Commons where the evidence of any person who had been present at such a marriage was rejected until the oath of absolution had been voluntarily taken. The *General Evening Post* reported in its issue of 27-29 June 1745 that a Fleet parson "being excommunicated for clandestine marriages, could not be received as a witness" in a case concerning a Fleet marriage, with the result that this particular case went by default as the evidence of the principal witness could not be utilised.

The ecclesiastical authorities made a visitation of the prison in 1702. It had little effect. A few years later the Lower House of Convocation, after governmental probing, complained to the bishops about the scandal created by the existence of these centres. This complaint had the effect of implementing the legislation of 1711 which drove the marriages out from the Fleet Prison, but this was the last effective step taken by the Church against clandestine marriages, though a draft set of canons to regulate the issuing of licences was produced in 1714, but lost by the death of Queen Anne. Convocation ceased to function in any case after 1717. In addition Bishop Compton of London, one of the most vigorous opponents of clandestine marriages, died in 1713. The State, however, took over the Church's role in this direction, especially as a result of the legislation of 1694-6. As the State had better machinery and more effective methods of ending or controlling the marriages and their centres, the Church appeared to have abdicated its responsibilities regarding them. This is clearly seen by the failure of the ecclesiastical authorities to proceed against those clerical offenders who publicly admitted their guilt at the various trials connected with the Fleet marriages.

It is hardly surprising, therefore, that there were many who maintained that throughout the eighteenth century the Church was more concerned with the abstract and theoretical side of marriage than with its practical and moral implications. Indeed, all that the Church seemed concerned about was that a marriage should not violate the essential nature of consent. An illustration of this attitude may be seen in the case of *Hill v. Turner* of 1737. An infant who was made drunk and abducted into a Fleet marriage was sent by his mother to Holland. The abductress, now his wife, instituted a suit in the ecclesiastical courts for the restitution of her conjugal rights and for alimony. In spite of the injustice of her claim, she was successful. Again, in 1752, the London Consistory Court accepted the validity of a marriage allegedly made 23 years earlier, though there was only one witness to it.

It was the State, therefore, which took over the effective prosecution of those who had been engaged in clandestine marriages. It did this only in so far as the clergy and clerks evaded the stamp duties imposed on licences and certificates, and also, at an earlier period, the tax on marriage. To better enforce these purposes penalties involving fines, suspension, and deprivation from office were imposed upon clerical offenders, and fines upon lay offenders. Several of the Fleet clergy and keepers were prosecuted under these enactments. It was alleged in 1720, however, that any clergyman who was prosecuted and fined could, "depending on the delay of write of error, carry on his offences with impunity for a year and a half when the gains amount to five times the sum of a hundred pounds [the statutory fine], then he runs away". There is no evidence that this was true. In 1717 Lilly was fined £5 for acting as clerk to a Fleet marriage, and Mottram was tried at Guildhall and fined £200 upon his conviction for not giving stamped certificates of marriage. In 1730 the *Grub Street Journal* recorded that:

> The clergymen who perform marriages within the rules of the Fleet Prison, are under prosecution at the suit of the Crown, for not giving their certificates upon stamped paper, pursuant to the statute in that case made and provided.

Seven years later, *Reed's Weekly Journal* reported that Gaynam, described as the "wry necked parson", was "attached at His Majesty's suit and carried to Wood Street Compter for £200, being the penalty for giving certificates of marriage that are not stampt with five shilling stamps according to Act of Parliament." Wyatt was similarly indicted. Presumably, it was an occupational hazard.

Prosecutions were few. This was because of several factors. The people best able to inform against the parsons were the clerks and the customers. But the act of 1696 placed penalties upon them for taking part in these marriages, and thus they would have no wish to initiate proceedings against themselves. Furthermore, in most cases the informer had to prosecute the case himself, and this, by reason of the danger of losing the case altogether as well as the costs incurred, was too lengthy and risky a business for many to undertake. Gally remarked that many prosecutors as a result had been "obliged to stop short almost at their first setting out". He also noted that while some of these trials had been "brought to issue", their effect had been minimised because of the poverty of the clergy (which made a fiscal penalty absurd), through their disregard for the penalty of excommunication, and their contempt of imprisonment.

It was also a civil offence for laity to be married at the Fleet, but there is little evidence to suggest that any were prosecuted, probably because the same difficulties applied to these prosecutions as to those of the clergy.

Although a House of Commons committee had commented upon the existence of many abuses in 1705, it was not until 1718 that a bill to end clandestine marriages was introduced into that house. Other bills were presented in 1735 and 1740. All these bills failed. This was partly due to the feeling that the main concern of these bills was to remedy the deficiencies in revenue from the stamp duties (in 1718 the loss was estimated at between £4,000 to £5,000 per annum), rather than to prevent the abuses these marriages created. In addition neither legal nor public opinion was then prepared to support the idea of voiding clandestine marriages as these bills proposed. Another factor may have been that neither bill had government backing. It is necessary, therefore, to conclude that, apart from providing legislation difficult to enact, and always with a fiscal aim in mind, the State did little to prevent the abuses committed at these clandestine marriage centres.

Another authority that was presumed to possess power to prevent the clandestine marriages at the Fleet was that of the warden of the prison. However, in view of the penal clauses of the 1711 act the prison authorities were careful to ensure that no marriages were performed within the prison house. Although a certain number of prisoners in the Fleet acted as parsons and keepers, their number was so few that their activity was probably due more to oversight on the part of the warden than to wilful compliance with their position. The warden could do little more than protest himself at the existence of these marriages, for they and their perpetuators had long since passed out of his jurisdiction.

In the absence of State and ecclesiastical interference, the attempt to regulate these marriages was left to the courts. In this the lawyers found themselves in a dilemma, for they had accepted a theory for the establishment of matrimonial proof which insisted that the parties should have had their marriages solemnized in the presence of a clergyman. The Fleet marriages, by complying with this provision, were thus regarded as valid marriages, however irregular their ceremony may have been or violent their performance. Consequently, the law courts were left with a negative function, namely, to punish those who had committed malpractices against the legal form of matrimony, to attempt to diminish the irregularities and abuses that resulted from these marriages, and to issue judicial comments against the continued existence of those centres where these abuses were tolerated.

It is possible to observe certain tendencies developing within the practice of these courts as they dealt with clandestine marriages. These made the legal theory of the common law lawyers a little less rigid in practice than it might otherwise have been. In general terms the result of these tendencies was that the courts declined to admit the rights of marriage where there was insufficient proof of marriage, or where there had been a clear violation of the principle of consent. In so doing, the law not only attempted to protect the essential nature of marriage, but it also began to see marriage as of fundamental concern to the family life and future prosperity of the nation.

The courts from 1732 onwards thus began to insist that more substantial proof was required for a marriage to be recognised than the mere production of a Fleet entry or certificate, for suspicions about their authenticity and validity had become concrete proof as a result of the evidence presented at many bigamy trials. In that year the case of *Green v. Luff* was heard. This concerned a woman who claimed the estate of an alleged and deceased husband by reason of a Fleet marriage. The court, however, declined to administer the estate since it "did not think it proper to give any credit to the proofs of the marriage", arguing that "such marriages ought never to be supported by law, but upon the most clear and common proofs". The precedent was noted and taken. Thus at Robert Hussey's trial for bigamy in 1735 the court insisted that the marriage should be proved by somebody who either gave the bride away or who saw "the book opened and read", and stated that a Fleet entry was not "sufficient without some solid proof of this kind". In the following year at the trial of Mary Sommers it was once again held that "all the proofs they can give, is this Fleet register, which ought to have no weight at all". In the case of Thomas Burrell it was again established that if the prosecution produced a Fleet register "it would not be a legal register, and so would be no register at all... ". This court also stated that the evidence of a Fleet register alone was not "sufficient to convict a man of felony", arguing that it would "be hard if such a person [as a Fleet parson] and his register should have the sanction of a court of law", while in the case of Mark Lutwich the court would not allow the register to be read "it being a Fleet register". There was also a tradition preserved in Westminster Hall that Lord Hardwicke, on one occasion, as judge, had torn up a Fleet register which had been presented to him as evidence.

Similarly, Fleet certificates were also regarded as worthless pieces of evidence. The Admiralty took its cue from these legal pronouncements, for, in the claims for bounty money it accepted without question the certificates of marriage signed by the parochial clergy, but it only accepted Fleet certificates if they were corroborated by the evidence of witnesses. Charles Yorke, Hardwicke's son, in his *Letter to the Public upon the Subject of the Marriage Act*, of 1753, was quite correct, therefore, in asserting that "the chronicles kept by these scandalous ecclesiastics of their own illicit practices [were] justly discredited in all courts of justice".

The courts even went beyond the strict limits of statute law in their application of it. Consequently, a court voided a Fleet marriage between George Morison and Christian Steward on the grounds of his lunacy, although this appears to have become apparent only some years after the solemnization of their marriage. The following report from *Applebee's Weekly Journal* of 13 August 1720 may also be a further illustration of this practice:

> We hear that a person has been committed to the Fleet Prison for lately advertising in the public papers a reward of £100 to any that should discover and prove the supposed marriage of two persons, by reason it might be an encouragement to subornation of perjury.

The law also strove to diminish the abuses and to remedy the evils arising from the existence of these marriages. Hardwicke's views on this subject may be illustrated by the statement in made in *Hill v. Turner*: "it is incumbent on this court to prevent as far as it can, persons from profiting themselves by such infamous methods ...". He argued that in particular:

> The Law of England is favourable to infants. No decree shall be had against them here, but that they may show cause for, when they come of age. This court will make strangers accountable to infants, in case they take it upon them to receive the profits of their estates ...

This principle was administered with legal ferocity. In that particular case the ecclesiastical courts had ordered the restitution of the matrimonial rights of the guilty partner. Hardwicke, on the case being referred to a secular court, issued an injunction which, while admitting the jurisdiction of the ecclesiastical courts, nevertheless declared that its procedure was being used contrary to equity and conscience. The woman was thus restrained from proceeding further in her suit against her "husband" and his mother. In the case of *Bennett and Spencer v.*

Wade of 1742 the settlement made on the marriage of the elderly and drunken Sir John Leigh, who was married to his apothecary's daughter, was set aside and his estate was conveyed to their heirs at law. In a similar way the property of minors who had been abducted and married at the Fleet was protected and tied up outside the control of the parties. This also occurred in the cases of *Edes v. Brereton* and of *Hughs v. Science.*

The courts also severely treated all those who came before them charged with matrimonial offences, particularly if the subject of the abuse was a ward of court. Consequently, several of the Fleet clergy found themselves imprisoned for contempt of court, amongst them being Wagstaffe in September 1727; Wigmore, who was detained in the Fleet by warrant of the Lord Chancellor until he had been cleared of his contempt arising from the case of *Hill v. Turner*; Ashwell, in March 1737, for officiating at the marriage of one Sophia, a ward of court, to James How; and Michael Barratt in October of the following year for his involvement in the case of *Edes v. Brereton*. In 1731 the Master of the Rolls committed a parson to the Fleet for solemnizing the marriage of a young Eton schoolboy possessed of a rich estate to a servant maid, as he did to others who assisted in this marriage, and also to two sisters who had been involved in the marriage of another youth while he was a ward of court. Several of the marriage house keepers also found themselves charged with contempt of court. Their number included Hodgkins and Joshua Lilly, who entered the Fleet as a result of his participation in the marriage of Elizabeth Gadsby, yet another ward of court, in 1745. He was not discharged until 1750, but probably had the benefit of the *rules* during that period.

It is appropriate to quote the various judicial comments made against these marriages, many of them by Hardwicke. They display his growing concern about their continued existence. In the case of *Harvey v. Ashton* he called clandestine marriage "one of the growing evils, introductive of much calamity and ruin to many families and complained of by considerable men as highly wanting a remedy". In the case of *Middleton v. Croft* he noted that the evil of clandestine marriage was:

> One of the growing evils of these times, and productive of many calamities and grievances to the community, and therefore we have thought it our duty not to weaken any power whereby it may be reformed and seasonably punished.

In the case of Sophia Moore, a minor, whose husband had gained a licence from Doctors' Commons claiming she was of age, but omitting to name the parish of residence, Hardwicke remarked "it is very surprising, considering the canons have laid down such particular rules in relation to marriages by licences, that clergymen should be so careless in observing them".

Similar comments were made by judges and juries in other courts. In 1735 the Grand Jury represented to the court that Gaynam, a witness in a bigamy trial, "was a scandal to his function; and requested that some method might be taken to suppress his iniquitous proceedings". Peter Symson was informed by a judge at the London Sessions:

> You might have exposed yourself more, had you gone on the highway; but you'd do less prejudice to your country a great deal, you are a nuisance to the public, and the gentlemen of the jury, it is to be hoped, will give but little credit to you.

Another judge "hoped to see this crime [bigamy] punishable with death".

By the end of the first half of the eighteenth century there was not only a practical change in the application by the court of the principles used to determine which marriages they could, or would not, support, but also a judiciary ready and willing for a legal enactment which would end these marriages once and for all, for, as Hardwicke observed, "the misfortune is, the want of a sufficient law to restrain such clandestine marriages". By the 1740s public opinion had also developed from indifference about the existence of these marriages to considerable concern about them. The long saga of *Muilman v. Muilman*, between 1722-48, as detailed by Lawrence Stone in his book, *Uncertain Unions*, helped contribute to this concern within the wealthier classes of society. This concerned the sham marriage of Con Phillips, a notorious courtesan, to Francis Delafield in order to avoid debt, but also involved Delafield's previous marriage to Magdalen Yeomans. It was a long, complicated and expensive case, and although only one of the four marriages implicated by it involved a Fleet marriage, it was used with great effect by Dr Gally in his "war" against these marriages, especially as the various cases involved in it revealed all sorts of duplicity, scandal and legal chicanery.

It has been argued that the marriage of Henry Fox in 1744 further raised public awareness and concern about these marriages. The duke of Newcastle even treated it as an affair of state, and Lord North termed it "this most unfortunate affair"; "making so great a fuss", wrote Cateret, "as if Mons had been betrayed into the hands of the French". The marriage had considerable political implications, however.

The opposition to these marriages took many forms. Some were disgusted by the way the ceremonies were conducted. "Virtuous", for example, wrote a letter of protest to the *Gentleman's Magazine* in which he complained about the scandals these marriages caused and the dissolute life of the parsons. Others were aware that the Fleet trade undermined the dignity of marriage, and Gally, for example, warned his readers that clandestine marriage was a "disgrace to any civilised nation". The upper classes began to realise the dangers to which their children, and their dynastic ambitions, were being exposed to by the continuation of these marriages, and others claimed that the marriages increased the number of beggars, rogues and prostitutes in the city. At least one concerned person began to warn the public through letters in the journals and newspapers about "innocent persons ... being ruined" by these marriages, and another person frequently advertised against these marriages in various periodicals over a number of years, mentioning their inconveniences and the penal statutes made against them. One such advertisement read:

> Whereas several inconsiderate and unwary persons consent to be married at the Fleet, May-Fair and other places by sham licences, by which the parties that think themselves properly married are much difficulated in the proof of their marriages are of the legitimacy of their children, ... it is thought proper to the well being, peace and security of such as intend to marry and to make it known, that besides the inconveniences before mentioned, there is an Act of Parliament made in the 7 and 8 years of King William cap. 35 ....

Indeed, the reputation of these marriages was such that an issue of the *Daily Post* in 1742 happily reported that:

> A gentleman near the middle of the Strand died last week possessed of a considerable fortune, which he bequeathed into the hands of trustees to his wife, but with this exception, that in case she married an Irishman the trustees were to pay her ten guineas for a Fleet marriage, a dinner, a ring &c., the remainder, which is about £8,000, to devolve to his nephew.

It is hardly surprising that the majority of literary references to these Fleet marriages, and the two major prints about them, noted the bawdiness, dirt and squalor that seemed to accompany them. The two engravings both have a Hogarthian tone to them. The just-married wife in "The Sailor's Fleet Wedding Entertainment" [illustrated on page 96] is no virgin, and Jack has been deceived, as the accompanying poem declares. All around the room are scenes of vice and promiscuity. The parson is making overtures to the procuress, a man places his fingers in the shape of a horn over Jack's head, the dog and the cat fighting indicate nuptial strife, and the painting of the Skimmington conveys the same. The broken pipes and the smashed glasses declare a state of discord, and the bailiff at the door, accompanied by a mercer with his bill of £70 for the bridal finery, adds further colour to this image of deception. Similarly, the engraving of "The Fleet Wedding" [illustrated on page 78] also indicates that not all is well. A herb seller offers bunches of rue, hinting the sailor will rue or regret his marriage, while a chimney sweep's boy dips a piece of bread with his sooty hand into a pail of milk, so ruining it.

Miles Ogborn thus makes the suggestion that these images of the Fleet were a major factor in the support Lord Hardwicke received for his desire to end these clandestine marriages. The Fleet area, associated with a prison and a market and, we might add, known as one of the major red-light areas of London, was clearly a place where many people were deceived and ruined for life.

It may be a strange coincidence that the full evils of the system were related to Englishmen by the French traveller, L'Abbé le Blanc. His *Letters*, written in the late 1720s, may well have helped awaken, strengthen, articulate and even influence public opinion against these marriages. He noted, for example:

> This is the country, where unequal marriages are the most common; the curb of decency hinders but few of the English from following their caprices, or indulging their passions ...

If unequal marriages took place:

> Some few people will laugh, but the rest will take no notice of it, and nobody will be surprised ... Decorum is little respected, and vice is rendered familiar ...

He added, "the laws of England ... tend to favour even the most indecent marriage".

It was a tragedy that the Church abdicated its responsibilities regarding these marriages, for thereby it incurred considerable hostility and subsequently lost much of its matrimonial privileges to the civil law; it was a pity too that the concern of the State was more for its financial resources than for the dignity of marriage, and it was unfortunate that the law could only attempt to remedy the abuses caused by these marriages rather than end them. Yet legal practice and public opinion by the 1750s were ready for an operative change in the law in order to end once and for all the scandals and misfortunes these marriages created. In the same way, Lord Hardwicke, as Lord Chancellor, having himself seen many of the tragedies which resulted from these marriages, was ready to provide that change when opportunity presented itself. In the next chapter we examine how this opportunity presented itself, and the use made of it by Hardwicke in his Marriage Act of 1753.

Lord Hardwicke, the architect of the Marriage Act

CHAPTER 12
LORD HARDWICKE'S MARRIAGE ACT OF 1754

It was amazing, in a country where liberty gives choice, where
trade and money confer equality, and where facility of
marriage has always been supposed to produce populousness, -
it was amazing to see a law promulgated, that cramped
inclination, that discountenanced matrimony, and that seemed
to annex as sacred privileges to birth, as could be devised in
the proudest, poorest little Italian Principality ...

Horace Walpole.

The Marriage Act of 1753, correctly titled *An Act for the Better
Preventing of Clandestine Marriage*, was accepted by most of its
critics and supporters as an act designed to prevent the clandestine
marriages performed at the Fleet and May-Fair. In its original version
the bill expressly referred to "marriages within any prison or the rules
thereof", and section viii of the Act stated that "many persons do
solemnize matrimony in prisons and other places without publication
of banns or licence of marriage first had and obtained". During the
course of its debates the only instances of clandestine marriages
recorded were those performed at these centres. Many comments were
made about them. These marriages, declared Lord Barrington, could
not "contribute towards making the vulgar believe that there is any
sanctity in the marriage contract", and Beckford suggested that they
were "a burlesque upon the marriage ceremony". Tindal argued that
the marriages at these places had become "as much trade as any
mechanical profession", while Lord Hillsborough asked:

Can anyone believe there is anything sacred in a ceremony
performed in a little room of an alehouse in the Fleet, and by a
profligate clergyman whom they see all in rags, swearing like a
trooper and higgling about what he is to have for his trouble, and
half drunk perhaps at the very time he is performing the ceremony.

166 The Fleet Marriages

Lord Hardwicke, who had so frequently denounced these marriages in the Court of Chancery that many accused him of having a personal vendetta against them, had clearly wished for earlier legislation on this subject. He remarked in *More v. More* in 1741 that "there are mischiefs that want the reformation and correction of all the legislature as much as any case whatever, and I believe it will very shortly come under the consideration of Parliament". Ryder, the Attorney General, defended Hardwicke's eventual bill as a reasonable extension of his judicial approach to clandestine marriage. Not for nothing, therefore, was the act termed Hardwicke's Act, for not only did much of its direction come from him, but much of the credit for its passing was due to his tenacity.

It is worth quoting Lawrence Stone's account of Hardwicke's involvement at some length:

He rewrote the bill and for the next six months personally masterminded its passage through both Houses of Parliament, in the face of some fierce opposition, by the use of rhetoric, logic, cajolery, and behind-the-scene threats, deals and lobbying. He bought off the peers by allowing the archbishops to retain the right to issue special licences for noblemen to be married how, where, and when they pleased. He satisfied the middling sort by allowing the surrogates to continue to sell ordinary licences to dispense with banns, despite the fact that it was the corrupt distribution of these licences which had been no small cause of the clandestine marriage problem. He tried to satisfy the parish clergy by arguing that the suppression of clandestine marriages would drive the poor into getting married in church, thus augmenting clerical incomes generally. He bought off the Scots by omitting Scotland from the bill, leaving it to be taken care of by another bill prepared by the Scottish Lords in Sessions. He bought the support of the squires by offering them the one thing they really wanted, which was a legal veto power over the marriages of their children up to the age of 21. He kept all the lawyers in both Houses lined up solidly behind the bill, partly by persuasion, partly by exploiting their desire to clip the wings of the ecclesiastical courts, partly by appealing to their exasperation at the problems of legal proof of marriage raised by the existing situation. When all else failed, he made it clear that any opponent of the bill would be punished by being excluded from the lord chancellor's extensive patronage.

Stone gives the impression that Hardwicke had carefully calculated the odds and had deliberately designed a bill to appeal to all the sections of society that might have opposed it. This is hardly the case, though he is certainly correct that Hardwicke pushed and shoved the bill through parliament. He made it clear that any opposition to the bill would be seen as an attack upon the law, its officers, the constitution, and himself. For Hardwicke, the bill became a personal affair, as befitted his egalitarian character.

In 1752-3 the case of *Cockrayne v. Campbell* was sent on appeal from the Scottish courts to the House of Lords. This was a case which involved the estate of a wealthy man, who had supposedly been married for twenty years with issue, but whose estate had been claimed, after his death, by another woman on the strength of a precontract performed in secret. Lord Bath took up the case, and on 31 January 1753 the House of Lords directed the judges to prepare and bring in a bill for the better preventing of clandestine marriages. As their drafts failed to give satisfaction, being of too general a nature, and by following earlier precedents, Hardwicke seized the initiative and brought in his own measure on 19 March, although it seems clear, as Outhwaite suggests, that he was not privy to the actual drafting of the final measure.

The aim of this new bill was so to regulate the order of matrimony that rash and hasty marriages would be prevented, to establish definite proof of a marriage, and to declare which marriages the State would support as such. To achieve these objectives it was decided, as a first preliminary, to make a marriage *in facie ecclesiae* the only form of marriage which the State would support, thereby accepting the legal rule of thumb that a clergyman was indispensable for a valid marriage. In addition, the ecclesiastical requirements of marriage as laid down in the canons of the Church were mainly adopted, although modified, for the sake of convenience.

The bill insisted that no marriage should be performed until the banns had been read for three Sundays beforehand at the parish church, churches or chapelry of the parties to it, and that the marriage be performed at one of the places where the banns had been called, provided that banns had previously been published at that place. This was to ensure that the credentials of the parties to be married were in order, to allow public knowledge of the forthcoming marriage, and to give an adequate time to the parties concerned to consider the seriousness of their intentions. Even greater difficulties were laid on those who wished to be married by licence, for, as Hardwicke wrote to the bishop of Oxford:

> If some difficulties are laid upon licences in consequence of this Act, I think there is no harm in it, for I always was of opinion, that the most desirable point of all was to induce the people of this country, as far as possible, to marry by banns, and therefore this new law has given certain advantages to that regular public method ...

Accordingly, a marriage by licence could only take place at the parish church of one of the parties, and each surrogate (an ecclesiastical official empowered to issue these licences) was required to make an oath and to give a bond of £100 that he would not abuse his authority. Furthermore, parental consent for the marriage of minors, while presumed in the case of proclamation of banns, was required in the case of licences. If parents proved unreasonable, were beyond the seas, or *non compos mentis*, an appeal could be made to the Lord Chancellor and other specified dignitaries, to examine and, if found fit, to consent to the marriage. An amendment ordered that register books be provided for both banns and licences, and that the marriage should be celebrated before two witnesses, besides the officiating minister. Any person found guilty of altering, forging, counterfeiting an entry in a register, or procuring the same, destroying any entry, or defacing or adding to a licence of marriage, was to be adjudged guilty of felony and suffer death as a felon without benefit of clergy. This particular amendment was not from Hardwicke's pen.

The foundation of the bill was preventative rather than constructive, for it was agreed that the only effective way to deal with those marriages which contravened its provisions was to refuse to accept them as marriages which the State would support. Ryder, the Attorney General, thus maintained that "nothing can ... be effectual for preventing clandestine marriages of every kind, but declaring all such marriages null and void to all intents and purposes". Consequently, marriages performed contrary to even one particular requirement laid down in the Act were held to be null and void.

A further clause banned any proceedings to compel or establish a marriage *in facie ecclesiae* by reason of any precontract entered into after the Act had come into force. Before 1753 these proceedings had caused vast amusement to society, as did the cases for damages for breach of promise which replaced them after the passing of the Act. Those clergy who offended against the Act, otherwise than the registration clauses, were to be judged as felons and be sentenced to transportation for a term of fourteen years.

It was Henry Fox, the Whig politician, who ridiculed Hardwicke under the name of "Dr Gally". This assertion had a great measure of truth in it, for Hardwicke made use of Gally's opinion that society had as much right as the Church to insist that its consent to a given marriage should be conditional upon the observance of its requirements, and without which the marriage could not be permitted to legally exist. Gally was careful to point out, however, that the State was not interfering with the ecclesiastical laws by making the marriage void on its own authority; rather, it was only stating what marriages it would support and protect as such. The marriage was only void, therefore, in its civil effects, which left the parties to it in a somewhat delicate position. The erastian Bishop Warburton extended this argument. He wrote that marriage was "in part a religious, and in part a civil contract", and it needed to be "entered upon on such terms as religion enjoins, and completed by such forms as the civil magistrate prescribed". Warburton inferred from this that the mutual agreement of the two parties alone was not sufficient to make a legitimate marriage, either in the sight of God or of society. He concluded, therefore, that if the State ended a clandestine union it was "only breaking an insolent and disorderly confederacy in licentiousness, where God's sanction and the magistrate's authority are equally insulted".

There were good precedents for this concept of voiding a marriage. These derived from the 1742 Act preventing the marriage of lunatics; the 1746 Act of the Irish legislature which voided all marriages of those under twenty one years of age made without parental consent, as well as marriages between Roman Catholics and Protestants solemnized by a Roman priest; and the 1751 Regency Act which had a clause inserted into it annulling any marriage by the heir to the throne made before the expiration of his minority and without the consent of the Regent or the major part of the Council.

These ideas, which deeply affected the compilation of the Act, were not far removed from the concept of marriage as a contract. This concept was the third major influence of contemporary legal opinion upon the Act, the others being the necessity of priestly intervention and society's right of consent. Charles Murray thus suggested that marriage was similar to a contract under the Statute of Frauds, and Dudley Ryder, the Attorney General, after stating in the debates on the bill that the idea that marriage could not "be annulled and made void by any human law whatsoever ... was a superstitious opinion", added, "thank

God, we have in this age got the better of this ... and the Reverend
Bench in the other House will deserve the thanks of later posterity for
consenting to render Christianity consistent with common sense".
Remarking "we may see what infinite mischiefs flow from this sanctity
and indissolubility which has been added to the marriage contract", he
continued:

> Nothing can be more inconsistent with common sense than to say,
> that the supreme legislature of a society cannot put contracts of
> marriage, as well as any other contract, under what regulations
> they think most conductive to the good of that society.

Nugent, in replying to Ryder, said:

> I hope the honourable and learned gentleman will excuse me when
> I call the marriage contract sacred, after he has been at much pain
> to shew, that it is no way more sacred than any other contract.

Beckford, in a later speech, also expressed his sadness at hearing "the
solemn and sacred contract of marriage put upon the same footing with
a contract for the sale of goods, or a debt without speciality". But it
was this "contract" theory which prevailed, so that Blackstone, one of
the greatest commentators on English law, could write later:

> Our law considers marriage in no other light than a civil contract.
> The holiness of the matrimonial state is left entirely to the
> ecclesiastical law; the temporal courts not having jurisdiction to
> consider unlawful marriage as a sin, but merely as a civil
> inconvenience.

It was this attitude which led directly to the nineteenth century divorce
laws.

It is possible to argue that many of these theories which underlined
the Marriage Act had themselves been brought into effect by the
existence of these clandestine marriages. The concept that the State
needed to approve of any union, and the requirement that such a union
be conduced *in facie ecclesiae*, may both be seen as attempts by the
civil lawyers to control the abuses in matrimonial matters which the
ecclesiastical law was powerless to prevent. In the same way, it is not
too great a speculation to assert that the concept of marriage as a
contract emerged because of the legal dislike of the sacramental theory.

For this theory caused that rigidity which lay behind ecclesiastical law, and thus allowed the validity of any marriage provided it had satisfied the Church regarding the basis of consent, however irregular or illegal its composition may have been, and furthermore prevented any effective escape clauses in the event of dissatisfaction or even of criminal proceedings. These matters, however, could only have become acceptable to the public because of the growing secularization of society which characterised the eighteenth century.

****

The bill aroused tremendous opposition, even though the newspaper reports about its progress through Parliament were very limited. This opposition was completely unexpected, though many thought, in words later expressed by Joseph Phillimore, that it had gone "from the extreme of laxity and negligence, to that of undue severity and rigour". If some argued the act was necessary to remedy the abuses caused by these clandestine marriages, others believed its remedies would be ineffective and unfair. A writer stated in the *Gentleman's Magazine* that "the only question therefore which could be debated was, whether it would not produce greater mischiefs than it would prevent". Yet care must be taken to distinguish between the opposition to the bill itself with its proposals, and those who made use of it as an opportunity to launch a strong attack upon the government.

First, the legitimate complaints. The main area of concern was the sanctity of marriage. Alarm was expressed by the denial of the sacredness of marriage and its definition as no more than a legal contract. The whole concept of voiding a marriage gave the ecclesiastics enormous concern as to whether a marriage voided by the State could yet bind in conscience. One Hawkins, preaching an assize sermon at Oxford asserted, incorrectly, that the bishop of Oxford had stated that those whose marriages had been voided might cohabit with a good conscience, to which statement Hawkins added his own comment, "that they were bound to do so". Men such as Hawkins felt that the State was making free "with the laws of nature and of God". Another sermon by the Revd. Marshall Montagu Merrick, also preached in an Oxford church, asserted that marriage was a divine institution and should not be tampered with by the state.

By and large the Church as an institution was remarkably quiet, even though it was aware that the bill when passed would end the ecclesiastical dominance of marriage, take most of the matrimonial jurisdiction out of the ecclesiastical courts into secular hands, and require offending clergy to be tried in the secular courts. On the other hand, it was aware that it would give the Church a near monopoly of the marriage market.

Much objection was made to the penal provisions of the bill, for it was held that the death penalty was far too harsh for offences connected with the registration of marriages, and it was also felt that when a marriage was declared void by the courts it would be the innocent partner who would suffer rather than the guilty seducer. An amendment to legitimise the children of such a union failed.

Three further points were made the subject of justifiable criticism. The first was the exclusion of the royal family from the bill's provisions. This was done, it was said, at the insistence of the King himself who had been aroused by the duke of Cumberland's fury and Fox's scorn that princes of the royal blood should be classed with the masses. Beckford observed, however, "it is more the public interest, and we ought to take more care, that none of them shall make an improper marriage, than we have with respect to any other family in the Kingdom". The Royal Marriage Act was passed to remedy this omission, by which time two of the royal dukes, Cumberland and Gloucester, had entered into clandestine marriages.

The second point was that the act only extended to England and Wales. Scotland was excluded from the original draft - rather surprisingly as the stimulus for the act had come from a legal case regarding a marriage under Scottish law. The House of Commons had added to this omission an amendment which excluded all marriages performed overseas from the bill's provisions. Only the duke of Bedford appears to have noted at the time that persons could easily pass over to Calais or Boulogne or journey to Scotland in order to be married clandestinely. Hardwicke, in fact, had hoped to establish a similar bill for Scotland, but after the clamours occasioned by the English bill he felt he could not embarrass the government any further.

The final point of criticism was one hardly mentioned at the time. This was the fact that all marriages, save that of Jews and Quakers, had to be celebrated *in facie ecclesiae*. This clause meant that the debate concerning the legitimacy of Nonconformist marriages was now terminated in favour of the establishment, while Roman Catholic marriages, previously accepted as valid due to their solemnization before a priest, were placed in an equally negative position.

It has already been noted that the Marriage Act was made the occasion by the "friends of Bloomsbury Square" of "a dark intrigue" against the administration of Henry Pelham, through the person of Hardwicke, the mainstay of the government, in the hope of establishing their own ascendancy. Their number included Henry Fox, Secretary of State for War, Charles Townshend, Robert Nugent, William Beckford, and the duke of Bedford. They had previously gathered around the Prince of Wales as a focus of opposition, but after his death allied themselves with his brother, the second son of George II, the duke of Cumberland. He was hostile to Hardwicke for the part he had played in the Regency Bill. Fox, in Walpole's phrase, "neither spared the Bill nor the author of it, as wherever he laid his finger, it was not wont to be light". His own clandestine marriage was suggested as the reason for this interest, although he does appear to have had a genuine concern about the bill. He wrote, for example:

> The Clandestine Marriage Bill ... will have sad effects. ... I verily believe that the legitimacy of the children of every family will come into question if the Bill passes as frequently as their estates do now.

The Marriage Act became a hereditary squabble with the Fox family.

The arguments used by Fox and his friends were designed to stir up the mob and to obtain the support of the rising middle classes. Their main concern was to aggravate the popular aversion to the bill, describing it as a patrician measure, and ascribing to it all kinds of injustice and cruelty. For a short time their views received a certain degree of popular acceptance. Mrs Bellamy remembers that Fox's popularity was so great that his "chariot was carried upon the shoulders of the crowd for several days together". Yet their only notable success was in preventing a similar bill for Scotland.

They argued that the abuses were not so frequent as to justify such violent legislation, even though some, such as the duke of Bedford and George Haldane, made clear their dislike of the Fleet marrying trade. Charles Townshend, by contrast, argued that the majority of clandestine marriages were not detrimental to society. As such these men would have agreed with Horace Walpole who wrote: "the new Act set out with a falsehood, declaiming against clandestine marriages as if they had been a frequent evil". Walpole, however, was no friend to Hardwicke, and appears to have harboured a personal animosity for him. Consequently they quibbled over the minor points and alterations of the bill, and suggested that the addition of the clause requiring the keeping of the registers would satisfy the object of the bill by itself, so that its other clauses could be abandoned. It was even thought by some of the bill's supporters that the various exclusions already discussed were added to the bill by Fox and his friends in order to make it unworkable.

One of the major assertions made against the bill by Fox and his friends was that the requirement of parental consent was detrimental to the established right of children to marry whom they pleased. If parents were to control this right, they argued, then the interests of love would be sacrificed to those of society and financial ambition. Rich heiresses would be reserved for the aristocracy: "for the rich man will always be for making his daughter a duchess or a countess, and will as certainly choose the richest that offers, without consulting in the least her inclination". The bill could be nothing less than a remedy for private families against unequal marriages. Fox declared, therefore, "and all these inconveniences, all these dangers, we are to expose ourselves to, lest the daughter of a noble or rich family should marry a footman or a sharper, or the son a chambermaid or common strumpet". If the bill passed, there was a danger that all the wealth of the country would be drawn into the hands of a few of the nobility, who would thereby buy their influence in the House of Commons and obtain the government for themselves. In short, the bill was an aristocratic plot designed to overthrow lawful government and create a powerful and oligarchical upper class, which would be "of more danger to our constitution than ever the military power was, which they in former times separately possessed". To prevent such a calamity of aristocratic enterprise, clandestine marriages should be permitted to continue as a running sore upon their schemes. Townshend even argued that these marriages were of public benefit, for they served "to disperse the wealth of the Kingdom through the whole body of the people, and to prevent the accumulating and monopolising of it into a few aristocratic hands". They also brought "good and wholesome blood" into these families, for otherwise, he continued:

> Our Quality and rich families will daily accumulate riches by marrying only one another, and what sort of breed their offspring will be we may easily judge, if the gout, the gravel, the pox and madness are always to wed together, what a hopeful generation of quality and rich commoners shall we have amongst us? What a fine appearance will they make at the head of our army, should we ever happen to be invaded by a foreign enemy?

This point was stressed so often that many jumped to the conclusion that the main motive of the bill was to prevent unequal and imprudent marriages, and to revive the old principle of absolute parental control over the marriages of their children during an age when individuality was being increasingly asserted. Walpole's sneer that the Chancellor had given "all his attention to a statute into which he had breathed the very spirit of aristocracy and insolent nobility", may have been clever, but it fell far short of the mark of accuracy.

The idea of an aristocratic plot was a negative statement on the part of the opposition, but it was balanced by the positive assertion that the lower classes needed quick and convenient forms of marriage. Ryder almost hinted at a compromise. Let there be, he argued, a distinction "between the marriages of persons of rank and fortune, and those of the people we usually call the vulgar". But, he then added, this "is impossible to do in this country". The poor would have to suffer for the convenience of the rich.

It was presumed that the motive of the "vulgar" for marriage was passion, and passion alone. Without these quick forms of marriage, it was argued, they would either be discouraged from marriage or they would repent before the process of calling their banns was completed. This was particularly so because the calling of banns was so greatly disliked: "we know how adverse our people generally are to a proclamation of banns, even in the present method", declared Colonel Haldane. "In fact," said Beckford, "there is one amendment, I am clearly of opinion, we should make to the title, which is that of leaving out the word 'clandestine'". Nugent summed up this argument in these words:

> The most pernicious consequence of the Bill will be, its preventing marriage among the most useful, I will not scruple to say, the best sort of our people ... It is from their labour our quality derive their riches and their splendour; it is to their courage all of us owe our security. Shall we, for the sake of preventing a few misfortunes to the rich and great among us, make any law which will be a bar to the lawful procreation of such sort of men in this country.

The whole issue was exacerbated by the contemporary Naturalisation Bill, contemptuously referred to as the Jews' Bill, which permitted the naturalisation of foreigners in order to keep up the population of the country. This aroused such violent opposition that it was withdrawn after one year.

It was also argued that by imposing a waiting period for marriage, immorality would be encouraged, and Nugent emotively argued that:

> If you render marriage among that sort of people so difficult and expensive, you must by public authority set up a common stew in every parish, if you do not, you will be the cause of the murder of many infants, either after they are born, or by abortion ...

Townshend added his own argument to this particular debate. He argued that once a couple had given the required notice for the publication of their banns, "they would begin to co-habit together". But the man might be "so cloyed with enjoyment before they are finished as to refuse to be married". Others argued that the new requirements would prevent the marriages ordered by a magistrate in the case of pregnancy, because if they now had to wait for the banns to be called the man "would march off and leave both the girl and the parish in the lurch".

It was claimed, in addition, that the many requirements proposed by the bill for a marriage to be regarded as valid were sufficient to put a weapon into the hands of the unscrupulous. They would be able to commit a legal form of polygamy by purposely ignoring one of the requirements prescribed, so that if they were prosecuted they could show that one of their marriages was void in law. This, and other considerations led Townshend to assert that the bill was

> One of the most cruel enterprises against the fair sex that ever entered into the heart of man, and if I were concerned in promoting it, I should expect to have my eyes torn out by the young women of the first country town I passed through, for against such an enemy I could not surely hope for the protection of the gentlemen of our army.

William Beckford echoed this thought, stating that it was "a bill for the ruin of the fair sex".

These arguments were readily answered in the House of Commons by Barrington, Bond, Hillsborough and Murray. They pointed out the absurdity of these suggestions, maintained that the arguments of an aristocratic plot were without foundation, and that a fear of a decrease in the number of marriages as a result of this legislation was ill founded. Such hasty marriages, declared Bond, were productive of nothing save poverty and despair. He and his colleagues held that care and consideration were required before two people entered into matrimony, while they believed that people were married for reasons other than ambition and passion. John Bond asserted, therefore:

> As to all those rash and inconsiderate marriages which are entered into between two poor creatures, sometimes before they have got clothes to their backs, and often before they have saved anything to furnish a lodging or cottage for themselves, or have got into the way of providing for themselves, much less for their children, I think they ought all ... to be prevented.

To this Hillsborough added his own sentiments:

> Every inconvenience which has been mentioned as the consequence of the Bill has for many ages been established, by the laws both of our Church and State, so that we not only have the wisdom of our ancestors, but the experience of many ages to convince us, that these inconveniences must be submitted to, rather than allow such a licentiousness with respect to marriage as .... by ... marrying in a clandestine and unlawful manner. ... The prosperity and happiness of a country does not depend upon having a great number of children born, but upon having always a great number well brought up and inured from their infancy to labour and industry.

This open attack of Fox and his friends was a great mistake. Pelham, a skilful political manager, immediately began to encourage the bill from a ministerial capacity, so that, as Walpole noted, "the numbers against the Bill diminished", and he and Hardwicke were able to "cram" the bill through parliament. Walpole noted a rumour that Pelham was informed by the Chancellor that he would "be supported in this, 'or I will never speak to you again", and he observed that Sir Richard Lloyd,

> Who had spoken against the Bill, voted for it afterwards, without assigning any reason for his change of opinion. Captain Saunders, who had said he would go and vote against the Bill, for the sake of the sailors, ... was compelled by Lord Anson, the Chancellor's son in law and his patron, to vote for it.

Henry Fox noted the same. In a letter to his cousin, Lord Ilchester, he wrote: "complaisance to the Lord Chancellor prevailed, and it is not to be believed how strong a point he makes of it, and every lawyer in the House was sent down to vote for it". Obviously, Hardwicke had no wish to see the bill lost after his efforts to procure its adoption. So great was his interest in the eventual Act that it is significant that Blackstone did not insert his strictures against it until the second edition of his *Commentaries on the Laws of England*, published the year after Hardwicke's death in 1765.

A bill with so many blemishes would probably not have passed into law were it not for the tactical error of Fox and his friends in opposing it in the way they did, so causing the government to come to its rescue. Hardwicke himself observed in the House of Lords that "their opposition had been attended with an event, which they had little intended, and had raised a zeal in favour of the Bill which had secured its success". The conduct of Fox was condemned in government and society circles and he incurred the royal displeasure; nor did Hardwicke disguise his contempt for Fox, even though Fox, on Pelham's advice, tendered some sort of an apology in the Commons. He had not meant to give offence, he stated, and when he applied the term "cruel" to the Bill he "was far from applying it to the author of it". Hardwicke replied to this in the House of Lords, and Walpole wrote of the scene:

> At last the Chancellor – not, as he has been represented, in the figure of *public wisdom speaking*, but with all the acrimony of wounded pride, of detected ambition, and insolent authority. He read his speech; not that he had written it to guard himself from indecency; or that he had feared to forget his thread of argument in the heat of personality; he did not deign an argument, he did not attempt to defend a Bill so criticised. He seemed only to have methodised his malice, and noted down the passages where he was to resent, where to threaten.

After alluding to the activities of the duke of Bedford and Townshend, Hardwicke referred to Fox, describing him as:

> Another, dark gloomy, and insidious genius, who was an engine of personality and faction, had been making connections, and trying to form a party, but his attacks had been seen though and defeated … Such attacks on the Chancellor and the Law were flying in the

face of the King: that this behaviour was not liked .... I despise his scurrility, as much as his adulation and retraction. This *Philippic* over, the Bill passed.

Lord Campbell, in his *Lives of the Lord Chancellors*, is compelled to admit that Hardwicke's conduct on this occasion "was not in great taste".

The bill, subject to some amendments, which Hardwicke accepted even though they weakened it, "since ... the substance of it was of so much moment to the nation, and those defects might be supplied by a subsequent one", passed the House of Commons on 5 of June 1753 by a vote of 125 to 56, and the Lords on the following day. It was enacted on 7 June, and took effect on 25 March 1754.

It was quite clear that this act would end clandestine marriage. But while it was confidently held that it was no more than a reiteration of the existing ecclesiastical and civil measures, it was in two respects a complete innovation. First, it made marriage a public affair, to be celebrated in the parish church. Secondly, although there were some precedents for voiding a marriage, the bill, by imposing this penalty upon every defaulting marriage, inaugurated a radical change in the legal conception of marriage, namely, from a sacramental concept to that of contract theory. Yet the Act must be seen as the logical conclusion of the English legal theories current at that time, and as probably the only effective remedy against clandestine marriage. Nevertheless, we should see the bill in its more positive light, which is often forgotten, namely that it declared what marriages the State would support, rather than in its more narrow sense of voiding those marriages which failed to reach the standard of proof required.

The Savoy Chapel (courtesy of The City of London, Guildhall Library)

13
REFLECTIONS, AND THE DISASTER OF THE SAVOY

The Marriage Act was ordered to be read from every pulpit in every parish church. If this ensured its publicity, it also gave it notoriety. When it was read at Kingston Parish Church in Surrey the *Gentleman's Magazine* reported, "almost all the congregation went out from the church". Such dissent was futile, for it was clear that the act would end the practice of clandestine marriages in England and Wales. Not unnaturally, there was a last minute rush to take advantage of the "old law" before the new act was enforced, and one Fleet register records 19 marriages in January 1754, 16 in February, and 28 in March, of which 12 were between the 22nd and the 24th.

The Fleet clergy disappeared into oblivion: none remained in the area of the Fleet or appear to have obtained ecclesiastical preferment, though, on the other hand, none became debt prisoners within the Fleet Prison as a result of poverty. The marriage house keepers lost both trade and profit, although several found a lucrative source of income by opening up their premises as registry offices, where their registers could be inspected for a fee. By purchase and amalgamation they augmented the size and usefulness of these collections, which were frequently advertised in the public press. One such advertisement, printed beneath the sign of a pen in hand, was as follows:

The original register books, being some hundreds in number, of the Fleet marriages, performed by all the ministers for upwards of one hundreds years past, are now purchased at upwards of two hundreds pounds expense; are to be seen, searched and certificates granted according to law, from the above and only original books, at Cope's Jerusalem Wine Vaults, opposite the Elephant and Castle, in Fleet Lane, near Fleet Market; the very great utility of this valuable collection, which contains upwards of three millions of marriages, is too well known in the cause of law, to need further encomiums. N.B. each search 2s.6d., whether relative to law, equity, or parish affairs, and letters (post paid) directed to the

Original Register of the Fleet Marriages, as above, will be duly answered from all parts.

Both Wigmore's wife and Lando's clerk kept similar "offices" at Half Moon court.

The ownership of these registers could be highly profitable. One unknown registrar in 1761 obtained £90 from search fees and the issuing of certificates. Many of these collections were purchased by a Mr Benjamin Panton in the 1780s. At one trial he stated that his collection weighed more than a ton in weight, and that he was in the habit of attending courts of justice with selected registers in order to present them as evidence. His daughter sold this collection to William Cox in 1813, and eight years later he sold it to the government for the sum of £160 6s.6d..

Panton's court appearances were more lucrative to him than helpful to his clients, for the courts continually challenged the legal authenticity of these registers whenever they were presented to them as evidence. Although in *Doe exdem Orrell v. Madox* of 1794 they were admitted as evidence upon the precedent of former cases, the court stated that this was "not to be understood as thereby sanctioning their admission", for "as a species of evidence of a suspicious and exceptionable nature he thought they ought not to be allowed". Other courts were more ready to repudiate their authority. Lord Kenyon, for example, in the case of *Reed v. Passer and others* of the same year, rejected these registers as admissible evidence, stating:

> The books of the Fleet, however corroborated by other circumstances, are not, in any case, received as evidence of a marriage; not because a marriage celebrated there was not good, for such it clearly was before the Marriage Act; but because the manner in which those marriages were celebrated, and the conduct of the persons who, without any legal authority, assumed the power of registering them, have thrown such an odium on those books, as to take from them even the authority of a private memorandum.

A similar statement was made by Mr Justice Le Blanc at a trial at Shrewsbury Assizes in 1803. "The entry", he stated, "is nothing more than a private memorandum made by someone who has not authority to make it and who might put down anything he pleased, whether true or false."

The question of the legality of these registers was finally determined by an act of 1840. This made it clear that the register books of the Fleet marriages could not be received as evidence of marriage in any court of justice.

****

There is much that can be said in favour of the Marriage Act. It demanded a regular and public form of ceremony, it established one clear and certain rule for marriage, and it ended the many noisome jactitation suits and precontract cases. Reason and not passion was to be the recognised ground for matrimony. The Act thus ended the tragedies caused by rash and hasty unions, as well as the frequent abuses perpetrated at the matrimonial centres. Above all, by giving the protection of the State to the marriages it recognised, and by securing their decent celebration and proper registration, it offered security and protection to the institution of marriage. Property rights were thus safeguarded, as well as the legitimacy of the issue of each recognised marriage. Consequently, because the interests of the family were so closely bound up with those of the State, the Marriage Act gave stability to the pattern of society and protection at large to national life.

Although the Act's broad structure and policy were sound and substantial, the amendments made to the original bill caused an erosion of its aim, while the necessity of giving absolute security to the majority could only be done at the expense of the few. Though William Coxe in his memoirs of Pelham's administration might write, "the evils of which it was represented as a fruitful source, have proved most imaginary", Tobias Smollett in his *History of England* could argue that the "abuse of clandestine marriage might have been removed upon much easier terms than those upon the subject by this Bill". The difference in viewpoint really depended on whether one gave preference to the security of marriage that the Act gave to the many, or to the hardships it caused the few in order to afford that security.

One of the most glaring of these hardships was that the marriage of an illegitimate minor was placed under substantial difficulties, for the consent of the parents to that marriage was not considered sufficient, and consequently that of a guardian was required. For such purposes a guardian had to be appointed by the Court of Chancery, and this procedure caused endless delay and much expense.

Even greater hardship was caused by the extension of the clause, which stated that the absence of any one requirement would void a marriage, to include the names given for the publication of banns. It was held that a calling in false or even incorrect names was no calling at all. In the case of *Puget v. Tomkins* of 1812 a marriage was voided because the banns had been published under the name William, whereas the person had been baptised as William Peter and was commonly known as Peter, and in the case of *Fellows, falsely called Stewart v. Stewart*, two years later, the insertion of an additional name was held to be sufficient to void the publication of the banns and thus the marriage itself. In *Johnson v. Parker* of 1819 a marriage of twenty-two years' standing was declared void when the husband revealed that he had sworn his bride to be six weeks older than she was in order to obtain a licence. That same year also saw the case of *Hayes v. Watt* in which a marriage was nullified after eighteen years' cohabitation because the father, who had been presumed dead, had not given his consent. In the case of *Reddall v. Leddiard*, heard in the next year, a marriage was ended because it was discovered that the guardians who had consented to it had been appointed under a will that had been invalidated as it had been signed by only one witness. An even more unfortunate case occurred in 1808, when Jane Wynn Hughes was cheated of her husband's Caernarfonshire estate and her daughter illegitimised. This was because her husband's relations, acting on some irregularity in the consent given to Jane as an illegitimate minor, had the marriage voided, fourteen years after the death of her husband.

In many of these cases there was a real suspicion that an unintentional mistake, or even a deliberate one made for good reasons, was made use of to end an alliance that had become unsatisfactory. The suggestion made by the Act's opponents that those who wished to void a marriage could make use of its severity to accomplish their purpose became a reality. These nullities were a constant irritation until legislation was introduced in 1822. This legalised those marriages, which could have been subject to a nullity action under the terms of the Marriage Act, where the parties had cohabited until death or until 22 July 1822, unless the marriage had previously been declared invalid, or in those cases where one of the parties had lawfully intermarried with another person.

However, an amendment to the original bill allowed a marriage by licence to be valid even if the couple gave a false statement about their place or places of residence. This was known as Lord Holland's amendment, and was important as many urban parochial boundaries were uncertain, although it could also allow a couple to evade the consequences of a deliberate attempt to obtain secrecy for their marriage. Another amendment allowed the validity of marriage by banns when one or both parties were under age so long as their parents did not register their objection to it.

The exclusion of Nonconformist and Roman Catholic ceremonies from the terms of a valid marriage by the Marriage Act, though not apparently resented at the time, became a standard grievance in later years. This was not remedied until the 1836 Civil Marriage Act.

The opposition to the 1753 Marriage Act had promoted two amendments in particular, both of which were probably introduced in an apparent attempt to make the Act unworkable. Although this aim did not succeed, these amendments certainly caused considerable problems. The first amendment had limited the operation of the Act to England and Wales. It caused much comment at the time. A bill to regulate Scottish marriages received a first reading in 1755, but was dropped because its opponents successfully argued that any such act would violate the religious section of the 1707 Act of Union. Richard Burn, in his history of the Poor Laws, published in 1764, commented on the situation so caused:

> It is astonishing, and what posterity will never believe, that their forefathers made a law, that people in England should not marry but under such and such circumstances; but if they would go into Scotland, they might marry as they pleased. Insomuch that it became fashionable to take a tour into Scotland to be married, and it was almost a reproach to a young lady to have been married and not to have been thought worth stealing. As if it were an honour to a noble family, that the heir can make out his title to the inheritance by virtue of a Scotch marriage, solemnized possibly by an ale-house keeper, in a very ridiculous manner, and that he can be able to boast, though not born, yet he was begotten, on the other side of the Tweed.

In 1757 a couple absconded to Edinburgh and were married there, as a newspaper report of that year recorded:

> Gloucester, September 17. A young man and a girl, of equal character and circumstances, in the parish of Upton St Leonard's, in this city, having contracted a mutual affection for each other, were inclined to unite in matrimony, but, as the girl was under age, their inclinations were opposed by her mother. Upon which they had the resolution to take a ride to Edinburgh, where their

nuptials were performed, agreeably to the laws of Scotland, by the Rev. Mr. Grant, minister of the English Chapel in the city; and last week they returned, to the great joy, and with the universal applause, of the neighbours.

Dr Grant appears to have commenced his matrimonial work at Berwick, according to John Penrose, a Cornish parson, who met him at Bath in 1766.

Gretna Green, the first convenient stopping place after the border had been crossed, soon became established in its own right as a centre for clandestine marriage. Here, until Lord Brougham's Marriage Act of 1856, a group of men acting as "priests" (though none was a blacksmith), performed the marriage ceremonies in private houses, bribed the postboys to act as plyers, gave certificates, and charged no fixed fee. Between 1811-39 one of these "priests", Robert Elliott, claimed to have married 7,744 persons. All that Scottish law required was that two people, with free consent, should declare their wish to marry before witnesses. There were some doubts expressed, however, as to the validity of these Scottish marriages so far as couples domiciled in England were concerned. Lord Mansfield, for example, advised couples married in this way in Scotland to be re-married in England. Guernsey, also excluded from the provisions of the Act by the same amendment, also tried to obtain similar advantages for itself, for in 1760 a note appeared in the *Gentleman's Magazine* which stated that boats were available at Southampton to take couples, for the price of five guineas, "into the land of matrimony", namely Guernsey. The Isle of Man also became a venue for these marriages, with the result that in 1757 its own parliament passed legislation similar to the Marriage Act.

Thomas Turner, the shopkeeper-diarist, noted in 1764 that an under-age couple who had married at Ypres, presumably to avoid parental refusal, were re-married in their parish church as they feared their foreign marriage would not be recognised.

The second amendment was that marriages were only to be solemnized in those churches where banns had been published before the Act had been passed. This produced an absurd position, for it prevented marriages being solemnized in many of the then fashionable centres for marriage in London, such as the Knightsbridge Chapel, Gray's Inn Chapel, Lincoln's Inn Chapel, and the Oxford Chapel in St Marylebone. Even worse, it was not until the act had been passed that it was realised that St Paul's Cathedral, Westminster Abbey, and several other cathedrals were also affected by this amendment. The position of those places of worship erected after 1754, or even rebuilt after that date, remained precarious until the decision in *Rex v. Northfield*. This declared that a marriage solemnized at Buerlyhill Chapel, erected in 1765, was void. A similar decision, upheld by the Court of King's Bench on appeal, was said in the House of Commons to have "bastardized thousands".

As a result of this amendment, and the failure of many clergy to realise its import, Charles James Fox, Henry Fox's son, said this in the House of Commons:

> All persons, who had solemnized marriages in any of these new chapels were at present liable to transportation. Under danger of that penalty stood ... a vast number of clergymen and some prelates in the Upper House ... and, by the bye, the House might have the mortification to see bishops in their lawn sleeves, instead of preaching the Word, heaving ballast on the Thames.

It was upon such evidence that Parliament anxiously and speedily passed *An Act to Render Valid Certain Marriages Solemnized in Certain Churches or Public Chapels in which Banns have not Usually been Published before or at the time of a passing of the Act 26 Geo. II, c. 33*. This act, of 1781, validated these marriages, indemnified the offending clergy from the penalties of the 1753 Act, and accepted the registers of those places as valid registers. As many commented at the time, there could be nothing more absurd than to pass statutes in order to protect people from the effects of technically disobeying the provisions of another statute.

The difficulties were not removed by the 1781 Act. Bishop Horsley of St Asaph spoke at great length to his clergy in his 1806 Visitation Charge regarding this matter. He spoke as follows:

> Now it is a notorious fact, that many churches and chapels have been erected and consecrated since the time when this Marriage Act was passed; and in such chapels there could have been no usage of publication of banns anterior to the Marriage Act; which was itself anterior to their existence. And yet in many of these chapels the officiating clergy have perpetually solemnized matrimony, not aware that they were doing anything unlawful. A short time before I was removed from the see of St David's it came to my knowledge, that in a very considerable town in that

diocese the irregularities of marrying in a chapel, in which, though indeed it was an ancient chapel, banns never in any one instance had been published, had gone to such an extent, that there was hardly a couple in the town, who, while they conceived themselves to be man and wife, were not actually living in the eye of the law in concubinage; nor a child in any family born in lawful wedlock; not a clergyman in the place, though the clergymen in the place were highly respectable, who had not, not once or twice, but repeatedly for many years of his life, been committing acts of felony.

Soon after my translation to this see, I discovered that the like irregularity had been going on here. The chapel at Forlas is a public chapel duly consecrated in the district of Tir Abbot, in the parish of Llanufydd in Denbighshire. But the first erection of it was of later date by many years, than the passing of the Marriage Act; consequently there had been no usage of the publication of banns in that chapel anterior to the Marriage Act: yet from the time of its consecration the perpetual curate went on solemnizing matrimony in the chapel, with as little apprehension of his own danger, or the nullity of the marriages so solemnized, as if it had been a parish church.

However, my dear brethren, you may put your minds at ease, and the parties so unlawfully married may put their minds at ease; if it may give ease to your minds to know, that all that is past is pardoned and obliterated; and to theirs to know, that the knot so loosely tied at first is now drawn tight and hard, and made indissoluble and that the legitimacy of the offspring is secured.

This was because the bishop had carried a bill through parliament in 1804, which repealed the enactment of the 1781 act, and brought it up to date. But, Dr Horsley went on to warn his clergy:

You will take special notice that the benefit of this statute comes down only to the 25th of March 1805. If since that date any marriages have been or shall be solemnized in chapels in which banns had not been usually published before the passing of the Act of the 26th of George II, all such marriages are still null and void, as they would have been if this Act of mine never had been passed; the clergymen so solemnizing them are not indemnified; and the registers are not evidence in any court of law or equity.

This Act was renewed again in 1806, and in 1830 a further act was passed which made legal all marriages in churches and chapels erected since 1753.

Although it appeared that the Church had won the day by the Act's insistence that all marriages should be celebrated *in facie ecclesiae*, this was not the case in reality, for the Act effectually ended all consideration of marriage as conveying or being an indissoluble union, and instead it introduced the concept that marriage was no more than a secular contract. By ending the concept of marriage as being formed by consent alone, and by voiding marriages which, in previous times, had been considered valid unions, the law of matrimony went from one extreme to the other and caused a virtual revolution in English marriage law. Indeed, the Marriage Act effectually ended the ecclesiastical domination of marriage, and marked the first breach in the secular privileges of the Church. Yet the bishops made no protest, even though the Church thereby lost the battle it had been fighting since medieval times to establish marriage as a sacrament. In future the State alone would decide not only the nature of marriage, but also the question of its dissolution.

Most of the Act's hardships and inconveniences were not to be remedied until the nineteenth century, although several bills were presented to parliament in order to modify it or even obtain its repeal. For some years, suggests Outhwaite, the "Act fought for its life". Bills for its repeal were presented in 1764-5, 1772, and 1781. In 1781, for example, the opposition proposed to amend the Act by remedying the clauses requiring the publication of banns, the restriction of the use of the licence to the parish church, and the voidation of all marriages made without the prior use of banns or licence. The bill proposed to validate the marriages of English people in Scotland, as well as the marriages of those couples who had married in places where banns had not previously been called. Charles James Fox proposed these amendments, presumably as a continuation of his family's long-standing resentment against the Act. He was so ably opposed by Burke, Sheridan and others in the House of Commons that he was forced to abandon the measure. Thus in spite of Hardwicke's expressed hope that the Act would be amended in some of its more restrictive particulars, no change was ever effected. This may have been due to the fact that the supporters of these amending bills made use of the now discredited arguments relating to population and "aristocratic plots" instead of concentrating upon the Act's real defects. The supporters of the Act alleged in reply, for example, that the Act had shown its utility, and should not be laid aside unless proofs could be brought forward that "it had done hurt".

However bad the defects of the Act may have been, two points need to be reiterated: firstly, the Act ended clandestine marriages and gave a general security and stability to marriage contracts, to an extent that had been unknown before, and secondly, that these defects were not due to Hardwicke's original bill, but to amendments proposed in the Commons. Hardwicke's aims and intentions are perfectly understandable, as is the severity of the measure, when its requirements are contrasted with the abuses practised at the Fleet and whose tragedies long occupied Hardwicke's judicial mind. It might even be argued that Hardwicke had managed by this legislation to create a balance between ending the abuses of clandestine marriage and creating as few inconveniences as possible.

****

The Savoy marriages provided the first opportunity of seeing the Act in operation. If this showed its necessary hardship, it also indicated that only by voiding all such marriages, and by transporting the offending clergy, could clandestine marriages be ended.

The Savoy centre arose soon after the Marriage Act became operative. John Wilkinson had been elected minister of the Savoy in 1728. In spite of his many pluralities, which included the rectory of Coety in Glamorgan, the stipendiary curacy of Wise in Kent, the rectory of Eastwell in the same county (where he had to wriggle out of the suggestion of its patron, Lady Winchelsea, that her maid was "always intended to go along with the living" as the wife of the new rector), and a chaplaincy to the prince of Wales, Wilkinson was frequently in financial embarrassment. In 1745 he mortgaged his emoluments at the Savoy to a hosier, and three years later entered the Fleet Prison as a debt prisoner. His stay was short. In the following year his stipend from the Treasury as minister was stopped due to his restrictive practices in connection with the German Calvinistic Church in the Savoy precincts, and from that date until 1754 he seems to have made a precarious living from the fees which still remained to him, and by serving as a Fleet parson.

The decay in his fortunes, and his extensive knowledge of the clandestine marriage trade, combined with the extra parochial nature of the Savoy, made Wilkinson realise the potentialities of his office after the Marriage Act had been passed. For his predecessors had always granted their own licences for marriage at the Savoy; indeed, one of them, Dr Killigrew, had granted these licences on an extensive scale, and as Wilkinson stated at his trial, he had himself occasionally issued them during the previous 28 years and there had never been any episcopal action taken against this practice. Consequently, Wilkinson, with these precedents and a large family to support, concluded "himself secure, and not within the reach of that severe Act", and persuaded himself and others associated with him that his licences were "as lawful a licence as any in England". It appears that he relied upon the clause of the Act which stated that "any archbishop, bishop or other ordinary or persons having authority to grant such licences" could continue to do so, without realising that this clause was governed by the other clauses of the Act which required that marriages should be performed in the parish church of one of the parties to the marriage.

He thus began, in the words of his son Tate, a celebrated comedian of the late eighteenth century, "the dreadful experience of exercising his supposed rights as Minister of the Savoy". He forestalled the introduction of the Marriage Act by an advertisement in the *Public Advertiser* of January 1754. This declared:

> By authority. Marriages performed with the utmost privacy, decency and regularity at the ancient royal chapel of St John the Baptist in the Savoy, where regular and authentic registers have been kept from the time of the Reformation (being two hundred years and upwards) to this day; the expense no more than one guinea, the five shilling stamp included. There are five private ways to this chapel by land, and two by water.

As his son wrote, "All was *rat, tat tat* at the street door ... So many persons were for the indissoluble knot being tied, that he might have made a fortune had he been blessed with patience and prudence, and been contented with publishing the banns of marriage only". Grierson, who assisted him, estimated that over 1,400 couples were married at the Savoy between 1754-6, of whom about 900 were "from the country big with child, some who could not be married elsewhere". J. S. Burn, the historian of parochial registers, states that there were 15 marriages performed at the Savoy in 1752 and 19 in 1753. In 1754 their number had increased to 342, and to 1,190 in 1755, but in 1756 this had decreased to 63 and in 1757 there were only 13.

The fact that Wilkinson celebrated these marriages openly, and publicly advertised his authority for so doing, meant that the authorities were not unaware of his activities. But he presumed that those who warned him of the consequences did so from "fears of his undoubted rights", and that this was the real cause of their leniency. When officers came to arrest him he escaped to the roof of the Savoy gaining access to the chapel by a private entrance. Eventually proceedings were instituted against him and he fled into Kent, obtaining the services of a former Fleet and May-Fair parson, Grierson, to act for him in solemnizing these marriages. Wilkinson continued to issue the licence himself, "thinking that Mr Grierson would not suffer for what he in his own authority, as Minister of the Savoy, was to be responsible for".

Grierson placed complete reliance upon the legality of these licences and "acted with great caution" so as not to offend against the Act. Unfortunately, he became involved in the marriage of Joseph Vernon and Jane Portier, whose marriage service he conducted in June 1755. The woman was under age, and had not received the consent of her father, although her mother had indicated that the consent would not be withheld. David Garrick, the actor-manager, to whose company the happy pair belonged, and who in Tate's phrase "ever loved to be meddling", discovered these matters and was instrumental in commencing the process by which Grierson was indicted for marrying a minor without full parental consent. His defence that he had not knowingly married against the laws, and that he was not aware of the lack of validity of Wilkinson's licences, was of no avail, and he was sentenced to be transported for a term of 14 years. Another curate, Richard Mason, was acquitted in a further trial.

Wilkinson eventually surrendered, claiming that he had been "pursued with unrelenting vengeance". He was charged with having married a couple without having previously obtained a licence "from a person having authority to grant the same". His argument that the Savoy licences were of sufficient authority was not accepted, and he too received the same sentence of transportation. Having spent all his assets on his defence, friends assisted him financially, but he died en route for America at Plymouth, his letters of credential given him by Henry Fox to enable him to obtain a living on the other side of the Atlantic remaining unused and unfulfilled.

The conviction of Grierson meant that all the marriages solemnized at the Savoy Chapel, under the authority of Wilkinson's licences, were declared null and void, to the possible number of 1,400. These marriages were at once plunged into confusion and uncertainty, and families were thrown into disruption. As many of the couples married were alleged to have come from the country, it might have taken years before the knowledge of their invalidity became known, by which time it might have been impossible to rectify matters by a "re-marriage". In all, as was said at the time, the decision to void these marriages was capable of causing much human misery and mental anguish. There was thus a slight decree of truth in Horace Walpole's assertion about the outcome of these trials, namely that:

> The Chancellor triumphed in punishing so many who had dared to contravene his statute; a more humane man would have sighed to have made such numbers suffer by a necessary law.

Wilkinson may have acted naively and rashly, but for the safety of every marriage celebrated after the year 1754 these Savoy marriages had to be declared void. It was a harsh requirement for such a great necessity.

A Fleet Register notebook (courtesy of the National Archives: RG7/819)

14
RETROSPECT

Throughout recent history, two views of marriage have prevailed. On the one hand there is the human desire for quick and convenient marriages, but on the other hand there is the legal view that marriage, by conferring particular rights in law, requires not only a more rigid definition but also consideration and reflection on the part of those who wish to enter its state. Similarly the Church, by considering marriage as a sacrament, requiring an indissoluble status, has stood out against much popular feeling to the contrary.

These tensions were clearly reflected in the existence of clandestine marriages, particularly those solemnized in the great centre of the Fleet. For those with little or no contact with any form of organised religion, such a centre provided them with the only available substitute to the full rigours of a marriage *in facie ecclesiae*. It was not so much a financial question that brought people to the Fleet, but rather what might be described as a subterranean view of marriage. In spite of centuries of teaching by the Church, it appeared that people still accepted the pre-medieval notion that a marriage was established by the promises exchanged between two people in present or in future time, followed (or even preceded) by a sexual relationship. The Church's teaching only appears to have penetrated in so far as it was believed that such an existing relationship needed to be blessed by a priest, or, possibly, that the priest represented the sanction of society at large upon the union, so that all things could be done decently and in order. In the larger cities and towns, where the parochial intimacy between priest and people had broken down, it was impossible to discover the violations of the ecclesiastical requirements of marriage, or to impose them with any degree of seriousness. In such areas the Church's insistence upon the indissolubility of marriage had been replaced by the ever popular concept of "fairness", namely, that if a marriage had failed, or one partner had deserted the other, then that marriage should be considered as "dead", and the parties to it allowed to marry other partners. This was undoubtedly the rule of life accepted by those who committed what the State and Church described as bigamy, although the number of "offenders" brought for trial for this offence probably represented the tip of the iceberg. In the next century it seems that many, including clergymen, took the same position in respect of men who had been transported for life, by allowing their legally married wives to marry another. Equally, common law marriage was for many people a way of life.

The lawyers with their systematic regard for the rights of property and legitimacy which they held derived from matrimony, and the Church with its insistence upon a sacramental concept of marriage, held a view of society in which the family was seen as the proper place for the upbringing of children. Thus they endeavoured to establish marriage as a more stable and mature relationship than the popular concept would allow. To establish this both authorities insisted that various procedures be adopted before marriage was entered into, partly as a delaying tactic in order to promote reflection, and partly to ensure that the marriage was recognised and properly recorded.

The Fleet marriages, by their rejection of these safeguards, and through the toleration by their operators of more flagrant abuses, earned the criticism and scorn of the judicial bench and lawmen. In the absence of effective ecclesiastical censure, in an age when the Church was weak and without any effective government of its own, the remedying of these marriages was left to the lawyers, and in particular to the Lord Chancellor. Hardwicke's concern in the subsequent bill was for the welfare of society at large by the prevention of the abuses which could destroy the stability of well-established marriages, and by ensuring that every marriage was properly conducted and regulated. Although the opposition regarded the bill as "an aristocratic plot", this was simply a popular device to win support for themselves. While the act was severe, creating a substantial gap between the legal and social definitions of marriage, and caused many problems and pressures in later years, it was desperately needed in order to ensure the safety and security of family life within the nation at large.

Yet it must always be remembered that for several generations of Londoners the services which the Fleet provided formed one of the principal structures of the life of the community and of the private life of the individual. This can be readily displayed by an examination of the marriage registers of various London parishes. St Andrew, Holborn, had an average number of 137 marriages between 1735-53, but between 1755-65, after the Marriage Act had enforced the canonical requirement that marriages should only be held in the parish church of the couple concerned, the average annual number increased to 268. St Sepulchre's and St Bride's were in a similar position: their respective average numbers for the same periods were 42 and 120, and 46 and 86 respectively. Outhwaite provides similar figures. A diocesan return of 1772 which required the number of marriages in parishes seven years before, and seven years after, the passing of the Marriage Act, revealed that St Andrew, Holborn, had 845 before, and 1,593 after, St James, Westminster 615 and 2,172, while the 34 London parishes had 1,786 before and 4,046 after.

These figures provide some coherence to the idea that there was a clerical pressure group behind the agitation to end the clandestine marriage trade, as well as a legal concern. It is significant that the leading clerical opponent of these marriages was Dr Gally, rector of St Andrew, Holborn, one of the incumbents hardest hit by these clandestine marriages, which must have reduced his fee income considerably. Clearly the clergy had a financial interest in ensuring that these marriage centres (as well as the abuses in the issuing of licences) were brought to an end.

The human desire for quick and convenient marriage is still apparent today. Four thousand clandestine marriages took place in Scotland during 1914-15, when soldiers, on leave from the front, found they could not fulfil the legal requirements of residence, and so resorted to "marriage brokers" who helped them to take advantage of the anomalies then existing in the Scottish law of marriage. Legislation rapidly brought relief. In 1966 the *News of the World* reported a state of affairs in Las Vegas which still continues, and which indicates that this kind of marriage is still popular. Under the heading *Instant Marriage: it's becoming big business*, a special correspondent wrote:

> Instant marriages are the new rage in America. The boom is so great that they have become the biggest business in Las Vegas except for gambling.
>
> They are performed round the clock in highly commercialised, pseudo "chapels", which stretch along the city's tawdry neon-lit strip.
>
> Some are rushed though in 90 seconds.
>
> Many of the chapels with names such as Candlelite Chapel, Chapel of the Roses, Gretna Green, and the Hitching Post are built alongside motels.
>
> A £180 package, de-luxe deal includes rapid ceremony, canned organ music, single-tier wedding cake, photographs of the guests,

a taped recording of the ceremony, copy of the marriage certificate embossed with hearts, bouquets of everlasting plastic flowers plus a one-night motel honeymoon in a room with a circular bed and mirrored ceiling.

Nearly 40,000 people flew or drove into the Nevada gambling resort last year to get married before cocktails.

And the instant marriage business now rivals the prosperous quickie divorce business of nearly Reno.

The routine is simple. You buy a licence and then, if you don't want to go to a chapel, you walk upstairs to the Justice of the Peace's office for a 90 second ceremony.

The Justice of the Peace's office is so lucrative that he is only allowed to hold the post for two years.

No time is wasted at the chapels either. A licensed minister stands by to perform the ceremony. If another couple is ahead, the happy pair may pass the time by playing the one armed bandits.

When I spoke to Mr Charles Starker, co-owner of the Silver Bells Wedding Chapel, he defended this money-spinning idea.

"We put on a nice wedding in our chapel," he said. "We have a minister, stained glass windows, pews, organ music and a little altar with flowers on it. We also light candles on the altar, and there is a Bible.

"Our service takes about five minutes. It is simple and short. The bride is not given away. Many couples only pay about £6, but others spend £13.

"We can arrange a longer ceremony as in a normal church if the couple ask for it. We find most couples come here so they can have a quick, simple wedding without all the complications of arranging one back home.

"I think most of the Las Vegas chapels are doing a good job that is appreciated by the people who are married here.

"I know many people criticise the speed with which you can get married in Las Vegas. But the way I see it is if a marriage is successful it's successful, even if the whole procedure took only a matter of minutes.

"Having to wait for days or weeks while banns are published won't guarantee success."

Times do not change.
A Fleet parson could have said almost the same.

APPENDIX 1: GENEALOGICAL CLUES

It has been suggested already that between two and three hundred thousand marriages took place at the Fleet. These marriages are recorded in over 850 registers and notebooks. Parson Gaynam entered his marriages into at least 90 different registers and a whole variety of notebooks. Eleven different registers record the marriages which took place at the Fleet during the year 1701. Thirty-five cover the year 1720, and four notebooks include details of further marriages. Fifty-four registers and nineteen notebooks record entries for 1730, and for 1740 the number is seventy-two and thirty-seven respectively. Some registers contain a few hundred marriages for each given year, others ten or less. These registers, taken as a group, are not in any chronological order, as would be the case of the marriage registers of a parish church. Rather, each marriage house and parson had his own register. It is not surprising that any person endeavouring to discover a particular entry is immediately daunted by the magnitude of the task. It will be necessary to give some account of these registers before proceeding to offer some advice as to their use.

These "Fleet" registers also contain the record of the Mint, King's Bench, and some of the May-Fair marriages. They are kept at the National Archives at Kew (the former Public Record Office) under the serial number R.G.7. A further register is at the Bodleian Library, Oxford, as part of the Rawlinson Manuscripts, and there are other strays known elsewhere, including two in the records of the Prerogative Court of Canterbury (National Archives, PROB 18/50). At a rough estimate about two thirds of the probable total number of the registers have survived.

The National Archives has issued a catalogue of its own collection of these registers. This records the first and last dates of entries in each register (though often the main chronological sequence may account for only a fraction of this period), together with the name or names of the parsons and marriage houses concerned, if known.

Many of these registers are duplicates of others. An entry may be recorded in four or more registers by reason of the fact that the parsons and the marriage house keepers both kept their own registers and notebooks. Some of these registers were then transcribed into larger compilations by so-called "registrars". It is not surprising that errors in transcription were frequent, the principal variations being in the spelling of proper names, and occasionally a difference of several days in the date of a marriage. In the worst cases names are completely muddled.

Entries within the majority of the registers are in chronological order. There was an almost universal practice of writing some entries on the inside of the covers and the fly leaves, and sometimes these entries are not re-entered into their correct position in the register. Baptismal entries are generally to be found, if included, on the last pages of the registers.

The Fleet registers may be divided into three distinct groups. The first and most important group consists of the actual registers, numbers 1-273. The second is a small group of indexes to the first group. The third group is a collection of notebooks, numbers 291-833. The first group may again be sub-divided into three divisions, namely, those that belonged to the parsons, those that were kept by the marriage houses, and various registers that appear to have been compiled later by these registrars. These registers range from rough drafts (so it seems) to neatly compiled books, for some of the parsons and register keepers employed professional scribes to write up their entries.

Most of the register entries give the full names of both parties, their marital status (bachelor or spinster &c), the parishes in which they resided, and the occupation of the groom. In the case of sailors the name of their ship is sometimes recorded. In a few entries additional information is given, mainly of a more sordid kind. However, many entries, for reasons already explained, record only the Christian names of the couples concerned.

Several of the registers, especially those of Parson Wyatt, are compiled on a rough alphabetical principle, the first letter of the male surname providing the key. The entries for each letter are then entered in chronological order.

The indexes, either contained in the separate group, or bound into the actual register to which they refer, use the same system as these alphabetical registers. Although the indexing is based on the male surname, the name of the bride is also given, but not indexed. These indexes refer to only a few of the registers, and there are none for the notebooks. J. S. Burn in the 1830s urged their amalgamation into one large index. This has yet to be done.

The notebooks are all of pocket size, and represent only a fraction of those originally kept. Most of those surviving date from 1710, but the majority relate to the period 1727-48. Several were used as common place books as well, containing not only the usual marriage entries and comments but also accounts and even recipes. These notebooks are important as they often contain additional material to that given in the register into which their entries were transcribed. Most of the surviving notebooks belonged to three of the Fleet parsons, Wyatt, Gaynam and Ashwell, and to one marriage house keeper, Burnford.

In spite of the considerable bulk of the Fleet registers, provided there is definite evidence to suggest that the marriage took place at the Fleet, and the names of the parties and an appropriate date is known, and that the register entry has survived, it should not be too difficult to locate an entry. If a Fleet certificate is available then the name of the parson and / or the marriage house will probably be recorded on it, and this will provide the initial clue as to which register should be consulted. It should be remembered, however, that the word "Fleet" is not always recorded on these certificates. Instead the marriages are recorded as having taken place in the parishes of St Sepulchre's, St Bride's, or St Martin's, Ludgate.

If an inspection of the indexes proves unsuccessful, the searcher should examine first the registers compiled by the parsons, for their books record far more marriages than the registers of the marriage house keepers. If an entry is found it is often rewarding to examine the notebooks in the hope that further, or even more correct, information may be found.

Mark Herber has set himself the ambitious task of transcribing, and probably indexing, the various registers. A number of volumes are already available.

This appendix has been adapted from my contribution to volume I of the *National Index of Parish Registers*, edited by D. J. Steele, "Clandestine Marriages" (pages 292-320), and published in 1968 by the Society of Genealogists, London.

APPENDIX II: A LIST OF THE
PRINCIPAL FLEET CLERGY

By this term is meant those clergy who married at the Fleet on a regular basis and over a significant period of time

Jerome Alley	1681-1702 fled	John Mottram	1708-31
Edward Ashwell	1733-46 died	Edward Roberts	1689-1702
Samuel Backler	1732-51	Nehemiah Rogers	1694-1702, 1714-15
Michael Barratt	1717-39 died	Thomas Ryder	1728-43
James Coulton	1690-1722	James Shaw	1723-6
Thomas Crawford	1723-48	Anthony Shellburn	1732-7
Robert Cuthbert	1717-35	Nathaniel Skinner	1713-22
William Dare	1735-49	Richard Sindley	1738-45
Francis Deveneu	1739-54	John Stainton	1730-5
.... Draper	1689-1716	Edward Stacey	1719-26
Robert Elborrow	c 1691-1704	James Starkey	1718-30
John Evans	1689-1730	Peter Symson	1738-54
John Floyd	1708-29 died	John Tarrant	1742-54
John Gaynam	1709-40 died	Jacob Townshend	1752-4
Henry Gower	1716-19	Jo Vyse	1707-18
.... Grierson	1747-54	James Wagstaffe	1688-1728
Anthony Hanson	1729-38	Clement Walker	1726-35
James Lando	1738-52	Daniel Wigmore	1725-54
Edward Marston	1713-14	Walter Wyatt	1720-50 died

APPENDIX III: A LIST OF
THE PRINCIPAL MARRIAGE HOUSE KEEPERS

This term is reserved for those whose "house" possessed a register, and / or a chapel. All dates given are approximate

Mrs Barratt	of Bride Lane	1740-5
Sarah Bennett	*Hand and Pen*, Fleet Market	1747-8
..... Blinkthorn	*The Ship*, Fleet Ditch	1740
John Burnford	*Hand & Pen & Noah's Ark*, Half Moon Court	1722-49
Mr Crampton	*The Cock*, Fleet Market	died in 1742
..... Crosier	*Hoop & Bunch of Grapes*, Holborn Bridge	1739
Thomas Cox	*Hand and Pen*, Fleet Ditch	1736-9
..... Demat	*The Cock*, Fleet Market	after 1742
..... Ewell	*King's Head*, Fleet Market	1720-32
Mrs Francis	*Queen's Head*	1730
..... Gillet	*The White Swan*, Fleet Market	1742-54
Thomas Hodgkins & wife	*Hand and Pen*, Fleet Lane	1714-29
Mrs Levy	*The Green Canister*, by Fleet Bridge	1743-4
John Lilly	*The Bull and Garter*	1713-48
Joshua Lilly	*The Hand and Pen*, Fleet Ditch	1720-54
	The Fountain, Ludgate Hill	
Thomas Owen	*New Chapel for Marriages*, Fleet Market	before 1740
	The King's Head, Fleet Market	1740
Samuel Pickering	*The Fighting Cocks*, Fleet Lane	1725
Mr Roberts	*The Lamb*	1724-8
	New Market House, Fleet Lane	1730
..... Rylance	*Wheatsheaf*, Fleet Market	1743-54
..... Sands	*Wheatsheaf*, Fleet Market	1728-43
..... Smith	*Two Sawyers*, Fleet Lane (ex Wyatt)	1740-2
	Rose Coffee House	1742-8
Henry Stebbing	*The Shepherd and Goat*	1748
Henry Tuftin	of Tuftin's	1709-20
..... Wheeler	in Turn-again Lane	1740
Matthias Wilson	*The Hand & Pen & Golden Pot*, Fleet Lane	1727-35
William Wyatt	*Two Sawyers*, Fleet Lane	before 1740
	Hand and Pen, Holborn Bridge	1741
	At Seacoal Lane	1749-54

APPENDIX 4: A LETTER TO DR NEWTON
Chancellor to the Bishop of London
"Concerning the Ill Practices at the Fleet Prison", 1702
(Guildhall Library, London, MS. 9657, box 2, bundle 3)

Sir,
I think it my duty to God and the Queen to acquaint you with the illegal practices of the ministers and clerk in the Fleet Chapel for marrying clandestinely as they do some weeks fifty or sixty couples. The ministers that are there are as follows, Mr Robert Elborrow, he is an ancient man and is Master of the Chapel and marries but very few now without banns or licence, but under a colour doth allow his clerk to do what he pleases, his name is Barth. Bassett. There is there also one Mr James Colton a clergyman he lives in Leather Lane next door to the Coach and Horses, he hath been there these four years to marry but no prisoner, he marries in coffee houses, in his own house, and in and about the Fleet Gate and all the Rules over not excepting any part of City or suburbs. This clerk Bassett aforesaid registers whatever Colton marries in the Fleet register and gives him certificates. Colton has a living in Essex but the Bishop of London deprived him for this and other ill practices. There is also one Mr Nehemiah Rogers, he is a prisoner but goes at large to his living in Essex and all places else, he is a very wicked man as lives for drinking, whoring and swearing, he has struck and boxed the bridegroom in the Chapel and damned like any common soldier, he marries both within and without the Chapel like his brother Colton. There was one Mr Alley, he was a prisoner and [had] the benefit of weddings but is gone to some other preferment. The aforesaid Bassett rents the cellars of the Fleet and pays for that and two watchmen £120 per annum, but he himself pays but £20 per annum for the clergy pay all the rest monthly and if they do not they are threatened to be confined or outed. This clerk hath been sworn in Doctors' Commons not to marry any without banns or licence unless it be such poor people as are recommended by the justices in case of a big belly, but have married since many hundreds as I and many can testify who are confined prisoners. The chief days to marry are Sundays, Tuesdays and Saturdays but every day more or less. The clerk Bassett keeps a Register Book as he pleases as you may see when you look over the Registers, he hath another at his son's. He does what he pleases, and maintains a great family by these ill practices, £200 per annum he hath at least. The ministers and clerk bribe one Mr Shirley, I think him to be collector for the Queen's taxes. I hope Sir you excuse me for concealing my name, hoping that you will inspect into these base practices.

BIBLIOGRAPHICAL REFERENCES
(the citations are to the bibliography)

CHAPTER 1

The anecdote regarding Dean Swift is taken from Colman's *Circle of Anecdote and Wit* of 1828. The case of *More v. More* is found in Atkyns, that of *Middleton v. Croft* in Annally and Atkyns; *Haydon's Case* in Salmon's essay, and the case of Samuel Harris is found in the Rawlinson MSS., Bodleian Library, Oxford, B382, fol. 271.

CHAPTER 2

The episcopal correspondence noted in this chapter is found in the Tanner MSS., 30 and 124, at the Bodleian Library, Oxford.

The material relating to the Savoy marriages is in the 5th Report of the Historical Manuscripts Commission, appendix, p. 139; and the Tower and Minories marriages from Tomlinson. A fragment of a Minories register is in the Guildhall Library, London, MS. 9242a. The registers of St James's, Duke's Place, were edited by Phillimore and Cokayne.

Dr Payne's commission is at the National Archives, S.P. 44-150, fol. 75. Compton's protest and other material relating to is in found in the same papers (S.P. 44-274), Rawlinson MS. C983 at the Bodleian Library, and Addit. MS. 28,879, fol. 68 at the British Library. His son's comments are noted by A. T. Hart in his *Country Counting House*, (London, 1962), p. 4.

The various bills relating to clandestine marriages are found in the Tanner MSS., Bodleian Library, MS. 55, fol. 121; Historical Manuscript Commission Reports, no. 9, item 395, p. 90; no. 11, app. ii, p. 276; no. 12, app. vi, p. 243; no 13, app. v, p. 253. Whatham's proposals are contained in S.P. 32-11, fol. 65. The three acts mentioned are 5 & 6 William and Mary, c. 21 (1694), 6 & 7 William III, c. 6 (1694), and 7 & 8 William III, c. 35 (1695-6).

The bills for matrimonial insurance are at the British Library, press mark 1190 b5. See also the article by R. Brown, "Insuring for Happiness", *Insurance Brokers' Journal*, June 1974, pp. 419-21.

Coulton's evidence is at the National Archives, IND 4622, fol. 96, and John King's warrant in the same place, S.P. 35-25, fol. 95.

CHAPTER 3

The first Fleet register was thought to start in 1668, but examination has shown this should be 1698. The registers are at the National Archives, Kew, catalogued under the reference R.G.7.

The trials relating to the 1729 enquiry into the Fleet Prison are in Corbett's *State Trials*, volume xvii. The Report of the Parliamentary Committee into the Prison was published in 1729.

The 1702 visitation of the prison is at the Guildhall Library, MS. 9657, box 2, bundle 3.

The 1705 parliamentary enquiry is found in the *Journal of the House of Commons*, xv, pp. 108, 169, 188.

The Convocation Report of 1710 is at the Bodleian Library, Tanner Ms. 282.

The 1711 Act is 10 Anne c. 19, clause clxxvi.

The case of *Morais v. Morais* is contained in the Rawlinson MSS., Bodleian Library, MS. B382, fol. 438. Beau Fielding's trial is in Howell's *State Trials* (1719 edition), iv, 755.

Warden Eyles's protest is at the National Archives, IND 4625, fol. 207.

CHAPTER 4

William Skelbech's petition is at the National Archives, S.P. 34-36, fol. 55. "A List of the twenty-four debauched clergymen" is at the Bodleian Library, Rawlinson MS. D1092, fol. 222. Savage's petition is at the National Archives, T1 no 276, fol. 76. Alley's orders (or lack of them) are chronicled in Bodleian Library, Tanner MS. 42, fol. 133. Ashwell's indiscretions are noted in the Lansdowne MSS. at the British Library, MS. 841, fol. 123, and the prisoners' denial at the Guildhall Records Office, MS. 84.21, fol. 5. Vyse's career is found in Lawrence Stone's *Uncertain Unions*, pp. 105-12.

CHAPTERS 5-10

These chapters utilise extracts from the Fleet Registers at the National Archives. It is impossible to record all these references, but they may be found by consulting an unpublished M.A. thesis of the University of London: R. L. Brown, "Clandestine Marriages in London, especially within the Fleet Prison, and their effect on Hardwicke's Act, 1753", 1972. A microfilm copy is at the Guildhall Library.

CHAPTER 7

The Fleet certificates are found in the Admiralty Bounty Papers at the National Archives, Adm. 106-3026.

The story of the Meyrick brothers is related in *Bye-Gones*, 22 April 1896, p. 324, as is the case of Beatrice Baker: *ibid*, 22 October 1930, pp. 226-7.

A study of the Clerkenwell marriages was undertaken by the Cambridge Group for the History of Population and Social Structure.

CHAPTER 9

The various trials recorded are found in the *London Sessions Papers* for the years mentioned, but the case of *Phillips v. Delafield* is found at the Guildhall Library, MS. 9184. This was part of an even more notorious case, mentioned below, which is chronicled by Stone, *Uncertain Unions*, pp. 236-74.

The autobiography of Francis Place is at the British Library, Add. Ms. 35,142.

The churchwardens' accounts for the parish of St Bride's are at the Guildhall Library, MS. 6552 iii.

The case involving John Vyse is related by Stone in his *Uncertain Unions*, pp. 109-110; and that of *Phillips v. Cresse* in *ibid*, pp. 170-4.

CHAPTER 10

The Mint marriages are recorded in the Fleet registers. The May-Fair registers were edited by Armitage. For a history of the Mint see R. L. Brown, "The Minters of Wapping", *East London Papers*, xiv, 1972, p. 77.

Keith's case is found in the Act Books of the London Consistory Court. One of his licences is in the British Library, Additional Charters 67370-1.

CHAPTER 11

Much of the information relating to Hardwicke in this chapter is derived from Yorke's life. The case of *Hill v. Turner* will be found in Atkyns and West.

Lawrence Stone in his *Road to Divorce*, p. 117, notes the London Consistory Court case of 1752 relating to Sophia Moore, while Con Phillip's case is to be found in his *Uncertain Unions*, pp. 236-74.

Thomas Turner's diary, edited by David Vaisey, is entitled "The Diary of a Village Shopkeeper" (London, 1998).

CHAPTER 12

The 1753 Act is 26 George II, c. 23.

Its debates will be found in Corbett's *Parliamentary Historian*, volume xv.

The quotation from Lawrence Stone is from *Road to Divorce*, pp. 122-3, and used by kind permission of the Oxford University Press.

CHAPTER 13

The register advertisement is at the Bodleian Library, Douce MS. 949, fol. 118.

The 1781 Act is 21 George III c. 53, and the 1840 Act 3 & 4 Vict. c. 92.

Jane Hughes's case is mentioned by Colin A Gresham in his *Eifionydd* (Cardiff, 1973), pp. 197-8.

The trial of Wilkinson and his associates is found in the *London Sessions*

Papers for 1756-7.

Thomas Turner is his diary for 1758 noted two clergymen had been imprisoned in Horsham Gaol for marrying contrary to the Marriage Act.

CHAPTER 14

The registers of the three churches mentioned are all at the Guildhall Library, London.

The First World War marriages in Scotland are noted in R. L. Brown, "The Last Clandestine Rush", *Local Population Studies*, no 26, Spring 1981, pp. 58-9.

The *News of the World* quotation is dated 13 February 1966, and is used by kind permission of that paper.

SELECT BIBLIOGRAPHY

Ambler, C: *Reports of Cases in Chancery*, London, 1790.

Annally, Baron: *Cases Argued in the Courts of King's Bench at Westminster*, London, 1770.

Armytage, G.J.: *The Registers of St George's Chapel, May-Fair*, Harleian Society, volume xv, London, 1889.

Ashton, John: *The Fleet, its River, Prison and Marriages*, London, 1889.

Atkins, J.T.: *Reports of Cases in Chancery*, London, 3rd edition, 1794.

Bannet, Eve Tavor: "The Marriage Act of 1753: 'A Most Cruel Law for the Fair Sex'", *Eighteenth Century Studies* 30, 1997, pp. 233-53.

Bellamy, A.: *An Apology for her Life*, London, 2nd edition, 1785.

Benton, Tony: *Irregular Marriage in London before 1754*, London, 2nd edition, 2000.

Blackstone, William: *Commentaries on the Laws of England*, Oxford, 5th edition, 1773.

Blanc, L'Abbé le: *Letters on the English and French Nations*, Dublin, 1747.

B.N.: *Collection of Trials at the Old Bailey*, London, 1718-21.

Boulton, Jeremy: "Clandestine Marriages in London: an examination of a neglected urban variable", *Urban History*, 20, 1993, pp. 191-210.

Brown, R.L.: *A History of the Fleet Prison, London*, Edwin Mellen Studies in British History, volume 42, Lewiston, 1996.

Brown, R.L.: "Clandestine Marriages in Wales", *Transactions of the Honourable Society of Cymmrodorion*, 1982, pp. 74-85.

Brown, R.L.: "The Rise and Fall of the Fleet Marriages", in *Marriage and Society: Studies in the Social History of Marriage*, edited by R.B. Outhwaite, London, 1981, pp. 117-136.

Burn, J.S.: *The Fleet Registers*, London, 1833.

Burn, J.S.: *The History of Parish Registers in England*, London, 2nd edition, 1862.

Campbell, Lord: *Lives of the Lord Chancellors*, London, 1846.

Carpenter, E.: *The Protestant Bishop*, London, 1956.

Chambers, J.D.: *Population, Economy and Society in Pre-Industrial England*, Oxford, 1962.

Corbett's *Parliamentary Historian*, volume xv.

Cooksey, R.: *Sketches of an Essay on the Life and Character of Philip, Earl of Hardwicke*, Worcester, 1791.

Coxe, W.: *Memoirs of the Administration of Henry Pelham*, London, 1829.

Coxe, W.: *Memoirs of Horatio, Lord Walpole*, London, 3rd edition, 1820.

Dickens, J.: *Reports of Cases in Chancery*, London, 1803.

Draper, W.H.: *The Morning Walk, a Poem*, London, 1751.

Elliott, Adam: *A Modest Vindication of Titus Oates, the Salamanca Doctor, from Perjury*, London, 1682.

Espinasse, I.: *Reports of Cases Argued at Nisi Prius in the Courts of King's Bench and Common Pleas*, London, 1802.

Gally, H.: *Some Considerations upon Clandestine Marriages*, London, 2nd edition, 1750.

Gaynam, J.: *A Submissive Answer to Mr Hoadly's Humble Reply to my Lord Bishop of Exeter* ("by a student of Oxford"), London, 1709.

Gaynam, J.: *Cato's Principles of Self Preservation and Public Liberty* (by "a Subject of Caesar's"), London, 1722.

Gaynam, J.: *Marlborough still Conquers, a Poem*, London, 1708.

Gaynam, J.: *The Use and Excellency of the Church Catechism*, London, 1709.

George, M.D.: *London Life in the XVIIIth Century*, London, 1925.

Gibson, E.: *Codex Juris Ecclesiastici Anglicani*, London, 1713.

Hammick, J.T.: *The Marriage Law of England*, London, 2nd edition, 1887.

Haw, R.: *The State of Matrimony*, London, 1952.

Herber, Mark: *Clandestine Marriages in the Chapels and Rules of the Fleet Prison, 1680-1754*, 3 volumes, continuing, London, 1999-2001.

Hickering, E.: *The Most Humble Confession of ....* , London, 1684.

Holdsworth, W.S.: *A History of English Law*, London, 1903+.

House, Anthony: "A Problematic Solution: Responses to the Marriage Reform Act of 1753". An Oxford University thesis found at www.users.ox.ac.uk/~chri2057/z2002thesis.htm.

Howell's *State Trials*, London, 1719.

Humours of the Fleet, a Scrapbook relating to the Fleet Prison and Marriages, at the British Library, press mark, 11633 h2.

Ilchester, Earl of: *Henry Fox, First Lord Holland*, London, 1920.

Jerrold, D.: *Birds in the Cage* [a play about Fleet Marriages], London, 1835.

Keith, Alexander: *Observations on the Act for Preventing Clandestine Marriages*, London, 1753.

Lane, J.: *Titus Oates*, London, 1949.

Lasch, Christopher: "The Suppression of Clandestine Marriage in England: the Marriage Act of 1753, *Salmagundi* 26, 1974.

Leman, T.: *Matrimony Analysed*, London, 1755.

Leneman, Leah: "The Scottish Case that led to Hardwicke's Marriage Act", *Law and History Review* 17, 1999.

Lloyd, Beric: *The Fleet Forgeries*, London, 1987.

Loftie, W.J.: *Memorials of the Savoy*, London, 1878.

Malcolm, J.P.: *Anecdotes of the Manners and Customs of London during the Eighteenth Century*, London, 2nd edition, 1810.

Marston, E.: *To the Most Noble Prince Henry, Duke of Beaufort, Palatine of the Province of South Carolina*, London, 1712.

Merrick, M.M.: *Marriage as Divine Institution and the Emblem of the Mystical Union between Christ and his Church*, London, 1754.

Misson, M.: *Memoirs and Observations in his Travels over England*, London, 1719.

Ogborn, Miles: "The Most Lawless Space: The Geography of the Fleet and the Making of Lord Hardwicke's Marriage Act of 1753", *New Formations* 37, 1999, pp. 11-32.

Outhwaite, R.B.: *Clandestine Marriage in England, 1500-1850*, London, 1995.

Paget, W.: *The Humours of the Fleet*, London, 1749.

Parker, Stephen: *Informal Marriage and Cohabitation and the Law 1750-1987*, London, 1990.

Payne, Jennifer: "From Fleet Street to Gretna Green: The Reform of 'Clandestine Marriage' under Lord Chancellor Hardwicke's Marriage Act of 1753", a paper found at www.geocities.com/Athens/Aegean/7023.

Peake, T.: *A compendium of the Law of Evidence*, London, 1822.

Peake, T.: *Cases Determined at Nisi Prius in the Court of King's Bench*, London, 1795.

Pennant, T.: *Some Account of London*, London, 2nd edition, 1791.

Phillimore, J.: *Speech in the House of Commons on Moving for Leave to Bring in a Bill to Amend the Marriage Act*, London, 2nd edition, 1822.

Phillimore, W.P.W., and Cokayne, G.E.: *The Registers of St James's, Duke's Place*, London, 1900.

Prideaux, H.: "The Case of Clandestine Marriages Stated", in the *Harleian Miscellany*, volume 1, London, 1743.

Probert, Rebecca: "The Impact of the Marriage Act of 1753: was it really 'A most cruel Law for the Fair Sex?'", *Eighteenth Century Studies* 35, 2005, pp. 247-62.

Probert, Rebecca: "The Judicial Interpretation of Lord Hardwicke's Act of 1753", *Journal of Legal History*, 2002, pp. 129-51.

Reasons for Passing the Act to Prevent Clandestine Marriage, London, 1719.

Representation of the Prejudices that may Arise in Time from an Intended Act concerning Marriages, A, London, 1692.

Roberts, Peter (edited by D. R. Thomas), *Y Cwtta Cyfarwydd*, London, 1883.

Sadler, F.: *The Exactions and Impositions of Parish Fees Discovered*, London, 3rd edition, 1742.

Salmon, *A Critical Essay concerning Matrimony* ("by a Gentleman"), London, 1724.

Saussure, C. de (edited by Madam van Muyden): *A Foreign View of England in the Reigns of George I and George II*, London, 1902.

Scrope, Miss: *Her Answer to Mr Creswell's Narrative,* London, 1749.

Select Trials at the Old Bailey, various editions.

Shebbeare, Dr.: *The Marriage Act: a Novel,* London, 1754.

Somerville, R.: *The Savoy,* London, 1960.

Stackhouse, T.: *The Miseries of the Inferior Clergy,* London, 2nd edition, 1722.

Stone, Lawrence: *Road to Divorce,* Oxford, 1991.

Stone, Lawrence: *The Family, Sex and Marriage in England,* London, 1977.

Stone, Lawrence: *Uncertain Unions,* Oxford, 1992.

Strange, J.: *Reports of Adjudged Cases in the Courts of Chancery, King's Bench, Common Pleas and Exchequer,* London, 1782.

Straus, R. (editor): *Tricks of the Town: Eighteen Century Diversions,* London, 1927.

Swinburne, H.: *A Treatise of Spousals, or Matrimonial Contracts,* London, 1711.

Sykes, N.: *Church and State in the Eighteenth Century,* Cambridge, 1934.

Tegg, W.: *The Knot Tied,* London, 1877.

Tomlinson, E.M.: *A History of the Minories, London,* London, 1907.

Walpole, Horace (edited by Lord Holland), *Memoirs of the Reign of George II,* London, 2nd edition, 1847.

Walpole, Horace (edited by A.F.Streuart), *The Last Journals of .... ,* London, 1910.

Walpole, Horace (edited by Mrs Paget Toynbee), *The Letters of ... .,* Oxford, 1903.

Warburton, Bishop: "On the Nature of the Family Union", in *The Family Chaplain,* London, 1775.

West, M.J.: *Reports of Cases in the High Court of Chancery,* London, 1827.

Whitaker, E.: "The Fleet Parsons and the Fleet Marriages", in the *Cornhill Magazine,* 1867.

Wilkinson, Tate: *Memoirs of his Own Life,* York, 1790.

Wrigley, E.A.: "Clandestine Marriage in Tetbury", *Local Population Studies,* 1973.

Yorke, C.: *A Letter to the Public upon the Marriage Act,* London, 1753.

Yorke, P.C.: *Life and Correspondence of Philip Yorke, Earl of Hardwicke,* Cambridge, 1913.